RAISING
VEGETARIAN
CHILDREN

Also by Joanne Stepaniak

Compassionate Living for Healing, Wholeness, and Harmony

The Vegan Sourcebook

Being Vegan

Dairy Free and Delicious (with Brenda Davis and Bryanna Clark Grogan)

Vegan Deli

The Saucy Vegetarian

Delicious Food for a Healthy Heart

Vegan Vittles

Table for Two

The Uncheese Cookbook

The Nutritional Yeast Cookbook

Ecological Cooking: Recipes to Save the Planet (with Kathy Hecker)

Also by Vesanto Melina

Becoming Vegetarian (with Brenda Davis and Victoria Harrison)

Cooking Vegetarian (with Joseph Forest)

The Good Cookbook by Yves (with Yves Potvin)

Becoming Vegan (with Brenda Davis)

Healthy Eating for Life to Prevent and Treat Cancer (with Neal Barnard)

RAISING VEGETARIAN CHILDREN

A Guide to Good Health and Family Harmony

JOANNE STEPANIAK, M.S.ED.,
AND VESANTO MELINA, M.S., R.D.

Contemporary Books

Chicago New York San Francisco Lisbon London Madrid Mexico City
Milan New Delhi San Juan Seoul Singapore Sydney Toronto

Library of Congress Cataloging-in-Publication Data

Stepaniak, Joanne, 1954–
     Raising vegetarian children : a guide to good health and family harmony / Joanne Stepaniak
and Vesanto Melina.
        p.   cm.
Includes bibliographical references and index.
ISBN 0-658-02155-9 (alk. paper)
     1. Vegetarian children.   2. Children—Nutrition.   3. Vegetarianism—Social aspects.
4. Child development.   I. Melina, Vesanto, 1942–   II. Title.

RJ206 .S835   2002
613.262′083—dc21   2002067448

1 2 3 4 5 6 7 8 9 0   DOC/DOC   1 0 9 8 7 6 5 4 3 2

ISBN 0-658-02155-9

Dedicated to the children in our lives and hearts.

Help us to create the peaceful world you deserve to inherit.

Contents

PART TWO: NOURISHING OUR CHILDREN

Chapter 6   121
Vegetarian Nutrition 101

Chapter 7   159
Getting a Great Start: Nutrition During Infancy

Foreword

Families today come in all shapes and sizes. Some families are composed only of adults who have no children or who have grown children living on their own. Other families are made up of one or more adults and one, two, or more children, who may or may not be related. Some families fluctuate in size due either to temporary or alternating living arrangements, as often happens with custody settlements, or because they function as foster homes to children in transition. Still others include adult sons and daughters—whether married, divorced, or single, with or without children—who reside at the family home. Children are growing up in one- or two-parent households and are being reared by their biological mothers or fathers (or both), adoptive parents, grandparents, other extended family members, same-sex partners, legal guardians, or foster parents. There is no precise way to define families, the term *parent*, or the environments in which children are raised.

As adults, we are responsible for the children in our community and our culture, whether or not they live under our roofs or even have daily contact with us. We all have countless opportunities to mentor, nurture, and encourage children, whether they are our own or someone else's. Joanne Stepaniak and Vesanto Melina bring a unique blend of experiences and perspectives to this book to provide advocacy, information, and guidance for any type of family that is rearing, or wants to rear or support, vegetarian children.

Joanne has been a vegetarian since the midsixties, having made the decision as a young girl during a time when vegetarianism was viewed with skepticism and hostility. She and her husband, Michael, became vegans in the early eighties. Joanne has firsthand knowledge of what it is like to be a vegetarian child, adolescent, and adult, having grown up in a family that did not share her inclinations. Joanne also has a master's of science degree in education and over twenty years' experience as a counselor, caseworker, and teacher working with multiply challenged children, teens, and adults. She has provided interim parenting care for profoundly disabled youth, directed preadolescent and teen educational and recreational programs, provided counseling for at-risk elders and their families, coordinated literacy programs, and most recently operated a private counseling business. Joanne also is trained and experienced in a variety of approaches to alternative dispute resolution, including community mediation, family and parent-teen mediation, and restorative justice for victims of crimes committed by youth offenders. She also is a professional mediator and coach. Joanne's online services have afforded her the rare opportunity to communicate directly with thousands of parents and youngsters around the world who are grappling with issues related to vegetarianism. Joanne's essays and articles have been widely published. In addition, she writes a monthly advice column for *VegNews*, an international vegetarian newspaper, and is the media coordinator for the North American Vegetarian Society. Joanne is the author of nine vegan cookbooks and three texts on ethics and philosophy, including *The Vegan Sourcebook, Being Vegan,* and *Compassionate Living for Healing, Wholeness, and Harmony.*

Vesanto is a registered dietitian and coauthor of the nutrition classics *Becoming Vegetarian* and *Becoming Vegan.* She has been a nutrition consultant to major vegetarian food manufacturers and various levels of government and has researched and written extensively on the topic of nutrition for both children and adults. She was a coordinator for the vegetarian section of the *Manual of Clinical Dietetics,* 6th edition, 2000, a joint project of the American Dietetic Association and Dietitians of Canada. Vesanto has been a nutritionist for the WIC Program (Special Supplemental Nutrition Program for Women, Infants, and Children) for the Seattle–King County Health Department in Washington State and for the Vancouver City Health Department in British Columbia. She has taught nutrition at Bastyr University in

Statistics on Families

According to the U.S. Census Bureau, 2001:

Percentage of births that are to teenaged mothers: 12.8 percent

Percentage of births that are to unmarried mothers: 32 percent

Rate of marriages per thousand people: 8 percent

Rate of divorces per thousand people: 4 percent

Marriages involving a remarriage for the bride, groom, or both: 45 percent

Homes with three or more generations living together: 4 million

Homes with grandparents responsible for a grandchild under age 18: 2.4 million

Increase in gay couples since 1990 census: 300 percent[a]

Average family size in 1970: 3.58 persons

Average family size in 1999: 3.18 persons

For parent-child families (distinct from families headed by grandparents or unrelated adults):

Percentage headed by married couple: 72 percent

Percentage headed by a single mother: 23 percent

Percentage headed by a single father: 5 percent

Living arrangements of the 72 million children in the United States:

Percentage of children living with two parents: 69.1 percent[b]

Percentage of children living with neither parent: 4.1 percent

Source: United States Census 2000: Census of Population and Housing, www.census.gov /prod/2001pubs/statab/sec01.pdf, page 53; and www.census.gov/prod/2001pubs/statab/sec02.pdf.

[a]Advocacy groups say most of this increase is because more gay couples feel comfortable reporting themselves to the government than they did a decade ago.

[b]The two parents may or may not be biological parents.

Statistics on Vegetarians

According to Roper Poll, 1995:

Percentage of teen vegetarians who are vegan (apart from use of honey by some): 33 to 50 percent

Percentage of girls aged 13 to 17 who do not eat meat: 11 percent

Percentage of women who do not eat meat: 7 percent

According to Zogby Poll, 2000:

Percentage of Americans who never eat meat, fish, or poultry (vegetarians): 2.5 percent

Percentage of Americans who never eat meat, fish, poultry, dairy products, eggs, or honey (vegans): 0.9 percent

Percentage of Americans aged 18 to 29 who are vegetarian: 6 percent

Percentage of Americans living in large cities who are vegetarian: 5.4 percent

Sources: "How Many Vegetarians Are There?" *Vegetarian Journal* (May/June 2000): 36, or www.vrg.org/journal/vj2000may/2000maypoll.htm; "Vegetarian Resource Group Conducts Roper Poll on Eating Habits of Youths," *Vegetarian Journal* (November/December 1995) 6–7, or www.vrg.org/journal/95nov.htm#kids.

Seattle, Washington, and as a faculty member in the School of Family and Nutritional Sciences of the University of British Columbia. She is a coauthor of the Position Paper on Vegetarian Nutrition for the American Dietetic Association and Dieticians of Canada. Vesanto has been a vegetarian since the late seventies and a vegan since the early nineties. She has two grown children: a daughter, Kavyo, who was a vegetarian long before Vesanto was, and a son, Chris (Xoph), who is good at vegetarian cooking, though not fully vegetarian himself. As a result, Vesanto has hands-on experience living with, and appreciating, a family with diverse dietary preferences.

It is our sincere hope that this book will provide reassurance for your choice to raise vegetarian children and will help answer any questions you may have as you proceed. We wish you and your family abundant health, joy, and peace.

Joanne and Vesanto

Acknowledgments

Vesanto would like to express her appreciation to her daughter Kavyo for insights and feedback on growing up as a vegetarian. Vesanto also wishes to acknowledge the great joy it is to have son Xoph in her life as a friend and a wonderful human being to know. Both of them are great sources of learning and pleasure.

Joanne extends her deepest love and gratitude to her cherished husband, Michael, and the many children and families she has had the pleasure and honor to work with, learn from, and enjoy throughout her career.

Special thanks to those who provided thoughtful reviews of specific sections and gave suggestions: registered dietitians Brenda Davis, Suzanne Havala, Helen Yeung, Shefali Raja, Anita Romaniw, and Dr. Janis Joneja. We are grateful for assistance and information given by staff at Dial-a-Dietitian (Vancouver, B.C.), staff at the Vegetarian Resource Group, staff at the Allegheny County Health Department, Stephen Walsh, Cathy Carlson-Rink, and Dr. Reed Mangels, and for Dave Brousseau's excellent artwork on the Vegetarian Food Guide.

We appreciate the feedback, reviews, and invaluable insights from Martha Hunting-Menchhofer (and family Dale, Madrona, and Luia); Susan McFee (and family Chris and Evan); John Borders (and family Cindy, Mattie, David, and Jack); Michael Koo (and family Maureen and Anna); Eileen and Anna Burkholder, and Keith Barker. We also warmly acknowledge Jeff Armour Nelson and Sabrina Nelson (and family Nina, Randa, and Willie), Stan and Rhoda Sapon, and Susan Roghair for their exhaustive generosity and resourcefulness.

Our gratitude goes out to those who allowed us to use their very special recipes: chefs Ron Pickarski, Joseph Forest, and Francis Janes; John Borders; and Shirley and Al Hunting.

We loved having the enthusiastic recipe tasters: Elaine Rutherford and Lionel; Jared, Joel, Susan, and Ken Collerman; Ben and Lani Evers-Staples; Jenise and Bob Sidebotham; Pam Lucke, Don Stron, and Heather Hall; plus Andrea Welling, Nygal Brownson, and their outstanding "Ladybug Organic" food. Vesanto would also like to specially thank dear friend Bhora Derry, healer and inspiration.

Part One

Approaches to Vegetarian Living

Chapter 1

Charting the Journey: Contemporary Vegetarianism

The best way to predict the future is to invent it.

—*Alan Kay*

Raising vegetarian children is an exciting and rewarding adventure. It presents a remarkable opportunity to help construct the future we all yearn to have for ourselves and our children—a world brimming with vibrant good health, loving kindness, peace, tolerance, and compassion for all. Vegetarianism is cause to celebrate. Regardless of our backgrounds, outlooks, or beliefs, vegetarianism offers a wealth of life-affirming possibilities to everyone willing to explore its bounties.

There are many reasons why people choose to be vegetarian: ethical convictions, spiritual views, religious tenets, environmental concerns, health issues, and political or economic matters. Most vegetarians cite several motivational factors for their choice and often add new ones the longer they practice vegetarianism and the more they learn about it.

The term *vegetarian* was coined in England in 1847 and refers to the dietary exclusion of meat, fish, and fowl. This definition still stands today. It does not contain concessions for part-time or semivegetarians, near-vegetarians, or vegetarians who eat certain animals but not others. The consumption of no animal flesh—regardless of color or species—has been the determining criterion for being vegetarian since the word's inception, and these parameters remain unchanged. This, of course, does not imply that shifting toward a plant-based diet is not commendable. It certainly is! In fact, most people who eventually become vegetarians begin by moving gradually down the path until one day the designation "suddenly" rings true.

Within the accepted denotation of *vegetarian* there are tremendous possibilities. If we consider the definition as a beckoning invitation rather than a restrictive prohibition, we discover an expansive world of plant foods that can actually broaden and enrich our repertoire. This palette of vibrant colors and tastes exposes us to an awe-inspiring range of healthful foods and teaches both children and adults to appreciate varying textures and zestful flavors.

Although the fundamental meaning of *vegetarian* is succinct, there are several classifications that fit under the vegetarian umbrella:

1. *Vegan.* Vegans adhere most closely to the vegetarian ideal in that they select their foods exclusively from the plant kingdom. This means that in addition to not consuming meat of any kind, vegans do not eat dairy products, eggs, or honey. Vegans also abstain from the use of animal products in every aspect of daily living, as much as is possible and practical, and avoid animal exploitation and cruelty for any purpose. The driving force behind vegan practice is an all-encompassing philosophy that champions a dynamic respect for all life. This makes veganism not just a way of eating, as is vegetarianism, but a consistent and ethical way of living.

2. *Total Vegetarian.* The total vegetarian diet, as with the diet of vegans, is based wholly on the bounty of the plant world. Unlike vegans, however, some total vegetarians consume honey and other bee products. Total vegetarianism usually refers specifically to dietary practice, rather than denoting a lifestyle that extends, for example, to the use of cruelty-free cosmetics, household products, and clothing. There is no unifying philosophy behind total vegetarianism, and people who follow this diet often have myriad incentives.

3. *Lactovegetarian.* The prefix *lacto* in *lactovegetarian* refers to animal milk. *Lactovegetarians,* sometimes called *lactarians,* are vegetarians who include dairy products, such as cow's milk and cheese, in their diets.

4. *Ovovegetarian.* The prefix *ovo* in *ovovegetarian* refers to the ova, or eggs, that are produced by birds. Those who observe this type of vegetarianism do not eat meat or dairy products but do include hen's eggs in their diets.

5. *Ovolactovegetarian.* People who are ovolactovegetarians, also known as *ovolactarians,* are vegetarians who include both dairy products and hen's eggs in their diets.

The vegetarian population is expanding daily, and with good reason. Global outbreaks of dangerous foodborne illnesses have made us question the safety and purity of our food supply and the wisdom of choosing a meat-centered diet, or even a mostly plant-centered diet that still includes animal-derived items such as dairy products and eggs. As we become more aware of the correlation between what we eat and the risk of certain diseases—such as obesity, diabetes, high blood pressure, heart disease, atherosclerosis, digestive disorders, bowel complications, and some cancers—we rightfully have begun to dispute the soundness of approaching mealtime as if it were "business as usual." What is most sobering to learn is that although many of these deadly diseases don't manifest until adulthood, they have their roots in early childhood, and a plant-based diet is one of the best protections that parents can offer their children.

Living according to one's convictions takes courage, vision, and the willingness to think independently. When we are responsible for the health and well-being of little ones who rely on us to make wise choices that could very well affect them for the rest of their lives, our mettle is put to the test. We want our children to be vital and fit—physically, mentally, and spiritually—and this can require making tough decisions that counter the persuasive strategies of the formidable meat and dairy industries, the strong-arm tactics of the fast-food culture, pressure from dissenting family and peers, and the pleas of young ones who want to blend in with everyone else.

Understanding why we have chosen this path, recognizing the health advantages it can afford us and our families, and learning how to prepare wholesome, delicious, plant-based meals will help us remain resolute and confident in our decision. The vegetarian journey is exhilarating and illuminating and presents a lifetime of discovery, enjoyment, and personal growth. Let's venture forth and begin!

Ethics and Ideology

> The true meaning of life is to plant trees, under whose shade
> you do not expect to sit.
>
> —*Nelson Henderson*

No matter what our rationale is for being vegetarian, there is an element of ethics involved. Even if our decision has no overt ethical connection and is based solely on the notion that vegetarianism is the most natural or healthful way to eat, it still is fundamentally grounded in the pursuit of practicing what we believe to be "right" for us and our children.

Most people do not spend a lot of time thinking about what they eat—where their food comes from, how it is grown and processed, what it contains, what is involved in getting it from farm to table, how it impacts the environment, and how it will affect their physical and mental health. Surrounded by skillful marketers and effective product placement, we are unconsciously drawn into seductive, mind-numbing campaigns that jade our palates and convince us that industry propaganda is fact. On a certain level, we *want* to believe the persuasive yet lopsided rhetoric about food that permeates our culture. It is convenient to buy what is easily accessible and trust what we are told, even when it comes directly from food industry representatives, merchandisers, governing bodies, or corporations—all of which have an economic stake in perpetuating our consumption of particular products. Even if we are sufficiently informed to question our food choices, by adulthood we already are psychologically and emotionally, if not physically, hooked on the overwhelming preponderance of animal fat, other highly processed fats, sodium, and sugar that are the primary flavorings in virtually all fast foods and processed snacks. It takes determination to confront these ingrained tastes, habits, and beliefs. Being triumphant in this challenge requires no small measure of determination and principled conviction.

The majority of people who make a lasting commitment to vegetarianism do so because they feel good about this choice, not because they are fearful of meat and animal products or necessarily have an aversion to their taste. Often former meat-eaters remark that they feel healthier, have more energy, feel "lighter," "freer," "cleaner," more clearheaded, or more peaceful than they did when they ate meat, while others report no obvious or significant changes. Nevertheless, nearly all vegetarians agree their diet is humane, is inwardly liberating because it eliminates their culpability for the needless death of animals used for food, and has a favorable effect on the environment. These points reinforce the positive emotions that vegetarians report about their choice. Consequently, even if we already were in good health and don't experience appreciable or dramatic physical or emotional changes when we become vegetarian, we can take comfort in knowing that our food selections are beneficial in many ways.

This point is pivotal, especially when it comes to dietary matters that involve young people. It's hard to convince healthy children of the value of a particular eating style when our arguments are based on the premise that certain foods (including many they dislike) are good for them and others (mainly those they prefer) are not. Children can no more escape the powerful influences of the corporate food giants than can adults, and in many ways children have it even harder. High-fat fast foods, empty-calorie snacks, sugary confections, and caffeinated soft drinks have infiltrated our school systems and neighborhoods as well as our homes. Unless parents take a firm and early stand against such fat-filled products and junk foods, our children unavoidably will be snared by them. Once they become accustomed to these so-called foods, it is nearly impossible to wean young people off them. The process could be compared to seizing an addict's stash.

As with adults, the majority of children are not enticed exclusively by the nutritiousness of food. Although some may be interested in the health benefits of their menu, most young people are concerned primarily about the taste, texture, color, and overall appearance of what they eat. They also are attracted to certain food products because of advertising messages that promise status or fun. If food manufacturers key in on these essential factors and determine the specific food attributes that predominantly appeal to youngsters, they can penetrate the entire group. It is irrelevant whether companies' products are nutritionally bankrupt, unhealthful, or physically or psychologically addictive. When profit-driven promotions are aimed squarely at children, parents become disempowered. Don't be deceived; the food industry is savvy. Its toys, gifts, games, and gimmicks are an alluring public ruse. The people behind these corporate concepts know that if they can sway youngsters, they will capture an entire generation of lifelong customers.

We may observe in many children an innate sense of morality and a clear appreciation for right and wrong. Sadly, this part of their character may be suppressed as they become acculturated. On the other hand, we can witness incredible zeal among youngsters when their ethical views are solicited. Given the chance, children are eager to voice their opinions and offer advice regarding moral behavior. Young people are perhaps more passionate and sincere about these ideals than any other age group. This is heady stuff, because if we can capitalize on our children's inherent moral aptitude and charitable inclinations, rather than deconstruct or suppress them, we will provide them with a far better chance of growing into principled and compassionate adults.

This is the beauty of vegetarianism: with parental prompting, it can foster goodwill and a selfless regard for others that most young people are eager to extend. Children don't need to know all the finer points of good nutrition in order to become or remain vegetarian. If they understand the moral implications of their diet, feel good about it, and are introduced to wholesome food from the outset, their ethical perspectives and their palates will be aligned. Once they know the basics, continual adult intervention to ensure healthful and humane eating habits will be, for the most part, unnecessary.

Children have a natural affinity for animals, so we don't need to work too hard to convince them that eating their friends is inappropriate. Young people often are horrified to learn the source of their burgers and nuggets, and those who choose vegetarianism during their teen years occasionally express anger and moral outrage that they were never told the truth about where meat comes from. If children question omnivorous adults about their diets, they likely will hear the same mechanical responses and clichéd phrases that their parents' parents asserted: "Animals are raised for food, so they don't mind being killed," or "We need meat to be healthy." Even fast-food enterprises are shrewd in their attempts to foil children's innate curiosity about the origin of their food: they tell them that burgers grow on trees! Not only do we as a culture dupe our little ones, we outright lie to them. Still, most parents don't feel remorseful about this, mainly because we just don't give it much thought or consideration. Tragically, this only demonstrates how hackneyed a betrayal it has become. We have numbed ourselves to the truth about meat production so that we are incapable of frankly explaining it to our children, due in great part to our lack of awareness and our willingness—indeed, preference—to remain in the dark.

Honesty is something we owe our young ones. We cannot expect to raise truthful, responsible adults if we cannot be forthright with them when they are small.

Learning the facts about food and being genuine in what we teach our children is an obligation of positive parenting. Many adults know very little about food production and healthful nutrition. In addition, most of us are caught up in the same cultural food traps as everyone else, so we must first overcome our own skewed indoctrination, unlearn what we think we know, acknowledge our limitations, and accept that we will have to change some of our own habits, tastes, and outlooks if we wish to instill more ethical and health-promoting ones in our offspring.

Children learn by example. If we do not truly believe what we tell them, they will grasp our insincerity. Then not only will we have missed the chance to convey what we intended, we will have taught our youngsters that it is acceptable to be dishonest. Before we can be successful at raising vegetarian children in a nonvegetarian culture, we need to evaluate all of the reasons we have chosen to go down this path. If the moral concern about killing animals is even remotely part of our rationale, and if we intend to incorporate this point when we explain to our children why they are vegetarian, we need to be sure we feel secure in our stance. When children are presented with moral certainties, there isn't room for flexibility. From a child's vantage point, if killing animals for food is wrong, then it is *always* wrong. Children have difficulty grasping ethical inconsistencies. Parental ideology that comes across as wishy-washy or compromised will be seen as hypocritical. It is equally important that our behavior match the standards we expect of our children. If we preach one thing but do another, our children will feel misled and will be inclined to imitate our actions rather than our words.

In explaining that "we don't eat animals" to little ones, it isn't necessary to delve into graphic detail. Children readily can understand the idea of not hurting others, particularly when those others are our animal friends. No young child should be exposed to the gore and horrors that are the realities of animal slaughter, as this is the substance of nightmares. However, mature teens with a strong constitution and an interest in exploring this subject should be encouraged to do so. Learning about the slaughter industries and how meat is produced will affirm their own volition to be vegetarian, bolster their consciences, and equip them with a powerful incentive to maintain their harm-free diets. Parents also should make the effort to become informed. The more knowledge we have, the better prepared we will be to defend and uphold our decision and answer questions from our children (and curious friends and family members) when they arise.

We need never feel defensive or obligated to justify our choice to raise our children as vegetarians. Although our decision may be questioned, its soundness is backed by a mountain of scientific evidence. Countless times a day parents decide what is in their children's best interests and determine how to protect them from harm. In most instances, there is no one outside of ourselves to consult, so we must rely on our own inner judgment and common sense. We do our best to instill in our offspring the values and moral codes we want them to sustain, irrespective of outside opinion. A plant-centered or plant-only diet certainly falls under the realm of keeping our children healthy and invulnerable. Furthermore, vegetarianism can be a valuable catalyst for promoting integrity, awareness, and a caring heart.

From Principle to Practice

> It is good to have an end to journey toward; but it is the journey that matters in the end.
>
> —*Ursula K. LeGuin*

For many families, it is easier to dive into vegetarianism wholeheartedly than it is to take incremental steps toward their ultimate goal of a vegetarian household. On the other hand, some people feel more comfortable moving slowly and gradually. Only you can determine the momentum and approach that will work best for you and your family. Either way, there usually is an interval of adjustment, a time when cupboards, pantries, freezers, and refrigerators are cleared of nonvegetarian foods and suitable replacements are found and purchased. Nonperishable items that contain animal products can be used up by the family, or they can be donated to shelters, community kitchens, or food pantries where they will be welcome. You also will need to evaluate and revise your menu plans and recipes, and you'll probably want to purchase a few vegetarian cookbooks that suit your taste and cooking style. This way you will have a blueprint to meet the demands of your family, along with plenty of ready ideas right at your fingertips.

Raising vegetarian children frequently includes an element of anxiety along with exuberance. We may worry that our children won't get adequate nutrition or won't like the foods we prepare, and we may wonder if a vegetarian diet is going to be more costly. Let's take a look at each of these concerns individually.

Well-planned vegetarian diets are eminently appropriate for children and can offer many long-term advantages. One of the keys to raising healthy children, regardless of diet style, is to make sure they eat plenty of fresh vegetables and fruits and that high-fat, high-sugar, and high-sodium snacks and beverages are minimized or excluded. For your convenience, we have provided nutrition guidelines for all stages of childhood, including infants, children, and teens, beginning on page 119. The Total Vegetarian Food Guide on page 124, sample menus on pages 184, 207, and 217, and recipe section that begins on page 231 will help you to create shopping lists, balanced menus, and nutritious meals for all occasions to ensure your children's optimum health.

Take comfort in the fact that eating habits are learned. If bad eating habits are acquired early on, it can be more challenging to modify them later, especially if the home, school, and social environments reinforce them. However, if children learn to appreciate wholesome foods—including a wide variety of vegetables, fruits, whole grains, and legumes—when they are young, there is an excellent chance they will carry these good habits into adulthood, despite any negative outside influences. Furthermore, if their palates are accustomed to pure, fresh food, then highly processed items, meat products, and other animal-based foods will taste strange and unnatural to them.

Parental example plays a highly significant role in determining toward which foods children will gravitate. If we want to cultivate sound eating habits in our children, we must exhibit healthful practices ourselves. It is unfair and impractical to ask our children to eat foods we find repugnant, so the first step in raising vegetarian children is to take a hard look at our own habits and examine what we unwittingly may be teaching our little ones by our own behavior and food choices.

We all are concerned about the health and welfare of our children and want to provide them with the best start possible, but few of us have vast resources to spend on groceries. The most cost-efficient vegetarian foods are those that are the least processed and closest to their natural state. For instance, dried beans are less expensive than canned beans (and are equally convenient when cooked in quantity and frozen in small portions), fresh fruit in season is less expensive than frozen fruit, shelled peanuts are less expensive than peanut butter, and flour is less expensive than bread. Granted, we don't always have the time, energy, or inclination to make everything from scratch, but it helps to know what our options are if we want to maximize our food dollars. The basic vegetarian staples of vegetables, legumes (peas, beans, and lentils), grains, nuts, seeds, and fruits are among the most abundant and most economical foods available to us. It isn't necessary to rely on costly processed products for the foundation of our family's vegetarian diet. Instead, we can use those items as "condiments" to our mainstays—tasty additions that add fun and flavor to our meals—while recognizing that they are not essential fare.

If saving on your grocery bill is important to you, check out your local natural food stores. Many alternative grocery stores and an increasing number of mainstream supermarkets have bulk food sections where you can purchase the exact amount you need of an item, and at a much lower cost, because you aren't paying for unnecessary packaging. Some natural food stores and food cooperatives even offer a small discount or rebate if you bring in your own containers and reusable cloth shopping bags instead of using the plastic containers and paper bags they supply.

Natural food stores also are more inclined to offer a wider selection of organic produce and products, although some mainstream supermarkets are expanding their organic offerings as more customers demand foods that are not genetically modified or laden with pesticides. Children tend to be more sensitive than adults to potential food allergens—such as agricultural chemicals, colorants, preservatives, and other food additives—so it is vital that we take this into account when we make food purchases and determine where to shop.

If you have the space, motivation, and time, you could plant a small backyard garden and enlist the help of your children. If space is an issue, you can "container garden" easy-to-grow plants, such as tomatoes and herbs, right on your balcony or patio. You even can grow herbs in a window-box planter or start a kitchen sprout garden (see page 306). As an alternative, some urban neighborhoods have community gardens where interested families can obtain a small plot of land to grow food. Fruits and vegetables are much more exciting and palatable to young people when they have a hand in growing them, and homegrown produce is the least expensive route we can take. Another option is to join a community-sponsored agriculture program (CSA). This is an arrangement whereby a local farmer sells annual "shares" of the farm to community members who, in return for their investment, regularly receive a portion of the farm's seasonal produce. Often the food is organically grown or grown with minimal pesticides. Some farmers deliver to drop-off points in various neighborhoods, while others have pickups on location at the farm. Depending on the CSA's policies, shareholders also may be required to invest a minimum number of volunteer hours working in the fields, boxing or delivering produce, or performing other chores as needed. This is a wonderful way to teach children how food is grown, and, with a CSA, we can share this fun, productive, and bonding experience as a family, even if we are unable to have a garden of our own.

If a CSA in unavailable in your area, talk to local farmers about purchasing their produce directly or, instead, visit farmers' markets, which often have stalls in convenient urban areas and frequently offer early evening or weekend hours. Children can meet the farmers, ask questions about farming and food production, and help select the fresh foods you'll be preparing and serving during the week. This is yet another way to connect children to their food sources, involve them in the process of food selection, and get them excited about eating fresh vegetables and fruits and participating in their preparation.

Vegetarianism is a lifelong journey. When shared between parents and children, it imparts a special closeness—a deep, unifying connection that blends food, values, and spirituality. Try not to put pressure on yourself to achieve all your vegetarian goals at once. Begin where you are, and proceed as your motivation and comfort level dictate.

Changing Directions

> He who would be a great soul in the future, must be a great soul now.
>
> —*Ralph Waldo Emerson*

It would be wonderful to begin raising vegetarian children from the moment of conception, starting with the mother's choice to be vegetarian before, during, and after her pregnancy, but this isn't realistic for every situation. Often the notion to be vegetarian or raise children as vegetarians is an afterthought, one that can occur years after children are born. For example, when caregiving is intermittent or children are adopted after infancy, it may be impractical to significantly alter children's diets until their circumstances change or they are a little older.

The earlier vegetarianism is introduced, the more receptive children will be to it. This way, even though a transition period still may be anticipated, there is greater probability that it will be reasonably brief and relatively painless. Sometimes, however, the idea to switch to a vegetarian diet doesn't occur to parents until children are well past toddlerhood or even puberty and their eating habits are fairly well ingrained. In this case, what should parents do?

Eating is not merely a reflexive response to the physiological symptoms of hunger. We eat for a variety of reasons, most of which go beyond our bodily requirements for sustenance. We eat to satisfy cravings, relieve boredom, quell emotional upheavals, celebrate special occasions, be sociable, and join in camaraderie with family and friends. As adults, when we exercise our right to indulge in or avoid certain foods, we maintain control over what goes into our mouths. But how would we feel if this option were taken away from us and someone else regulated what we could and could not eat? When others impose their will on us by overriding our fundamental right to choose what goes into our bodies, we are left feeling powerless and understandably irate.

After children's eating habits and tastes have been firmly established, an abrupt alteration of the "food rules" can make young people feel every bit as angry and resentful as adults would be if the tables were turned. As parents and caregivers, we need to be sympathetic to children's emotional and social connections to food. Young people, just like adults, want to eat foods that are familiar, make them feel loved, provide a sense of comfort, taste like "home," are delicious, and are similar to the foods their friends are eating.

Still, caring about children's feelings doesn't mean we must yield to the pressure of our little ones' demands. Parents are responsible for determining what kinds of foods they want their children to eat. Our money funds the grocery bills, so we have the right to oversee how it is being spent and what is being purchased. It will not make youngsters happy to discover that their favorite meat products and junk foods no longer are permissible, but as guardians we realize that their greater welfare is at stake.

Inform children about the dietary changeover beforehand, so they do not feel caught off guard and unprepared. Be honest with them and sensitive to their concerns. Depending on their ages, they may have many questions about what they now can eat and whether they will like it. Becoming vegetarian is a chance to try new foods, experiment, and explore. If parents make it sound like an ultimatum or punishment, you can bet the children will react negatively. However, if we show genuine excitement about the switch to vegetarianism, our children will demonstrate enthusiasm, too.

Once we have made the decision to raise our children vegetarian, it makes sense that we would want to dive in headfirst. Some children will be ready to join us at once; others may balk at being expected to instantaneously transform their diets. Few of us are that adaptable, regardless of our age, so a little patience, flexibility, and empathy can go a long way in helping young people adjust and be more open to giving vegetarianism a try.

If everyone in the household is primed to launch into a vegetarian diet, we are in luck. The conversion can be reasonably quick; it may only require the time it takes us to devise meatless menu plans, restock the cupboards and refrigerator, and test out new recipes. On the other hand, if some members of the household are willing and others are not, or if no one besides us is prepared to move forward at a rapid pace, a different strategy is required. To entice the family, start off slowly. You could begin by having "vegetarian day" one or two days a week. This can be less threatening than asking children to give up many familiar items all at once. As you come upon recipes that everyone enjoys, serve them with more regularity. With repeated successes, you can gradually extend "vegetarian day" to three, four, or five times a week. Before they even are aware of how it happened, your family will be enjoying meat-free days the majority of the month, and meatless meals will no longer be an anomaly.

Using this method, you can progressively wean your family completely off animal-based foods in just a few months—maybe sooner. How rapidly your family advances toward vegetarianism will depend mainly on how amenable they were to the idea in the first place. Nevertheless, don't discount the fact that even the most stubborn people can have a change of heart once tasty recipes win them over.

An alternative approach is to serve one meal a day that is vegetarian. Breakfasts are easy to make meat free, so that might be a good place to start. If breakfast turns out to be a cinch, you could institute two meat-free meals a day, perhaps breakfast and lunch or breakfast and dinner. Another option is to have one week each month designated as "vegetarian week," or you could earmark every weekend as meat free and slowly increase the number of vegetarian days or weeks from there.

Whichever way you go about it, move forward at a pace with which you and your family are at ease. Vegetarianism is a climactic decision, a turning point, a milestone. Make this a time of joy rather than a time of anxiety. There is no "right way" to become vegetarian. Everyone's circumstances and motivations are unique, so your approach and time frame will be unlike anyone else's.

Serving new recipes, whether vegetarian or not, always is a bit worrisome because we don't know how receptive our families will be to them. As much as we dread the possibility of everyone turning up their noses and pushing away their plates, there also is the very real chance they will thoroughly enjoy and appreciate the new dishes we make. We won't be able to expose our families to unfamiliar foods and eating styles unless we occasionally risk preparing something out of the ordinary.

It's quite possible that a large number of our mainstay dishes and signature recipes already are vegetarian or close to it. Many common children's staples are naturally meat free, such as peanut butter and jelly sandwiches, tomato soup, vegetarian baked beans, or spaghetti with tomato sauce. In fact, most children's favorites that traditionally contain meat or other animal products—for instance, burgers, hot dogs, pizza, macaroni and cheese, tacos, burritos, and lasagna—can be made totally vegetarian, with no meat, dairy products, or eggs. (See the entrées on pages 308–327 in this book.) You even can find vegetarian counterparts to these and other popular foods ready-made at your supermarket or natural food store, along with vegetarian nuggets, luncheon "meats," soy yogurt, plain and flavored fortified soymilk and rice milk, dairy-free frozen desserts, animal-free jelled dessert mixes, and frozen TV–style dinners. Moreover, these foods typically are free of saturated fat, cholesterol, and animal protein; generally are lower in total fat, calories, sugar, and sodium; are higher in vitamins, minerals, and fiber; and rival their nonvegetarian cousins in taste, adaptability, and price.

Of course, purchasing a large percentage of convenience foods on a regular basis can wreak havoc on the weekly budget. Furthermore, many of the so-called natural snacks and beverages sold in alternative food stores—including chips, sodas, and cookies—often are no more health supporting than their mainstream counterparts. It usually is far less expensive and much more healthful to prepare recipes at home, where we control the ingredients, than to rely on prepared products and frozen foods. Still, if we keep a few of the more wholesome packaged items on hand, they can be a welcome boon on hectic days when time seems more valuable than money.

There are advantages and drawbacks to replacing familiar animal-based foods with similar vegetarian versions. Some children won't notice the change; they will be more concerned that the dish looks and tastes like the "original." Others may observe an unusual aroma, mouth feel, chewiness, or flavor. Whether or not they find these aspects appealing will influence how willing they will be to try other new foods. Generally, it is best to be honest with our families from the outset and let them know in advance that we have replaced a few of the ingredients in their old favorites. If they detect the switch before we alert them, they may be angry, feel deceived, and could easily become mistrustful of our cooking (and us!) in the future. At the same time, if they like the revised recipe, or even prefer it, we will have a new dish to add to our repertoire and the family will have taken a big, comfortable step in the vegetarian direction.

But what if our families don't like our vegetarian versions of their previous favorites? We each have our individual quirks when it comes to food, and children are no different from adults in this regard. All people, young and old alike, deserve to have their preferences respected. Unlike adults, however, children's tastes are in a state of perpetual flux. When they are very young, children commonly experience stubborn food jags when only one or two foods are acceptable to them. Fortunately, as children mature, so do their palates. Foods that once were detested often take on an entirely new appeal. This attitude toward food can change week to week, even day to day with children, so it can be difficult to predict when an item once considered "gross," "disgusting," or "nasty" will become the most requested dish of the house.

Give your family members time to adapt to the changes you are asking of them, and be prepared for some resistance. Demonstrating understanding, respect, and appreciation for each degree they move forward can give them the boost they (and you) may need. Bear in mind your purpose for switching the family's diet, and let the love you feel for it flavor your comments and observations as well as your food.

Encountering the Unexpected

> Even a minor event in the life of a child is an event of that child's world and thus a world event.
>
> —*Gaston Bachelard*

Although many adults may be reluctant to admit it, children have much to teach us. Young people often see the world more clearly than adults because, at least for a while, they are free of the perceptual distortions and limitations we tend to accrue as we get older and become indoctrinated into our culture. Children sense their world intensely, and they are inclined to live more deliberately and with greater awareness than most of their elders. Parents might think of their children as little sponges, absorbing everything in their midst, and to a large extent this is true. At the same time, children have minds of their own, along with opinions, impressions, ideas, and convictions that spring solely from the depths of their own spirits. Yes, some children are easily influenced and swayed, and at tender ages they are especially malleable. But this doesn't discount an ever-present inner life that is uniquely their own.

Teens, adolescents, and little ones, sometimes as young as age ten or even younger, may suddenly announce to their families, "I don't want to eat animals anymore!" or "I am a vegetarian!" Remarkably, young people frequently resolve to stop eating meat long before the notion of vegetarianism enters their parents' conscious imaginations. Although it is possible that these children hear about vegetarianism from friends, school, television, magazines, movies, or elsewhere, it also is conceivable that something in their hearts is stirred and they come to this realization of their own accord.

Children have an unshakable allegiance to their beliefs, whether these are ideals that have been taught to them or are others that have no apparent origin. During the typically unruly and often rebellious teen years, generally between ages thirteen and seventeen, young people commonly experience a period of fiery emotion. This is an age of much experimentation, of trying on various personas to see which ones fit best. There is a significant amount of "testing the waters," personal investigation, proving oneself, and seeing "how much I can get away with." Although it can drive parents bonkers, much of this falls within the realm of what is considered "normal adolescent behavior."

So when teenagers come home and make the startling declaration that they now are vegetarians, it is no wonder that many parents brush it off as "just another fad," "a phase," or "the influence of friends." We are eager to dismiss young people's independent conclusions when they conflict with our lifestyles and values—the lifestyles and values we were intent on instilling in them. Even when we know we aren't being fair to our children, it still seems easier to sweep their controversial sentiments under the rug and hope these "silly notions" will evaporate.

Young people's convictions are vitally important to them, and if we discount them they will be magnified out of proportion. Not every unanticipated or seemingly "radical" concept they take up will be fleeting. Many deep-seated principles that children hold dear will remain with them all of their lives.

Even when an ideal is short-lived, we want it to be respected by others. We are most fervent and protective of a new way of being when we first try it on for size; this is when our enthusiasm is at its peak. Normally our excitement tempers over time. The exuberance our children display when they first discover vegetarianism and adopt it as their own will wane as it becomes integrated into their daily routine. This doesn't mean that their vegetarianism is less important to them, but that they have accepted it as just one of the many attributes that make them individuals.

If your children decide on their own to become vegetarian, acknowledge their decision. Here are just a few ways you can let them know you care about them and respect their choice:

- *Reinforce your children's self-esteem by affirming their right to choose a meat-free diet.*
Nothing promotes defiance more readily than when a parent says "no" to a child. Whether your children's decision to be vegetarian is fleeting or long-lasting, your acceptance of their choice will affirm your respect for them. When children feel their ideas are heard and given thoughtful consideration, they are more willing to be open about other concerns, knowing they can trust you to listen to their views without judgment or condemnation.

- *Demonstrate your support by offering to help your children plan healthful, plant-based meals.*
If your children are the only vegetarians in the house and you do not want to make separate dishes for everyone, you will need to determine a workable mealtime strategy. Some dishes can be made by adding meat near the end of the recipe, as with spaghetti sauce. It may be possible to set aside a meat-free portion of sauce for the vegetarians and add meat to the remainder for the rest of the family. If the other dishes served during the meal are vegetarian, this may be the only adjustment necessary. Another idea is to make a protein-rich item, such as Crispy Tofu Fingers (page 315), serve a veggie "meat," or heat up a frozen or packaged entrée for the vegetarians, as long as there are enough vegetarian side dishes to supplement and round out their meal. A third option, if the children are old enough, is to have them prepare their own meal. A drawback to this, however, is that they will not be sharing the same foods as other members of the family, which can lead to feelings of isolation and rejection. Closer bonds are forged when families can have meals together and partake of the same foods.

• *Show your sincerity by teaching your children to cook vegetarian dishes, even if it means learning as you go.*

Words of encouragement are much more credible when they are backed by action. Learn how to cook vegetarian meals by reading books, watching videos, or taking cooking classes, preferably with your children. Shop together for the food you will prepare. Make cherished memories by having fun in the kitchen together and enjoying the experience of shared effort.

• *Advance your children's knowledge by purchasing age-appropriate vegetarian cookbooks or gift subscriptions to vegetarian magazines.*

Take the time to investigate the various vegetarian books and periodicals that are available (see the Resources section) and determine which kinds of recipes, information, and articles your children would most enjoy. Publications that reinforce their choice to be vegetarian are tangible offerings of love that children deeply appreciate.

• *Encourage responsibility by teaching your children about vegetarian nutrition.*

Most books on nutrition are written for adults, so the information contained in them may need to be adapted to your youngster's level of comprehension. As you explore the science of nutrition and explain it to your children, you will all learn how to keep your bodies healthy. Sound nutrition information is applicable to vegetarians and nonvegetarians alike and will benefit the entire family. (See Part Two: Nourishing Our Children, beginning on page 119.)

• *Promote independence by allowing older children to occasionally prepare meals for themselves or the whole family, when appropriate.*

Learning how to make tasty, nutritious, vegetarian meals that everyone can enjoy will boost your children's confidence and self-reliance. It also will reassure them of your faith in their abilities, as well as provide a welcome night off from cooking for the adults.

• Express your love by periodically cooking and serving vegetarian meals for the entire household.

To thoroughly understand vegetarianism, it must be given equal regard. Put out the welcome mat for your vegetarian children and invite the nonvegetarian family members to broaden their gustatory experiences by regularly serving vegetarian meals to everyone. (See the recipe section beginning on page 231.)

• Stock the refrigerator, freezer, and pantry with wholesome vegetarian foods and snacks.

Your children will be happier and healthier if they have ready access to nutritious foods they can eat with little preparation. If feasible, take the children with you when you go grocery shopping, or visit a natural food store together. Help your children learn how to select products that are nutritious as well as tasty. It will be fun and educational for them as well as for you.

• Champion your children's choice by selecting vegetarian or vegetarian-friendly restaurants.

It is frustrating for vegetarian children to be placed in the awkward position of trying to figure out if there is anything on a restaurant's menu they can eat. It also can be difficult or embarrassing for them to request a special meal or attempt to explain their requirements to the waitstaff. Instead of allowing children to feel hurt, perplexed, or left out, find a restaurant that has suitable options for everyone in the group.

• Be considerate by ensuring that vegetarian foods are plentiful for holiday meals and family gatherings.

Children want to feel a part of family celebrations and events, and food is an important unifying element. When there is very little for vegetarian children to eat, they can feel that no one cares about them or wants to include them in the festivities. Make it a point to ensure that lots of delicious vegetarian food is available no matter what the occasion, without the children having to make a special request for it.

• *Be thoughtful by not engaging in or allowing others to engage in hurtful humor or deriding comments regarding vegetarianism.* Humor is a common way to make an uncomfortable situation more bearable. As much as humorous comments can help to relieve tension for the person who initiates them, humor with a barb often does the opposite for the person at whom it is directed. Most vegetarians, especially young ones, take their dietary choice very seriously. If their vegetarianism is motivated by ethical convictions, there is little for them to laugh about regarding it. Being "different" because of their diet is hard enough for most young people to handle, and being ridiculed or having their food choices poked fun at is usually painful, not humorous. Be sensitive to your children's feelings and determine if they enjoy a little teasing or not. If you sense that joking about vegetarianism is not appreciated by them, intervene and terminate it. Let others know that humor at the expense of your children's dignity is not welcome.

When children decide to be vegetarians, it can be a wake-up call for the whole family and an extraordinary opportunity to investigate an option that you may not have considered previously. Try to stay open to your children's choice and, if you are so inclined, join them in the adventure.

Mountains and Rivers

> Spend the afternoon. You can't take it with you.
> —*Annie Dillard*

Raising vegetarian children is exciting and has many rewards, but it does require that parents be informed, supportive, adaptable, and creative. Of course, that's not much different than what is involved with raising nonvegetarian children. All parents realize that there are times when they must stand tall and hold firm like a mountain and other times when they must be as fluid as a river. What makes being a parent of vegetarian children distinctive is that vegetarianism is a special way of dealing with a physiological necessity and social activity that we and our children engage in several times a day: eating.

Our food preferences are personal and are intimately tied to our emotions. Consequently, everybody has strong opinions on the subject. We all believe we are experts when it comes to food because we all eat. Certainly, we are authorities on our *own* style of eating, but we rarely know much about other people's or even think about what fuels their choices. Most of us inherited our food inclinations from our families, and they from theirs. What we think we know about healthful eating has more to do with habit, convention, taste, familiarity, economics, marketing, and convenience than with nutrition science.

The foods we grew up with hold a special place in our emotional centers. These are what we call "comfort foods"—foods that make us feel safe, consoled, and secure. They may not be particularly nutritious, they may even be considered unhealthful, but they evoke warm memories and soothing feelings, making it difficult for us to give them up. Parting with animal-based foods that are a piece of our own childhood, heritage, culture, or ethnicity is a palpable loss, and being tempted by them can threaten our commitment to raising our children as vegetarians.

It is surprisingly easy to transform most animal-based recipes into vegetarian versions, and this is one technique that some vegetarian families employ to retain a sense of history and culture: simply stick with the old standards but make them plant based and more healthful. With this approach, vegetarian children can experience the traditional cuisine of their ancestors, with just a little tweaking, and parents can continue to enjoy adored dishes from their own childhoods. Typically, it is not the meat products in traditional and conventional foods that we miss but rather the seasonings, textures, and flavors, all of which are easily replicated.

Few consumers are aware that meat as a daily staple of the American diet is a relatively recent phenomenon. Prior to the Civil War, meat was a luxury item, and everyday consumption was limited mostly to the very rich. The slaughter of animals for food was purely a local business, primarily because the animals could not travel far without suffering serious weight loss. Cattle and hogs were driven in herds to local butchers who killed them using crude hand methods. The flesh of these dead animals could be preserved only by salting and smoking; but even in that form it could not keep long. As a result, each slaughtering center was capable of serving only a small territory. In most parts of the world, the availability of meat was unpredictable and seasonal. In North America, the average individual managed on a diet consisting chiefly of bread, homegrown potatoes, corn, and other vegetables from the garden.

It was not until the late 1800s, when the Armour clan—comprising brothers Herman Ossian (H. O.), Phillip Danforth (P. D.), Joseph, Simeon, and Andrew—engineered the first factory-style farm, "kill floor," assembly-line meatpacking facility, and refrigerated train car that the common man could afford to eat like the very wealthy. Despite unscrupulous business practices (among them the formation of the first United States monopoly, which inspired the enactment of the Sherman Antitrust Act), the Armour brothers secured a prominent position in the annals of human history: they ensured a legacy of meat consumption and dependency that has endured into the twenty-first century and has spread throughout the world.

Today, meat continues to be associated with affluence. The prevalent myth persists that to ensure good health it is essential to consume meat several times a day and, according to the dictates of convention, it must be featured front and center for holidays and celebrations. It is time to dismantle the legends surrounding meat and other animal products and denounce them as fiction. A more honest account of culinary history is that a preponderance of vegetarian dishes abound in virtually all cultures around the globe, and they have always been the principal fare for the majority of the world's populations. Among the most valuable inheritances we can bequeath our children is healthful vegetarian cuisine borne of the rich heritage of our own cultural traditions and those of many others.

With such an expansive legacy of vegetarianism worldwide, we can use international recipes for inspiration and innovation in our own kitchens. There is no formula for how vegetarian families must cook or eat, so we have a wide array of options available. Nothing is carved in stone. We can base our vegetarian menus on the standard American diet—for example, cereal, toast with peanut butter and jam, and juice for breakfast; veggie burgers with condiments on a bun and French fries with ketchup for lunch; apple for a midday snack; and spaghetti with marinara sauce, steamed broccoli, and a tossed salad for dinner—or we can explore the bounty of ethnic specialties that can make every meal every day fresh and exciting.

Evaluate your needs and the needs and preferences of your children and other family members. For ideas, look over your own heirloom recipes, peruse the shelves at your natural food store (don't miss the frozen food section, coolers, and deli counter, too!), read vegetarian cookbooks, join a vegetarian club or society, visit vegetarian restaurants, subscribe to vegetarian magazines, and gather recommendations from vegetarian friends and Web sites. Sign up for a vegetarian cooking class, perhaps with your children, partner, parent, or a friend. Input from others with more extensive experience can help you sort out your options. Nevertheless, remember that however you and your family choose to approach vegetarianism, the path you carve, the grade of the slope, and the flow of your progress always will be custom designed.

Chapter 2

The Inner Landscape: Psychological Perspectives

Although vegetarianism is associated with numerous positive aspects, it nevertheless demands the same psychological adjustment as any other shift outside the cultural norm. When we make choices that counter mainstream culture, it's not uncommon to undergo a period of emotional upheaval. For most of us, this experience is private and internal. With some people it is short-lived and negligible; for others, the feeling of not fitting in can be enduring and overwhelming. To preserve mental well-being—whether our own, our partner's, or our children's—it is sensible to learn to recognize, acknowledge, and deal effectively with the myriad emotions that can arise from "being different."

Even if we are elated about our or our children's decision, we can't ignore the fact that none of us wants to feel like an outsider, especially in our own homes. This chapter explores the multitude of ways we can provide emotional support for ourselves, our children, and our families, while nourishing relationships that foster balance and inner harmony. It also focuses on strategies of prevention, so that we can clearly identify and correct hurtful ways of interacting and avert potential problems before they take root. By molding a foundation of trust, receptivity, tolerance, and compassion, we will provide our children with the necessary tools to advance inner peace and self-acceptance.

Family Unity

> A great man is he who does not lose his child's heart.
>
> —*Mencius*

A family is more than a group of people who are blood relatives, or housemates, or people constrained to live together by law. A family consists of two or more individuals—young, old, or in between, related or not—who share many things, both tangible and intangible. Family members might occupy the same house or reside in the same neighborhood or town, but they also can live many miles apart, sometimes in other cities, states, or countries. Still, if the bonds of kinship are strong, they will remain intact despite prolonged separations or vast distances. Why do some families endure while others break apart?

The foundation of any solid relationship rests on three indispensable elements:

- Mutual respect
- Parallel trust
- Shared values

This triad is as vital to the endurance of families as it is to the steadfastness of life partners and friends. If one or more of these components is breached, a relationship—regardless of its nature—will be traumatized, sometimes irrevocably. To cultivate lifelong family alliances, we must plant and water the seeds of respect, trust, and common values when our children are very young, and continuously nourish them as children grow.

Parenthood and childhood are not balanced roles; parenting involves responsibilities for and obligations to children that they cannot reciprocate. Children can give us much joy, although it is not their duty to do so. They also can give us challenges and heartache. It is our job as guardians to provide a safe home for young ones—to protect, clothe, and feed them healthfully, as well as furnish them the tools with which they can become confident, caring, responsible adults. Loving children through the rough times, even when they seem unappreciative or antagonistic, goes with the territory. The unconditional love that parents extend to children means exactly that: love without provisos or limitations.

Parents get back from their relationships with their children (or anyone else) exactly what they put into them. If we want our children to respect us, we must offer respect to them, even when we disagree with or disapprove of their behavior or points of view. Learning how to treat our children with respect is a multifaceted task, and one that is particularly relevant to raising vegetarian children. The vitality of our family greatly affects our ability to swim against the dietary tides of our culture. Respect among family members contributes to unity and helps form a mighty network that gives rise to more assurance and resilience than any single member could summon alone. Here are just a few of the ways we can uphold family unity by manifesting respect for our children:

- *Listen.* Children wish to have their feelings heard the same as adults. Although they may not have the vocabulary to express their emotions precisely, they want their feelings to be acknowledged all the same. The events in young people's lives may not seem as complex or earth shattering as those of grownups, but their self-esteem, hopes, fears, and aspirations hinge on comparable desires and concerns. If their experiences are dismissed or trivialized or if parents are too busy to truly listen to them, children will feel demeaned. Foster respect for your children by allowing them to express their feelings to you without being rushed and without the fear of being ridiculed, put down, or judged. When they feel fully heard and understood, children are more willing to listen to what we have to say in return.

- *Cool off before speaking or acting.* Too often we say or do things we deeply regret when we are in the blaze of intense disagreement or anger. Whenever you get into a heated argument with one of your children, physically remove yourself from the room or building the moment you become aware that you are losing your temper. Do not return or resume the discussion until you have calmed down and can proceed with greater equanimity and presence of mind. If you are engaged in a fiery telephone conversation with older children, agree to hang up and speak later when you each have cooled off and are more levelheaded. Time and distance bring clarity to quarrels and charged debates. A composed demeanor allows us to gain objectivity, avoid being sidetracked by irrelevant issues or past disagreements, delve to the heart of the matter, and be an exemplary role model for our children for how to deal peacefully and responsibly with upsetting situations.

• *Find nonviolent solutions.* Never hit children or your partner under any circumstances. Hitting, slapping, spanking, punching, and other forms of corporal punishment are an endorsement of violence and promote bitterness, resentment, and mistrust. They divide rather than unite families, and their use teaches children that violence is an acceptable way to solve problems. When we use physical discipline in response to what we view as our children's misconduct or disobedience, we train them to inflict similar harm on others. Extending a child's logic on this, corporal punishment makes it permissible for children to strike back at their parents or hit other adults, their siblings, their peers, or anyone with whom they disagree. It also can incite them to trounce anyone smaller or less capable of defending himself or herself on whom they can unleash their anger or aggression, including younger or smaller children, animals in the neighborhood, or the family pet. Resorting to violence impedes our potential to patiently and creatively seek more conciliatory alternatives. Although finding diplomatic options might involve more time and effort, the process as well as the end result brings families together and cements long-lasting and mutually respectful relationships.

• *Strike a balance.* How we want our children to look, think, or act isn't always in sync with what our children want. We might be mortified or incensed by their preferences, but they undoubtedly are as adamant about them as we are about our own. Instead of knee-jerk opposition to our children's perspectives, we can stay open to considering new possibilities and differing points of view. There might be better ways to approach an issue, solve a problem, or face the world than what we have been accustomed to, but we will never know if we are unwilling to investigate beyond our comfort zones. Sometimes there are solutions that can appease both children and parents if we take the time to search for them. Compromise is a point of agreement where both parties concede something of value while simultaneously gaining something of value, too. There are many opportunities for parents to good-naturedly encourage children to comply with the adults' wishes through skillfully employing the art of compromise. This does not mean that parents should resort to manipulative or devious tactics, but rather that we provide internal space to welcome children's contrary outlooks and pursue the common points where parental hopes intersect the hopes our children have for themselves.

• *Honor choices.* Allowing children to make age-appropriate decisions nurtures independence and accountability. Young people may not always make the choices we would most prefer, but as long as what they choose is reasonable and harmless, there is no practical reason to override it. Children develop positive self-esteem and feelings of accomplishment and self-determination when they are given the freedom to make certain decisions about their lives. This not only teaches them how to be self-reliant, it demonstrates that parents respect their children's judgment. Of course, it would be foolhardy and negligent to turn over all decision-making to our children. Nevertheless, we can teach young ones how to choose wisely by giving them incremental responsibility for particular areas of their lives and by exploring the potential outcomes of these choices and the consequences that might follow.

Trust is the next element in the foundational triad that comprises sound relationships. Children instinctively trust their parents to protect them and make choices that are in their best interests. This faith holds fast unless something intervenes to damage or destroy it. When people feel deceived by those they trust, it is a herculean task to rebuild the relationship. Even if it can be repaired, it may be impossible to restore the level of trust that previously was enjoyed. The only way to safeguard the bonds of trust is never to violate them. Here are ten simple ways you can build trusting relationships with your children:

- Practice what you preach.
- Always keep your word and follow through on your promises.
- Have reasonable expectations.
- Ask only what you would ask of yourself.
- Never belittle, shame, or embarrass—publicly or privately.
- Build up rather than tear down.

- Praise often.
- Do not mock, swear, mimic, or use sarcasm.
- Use words your child understands.
- Request and invite rather than demand and push.

The following ten "Bs" are the defining qualities of trusting relationships and reveal how trust is communicated from parent to child:

- Be sincere.
- Be honest.
- Be tactful.
- Be consistent.
- Be reliable.
- Be appreciative.
- Be considerate.
- Be reasonable.
- Be kind.
- Be fair.

It is equally important for parents to model the behavior they expect of their children by exhibiting respect toward each other as well as toward other members of the family. Hurting someone a child loves—whether it is another parent, guardian, sibling, relative, friend, or animal companion—is as much a transgression of trust as any other type of betrayal, and it will produce similarly devastating results.

Trust is not one-sided, however. For trust to be engaged effectively, it must be reciprocal. Certainly the scope of responsibility for trust that is held by parents and children differ in both quantity and quality. Nevertheless, children must be held accountable for their actions and their commitments, and parents must come to trust their children, especially in their absence. Trust builds over time and should deepen and broaden as children mature. When we nurture trust in our children and teach them its value by honoring and exemplifying it in all our interactions with them and with others, children discover their role in maintaining the trust in our relationship and comprehend its significance.

Sharing similar values is the essential third and final element that constitutes sound relationships. Parents impart values to their children both overtly and subtly. Verbal instruction is one method for conveying values explicitly, but it isn't always sufficient, especially if children hear us say one thing but see us practice another. The moral principles we wish to instill in our children are imparted most effectively when children witness congruity between what we say we believe and what we actually do. Although behavioral observation is a more subtle form of learning, it holds great power. We substantially reinforce our messages when our actions reflect our verbal assertions. As a result, what we profess to our children will appear more credible and sincere.

Essentially everything we do mirrors our values, and children are very astute at picking up our cues. Although we might not usually think of eating as being an activity laden with ethical considerations, what we choose to eat or not eat in the presence of our children speaks volumes regarding our views about food, eating, and health. If we make poor choices, our little ones will notice. They will emulate our behavior more readily than they will comply with our verbal requests. By watching parents eat, children learn how to determine:

- what to eat
- when to eat
- how much to eat
- when to stop eating
- the purpose of food
- the value of food
- when food is used as a substitute for emotional gratification

What, when, and how our children see us eating shape the choices they will make about food later in life. When family members share meals and similar eating styles, the bonds of their relationship are fortified along with their food habits. Mealtime then becomes a worthy tool for developing camaraderie and familial closeness.

Many vegetarians have an ethical component to their dietary choice that includes nonviolence and respect for all life. Whether we are motivated mainly by an ideal of compassion, or whether this is one among many rationales, these ideals can give us a sense of inner peace and connection with other beings. Choosing harm-free foods is an excellent way to acquaint children with a practical means of implementing these valuable principles several times a day. Showing gratitude at mealtime for our food and all that was involved in getting it to our tables is another way we can strengthen these values.

Take advantage of the unique opportunities vegetarianism provides for informing our behavior, solidifying parent-child relationships, promoting family unity, and augmenting moral instruction regarding kindness and compassion.

Emotional Isolation

> Discovery consists in seeing what everybody else has seen and thinking what nobody else has thought.
>
> —*Albert Szent-Györgyi*

Being vegetarian and raising vegetarian children may set us apart from others who are not vegetarian. We don't serve the same foods as other families, special arrangements for meals and refreshments must be made for us when we are invited to social gatherings, we are more discriminating about the restaurants we patronize, and we must oversee the provisions that are available for our children when they attend school outings or visit nonvegetarian friends and relatives. These are not major ordeals in and of themselves, but they can contribute to making us and our children feel separated and emotionally disconnected from others.

It is critical that parents not allow their vegetarian children to become distanced from other people simply because they do not eat the same foods. It also is essential that vegetarian families immerse themselves in ordinary, everyday activities, and preserve the friendships, family relationships, and social contacts they had prior to becoming vegetarian. Although it is true that values and perspectives often shift when we adopt a vegetarian diet, the basic attributes we admired in our nonvegetarian friends prior to our changeover remain firm. If we liked certain people before we became vegetarian, chances are we will continue to like them even after we modify our diets.

Rifts in relationships commonly are caused when one party embraces an entirely new set of values or behavioral standards that aren't collectively shared. This can happen whether the impetus is religious, political, or personal in nature. If we assume that our new perspectives are right not only for us but for all with whom we come in contact, we surely will alienate everyone. Sometimes it is hard to restrain ourselves, particularly when we feel we've come upon something of great magnitude that could positively affect many others. It's tough to remember that as much as we think (or feel certain) we are right, other people are entitled to their contrary points of view, which are deserving of equal regard. Pushing our opinions on those who aren't interested, or who reject them, not only will drive away our support systems, it will leave us feeling ostracized and misunderstood.

This is all the more reason to retain our nonvegetarian colleagues, friends, and acquaintances and look for ways to relate to them that don't necessarily involve food. Hopefully, there are people we know who will generously extend themselves and make every effort to include and accommodate us and our families. Nonvegetarian friends who are especially close to us may be willing to act as advocates on our behalf, making sure the restaurants selected have vegetarian options, our children have vegetarian snacks and food when visiting them, and events and gatherings provide at least a few appropriate vegetarian choices. Occasionally, good friends may offer to step into the role of educator and inform other parents of our families' vegetarian requirements. They might even be willing to host an all-vegetarian holiday meal or get-together. These are rare individuals, but they do exist and are worth their weight in gold, even though they don't share our vegetarian leanings.

Without fail, there always will be a few associates and acquaintances who misconstrue vegetarianism and interpret our choice as a judgment levied against their own lifestyle and approach to childrearing. Often people who lash out at vegetarians, brush off our requests, or make arbitrary or senseless statements do so because they feel defensive. They are concerned that their way of eating is under siege. Vegetarians seldom have to say much about their diets in order to elicit spirited responses—just the mention of the word *vegetarian* incites a commotion. This actually has little, if anything, to do with the reality of vegetarianism or the particular vegetarian in people's midst. Rather, it is a demonstration of how attached people are to their habitual diets.

Don't take it personally. When people respond harshly to our vegetarianism, they merely are deflecting their own misplaced feelings about the foods they eat and serve to their children. No matter what we might say to certain people, they still will misunderstand or be unwilling to respect our choices. As much as this kind of reaction would make anyone feel deserted by those whom they thought were their friends, we must bear in mind that these individuals are not intentionally pushing us away; instead, they are objecting to the ideals they believe we represent. They are fearful of the path we have elected for ourselves and our loved ones and are apprehensive about what this might mean in terms of their own food choices for themselves and their families. Realize also that some relationships—especially those that are unsupportive, stifling, or destructive—simply may not be worth hanging on to. Because of its unsettling impact on others, vegetarianism can propel us to make an honest appraisal of our relationships and identify and weed out those that may have been choking us all along.

Deflecting Guilt

> The trouble with most of us is that we know too much that ain't so.
>
> —*Mark Twain*

When people make choices that are out of the mainstream, they and those around them have a tendency to blame these choices for any problems that come their way. Nonvegetarian friends, relatives, teachers, and even uninformed health care professionals often rush to judgment about a vegetarian child's diet at the first indication of an earache, the sniffles, or any other common childhood nuisance. It is easy for parents to get sucked into loaded scenarios because we are sensitive to being out of step with the majority. Though other aspects of our children's lives are "normal," we might fear that an unconventional diet will make them easy targets. Take heart that instead we may be giving our children and their friends a chance to realize that differences are commonplace and acceptable.

> Today's mighty oak is just yesterday's nut that stood its ground.
>
> —*Anonymous*

If you're vulnerable to feelings of guilt when your ideas differ from those of others, take back your power. Often the people with whom we interact are poorly informed about nutrition or are clinging to outdated notions about diet and health. They may have the most noble of intentions at heart—our children's well-being. They might speak with an air of authority, and they truly might have great faith in what they profess, even though it is inaccurate. Still, when vegetarian parents are interrogated by those unfamiliar with vegetarianism, it is easy to stir up the emotion of guilt. We secretly ponder the question: Are we harming our children by raising them as vegetarians?

One of the biggest worries facing parents is that we will make a poor choice for our children that will mar them for life. What is ironic about meat-eaters who criticize vegetarians is that most vegetarians, especially vegetarian parents, give their diets and the diets of their children considerable thought—significantly more than most nonvegetarians, who typically do not question cultural assumptions about food.

When we survey the typical American city or town, we see a profusion of fast-food restaurants that cater to children and families, each offering a menu saturated with fat-filled, cholesterol-rich animal products—foods that are a scourge on our health and major contributors to the top killers in the West: obesity, heart disease, stroke, and cancer. Open any newspaper or turn on any television station and we'll find advertisements for these establishments that are designed to bait children and lure parents with the promise of clever "prizes" and "gifts," fun food, and cheap prices. What we don't see are promotions that plug the healthfulness, minimal fat grams, and low caloric content of fast foods, because if such efforts were honest, they ultimately would be counterproductive. If we were openly and routinely exposed to the truth about these foods, we would be appalled and repelled. Yet greasy burgers, deep-fried foods, fatty shakes, sugary sodas, and oily pizzas are what most kids in North America are eating. These foods form the foundation of the average omnivorous child's diet, a fact that is untrue for most vegetarian children.

In addition to advertisements, parents obtain nutritional information from schools, physicians, and governmental bodies that are profoundly influenced by the commanding lobbying efforts of the dairy and beef councils, organizations that were formed for the purpose of swaying public opinion about and encouraging greater consumption of their products. In fact, the National Livestock and Meat Board (NLMB) was formed in 1922 by the Armour brothers and fellow meatpackers. The NLMB (whose name was changed to the National Cattlemen's Beef Association in 1997) was protected under the auspices of the American Medical Association, which was employed by the NLMB to review certain of the meatpackers' practices. This was the precursor to today's long-standing economic interests and commercial alliances between the nation's meat and dairy monopolies and U.S. governmental agencies, including the United States Department of Agriculture (USDA), meat inspectors, those who set food policy, and those who develop allegedly objective models for our purported nutritional needs.

Indeed, the well-known but now retired Basic Four Food Groups model, although developed at the prestigious, well-respected Harvard University Department of Nutrition in 1955, was by and large funded by animal-agriculture industries and their related trade councils and was in large part a campaign to market animal products in all their various forms. This cemented the relationship between animal agribusiness and local and national government officials and politicians, who today are lobbied aggressively and frequently are offered sizable campaign contributions, future employment, or board positions in exchange for industry support. It is not uncommon that executives for meat and dairy concerns take on dual roles, becoming government consultants, and that government officials become paid advisers or stockholders in the animal foods industry.

In the 1940s and 1950s, the National Dairy Council produced its *Guide to Good Eating*, which was used in elementary schools throughout the United States to teach children the basics of nutrition. With the Basic Four Food Groups as its anchor, this guide portrayed dairy products as one of the four "essentials" of a balanced diet. Unquestionably, this concept was a thinly veiled marketing coup for the dairy industry, a business that has reaped enormous financial benefit (not to mention federal subsidies) from its prominent position and government endorsement.

In 1980, the USDA and Health and Human Services (HHS) jointly published the first Dietary Guidelines for Americans. The intent was to provide advice to all age groups regarding food choices that promote health and reduce risk for disease. Although the USDA's primary purpose has been to support American agriculture, it now is giving nutritional advice to the American public via the Dietary Guidelines, despite a clear conflict of interest.

Critics take the position that the Dietary Guidelines, the cornerstone of federal nutrition policy, should have but one role: not to market commodities, but to recommend the best possible diet for Americans. The scientific evidence condemning animal products has been mounting. Instead of pointing directly at meat and other animal products as the sole providers of dietary cholesterol and primary sources of saturated fats, the voice of the Dietary Guidelines is seen as muted and lagging far behind our knowledge of the origins of chronic disease.

In 1996, an alliance of food industry and health organizations, in concert with the federal government, was formed to develop materials that would help consumers better understand and make practical use of the Dietary Guidelines. The group, called the Dietary Guidelines Alliance, includes the USDA, HHS, the American Dietetic Association, the Food Marketing Institute, the International Food Information Council, the National Dairy Council, the National Food Processors Association, the National

Cattlemen's Beef Association, the Produce Marketing Association, the Sugar Association, the Wheat Foods Council, and the National Pork Producers Council. So much for nutritional objectivity. When we recognize and challenge who and what are behind the dietary paradigms we are taught to accept as valid and true, we will be better equipped to deflect the guilt that well-intentioned but misinformed others project in our direction.

Sibling Interaction

> Laughter is the shortest distance between two people.
> —*Victor Borge*

The number of children in a household dramatically alters the dynamic interplay among family members and can extend the support systems available to children both inside and outside the home. When siblings have vegetarianism in common, are reasonably close in age, and get along well (at least most of the time!), they can lean on or bail out each other in sticky situations that involve food or teasing about their diets from peers. Even if your children have no other vegetarian friends, they can feel comforted and less alone if they have vegetarian siblings on whom they can depend.

Of course, there is no guarantee that vegetarian sisters and brothers will be chums or even like each other simply because they live under the same roof and have similar diets. Sometimes siblings are pals when they are younger and drift apart when they mature, or they are distant when they are children but become good buddies when they grow older. All families and groups of children have their own special styles of interacting. Their relationship is put to the test, however, when one child is vegetarian and the others are not.

Parents play an important role in sibling relationships. Children often pattern their behavior toward their siblings based on how their parents treat the children in the family and also how the parents treat each other. In some families, good-natured kidding is commonplace and accepted in the playful manner in which it is delivered. Through this interaction, children learn to differentiate between innocent ribbing for fun and strident wisecracks that are intended to sting. In many homes, light, harmless humor has the effect of drawing family members closer. It helps us discover how to laugh at ourselves and take ourselves less seriously.

Nevertheless, some children are distressed by teasing, especially when it involves something of great value or significance to them. When a child is the only vegetarian in the family, and the choice was founded on personal or ethical beliefs, or is a necessity due to health reasons, it is no laughing matter. Regardless of how gentle and friendly the banter may seem to the person delivering it, the recipient may view it as inconsiderate, hard-hearted, and offensive. There is nothing quite as painful as feeling that your family has turned against you, yet this is exactly how it may be perceived by children who are teased about dietary decisions that are very meaningful to them.

Sometimes parents are oblivious to how siblings behave toward each other, whether at or away from the dining table. When parents aren't looking, brothers and sisters are apt to make faces at each other while they are eating, stick out their tongues, or chew with their mouths open. This kind of juvenile humor is prevalent even in the most conservative households and generally is harmless. Sibling interaction around food becomes problematic, however, when the behavior is mean-spirited or when quips are derisive. Putting animal products on the vegetarian child's plate, discussing how tasty the animal-based foods are, making animal sounds (such as "moo" or "oink oink"), passing a platter of meat in front of the child or asking the child to pass the platter, or waving a forkful of meat under the child's nose and saying "Mmmmm" borders on cruel, and parents should intervene and put a stop to it.

It is emotionally hard on children to feel as though they don't belong, and when they are the only vegetarian in the family, those feelings can grow or magnify. However, if family members embrace the solitary vegetarian by including vegetarian food at meals and family events, prohibiting taunting by siblings, and remaining sensitive to the child's feelings and needs, the family will be a source of comfort and peace—something all of us value, vegetarian or not.

Team Building

> Within your own house dwells the treasure of joy; so why do you go begging from door to door?
>
> —*Sufi saying*

Strong families can weather the fiercest storms. No matter how cold the world may seem, if we have a haven of warm people to whom we can return, we will feel safe and protected. Home isn't just a box where we reside; it is a place where love flourishes and support awaits. It is the people who transform a house into a home, and the people within those walls who create a family, whether or not they are blood relatives.

In the security of our homes, we can test our values and ideas and receive critical but caring feedback before we unveil ourselves to strangers. We can comfortably experiment in our kitchens as we investigate alternative ways of eating, with no one standing over the stove judging what we are doing. In the confines of our homes, we are unafraid to try on new personas and examine how they fit and feel. Home provides a sanctuary, a place where we can face our fears and explore new frontiers without worrying what others might think about us.

Children need the refuge of home as much as adults. For children, the world outside the home can sometimes seem overwhelming, even scary. They need a place where they can feel shielded and validated, where there is a circle of arms ready to catch them if they should fall. Of course, this is what all people crave, regardless of age.

Home and family form the team that is behind us, cheering us on, patting us on the back, and helping us find our way even when we are apart or go astray. They constitute our safety net. Without the anchor of home and family, children feel lost. The home team becomes especially important when we choose a path for our children that is out of the ordinary, such as vegetarianism. Although it is not difficult to be vegetarian, others who are not vegetarian sometimes can make it trying for us. No matter what the cause, when we face a tough day, it is a relief to have the sanctuary of a sympathetic family to whom we can come home.

When children are young, the fibers of this safety net—home and family—are intricately woven. The tighter the weave, the more secure, durable, and resilient the net and the more easily children will rebound when they stumble. Families that are vegetarian before children are born, or those that become vegetarian shortly thereafter, have an inherent opportunity to provide an embracing support system for vegetarian children. For youngsters who grow up in a vegetarian home, vegetarianism will be the norm; it is the rest of the culture that will seem out of step. If children feel good about being vegetarian, coming home to a vegetarian family can be quite comforting. The key to building positive esteem about our dietary choice is to have a home team that makes sure the entire family, especially the youngsters, know precisely why the family doesn't eat animals. When we understand and are contented with our dietary choice, we will be equipped to face any odds that challenge it.

Helping children appreciate why they and their family are vegetarian gives them confidence in who they are and faith in their values.

But what approach should parents take if they choose vegetarianism for the family when the children are school-age or older, or if they adopt or foster-parent non-vegetarian teens or preteens, or if they provide intermittent care and the alternate home or homes are not vegetarian? When parental values change midstream, it is perplexing how to best introduce them to the family. If habits and tastes are well entrenched, young people are bound to be resistant. If they don't want to comply with these changes, what choices will they be given? Is it realistic to assume that children can have a diet and perhaps other values that clash with the rest of the family and continue to be included on the team?

Despite any differences between children and parents in terms of diet or opinion, children still need to feel a part of the fold and know that they are loved and valued for who they are as individuals. The same is true for children who choose to be vegetarian while their parents do not. We can set the standards for the behavior we expect of our children, but we cannot force them to comply with our eating style or with the rationale that inspires it. We also should never insist that children eat foods they find repugnant or demand that they eat meat when they have made a reasoned decision not to do so. This reverts to the issue of respect, for both our children's points of view and the ownership of their own bodies.

Nonvegetarian parents whose children choose to be vegetarian may need to explore their own dietary choices so they can discuss them intelligently with their children. For most people who eat a meat-based diet, this will be a peculiar undertaking, because many meat-eaters never question the validity of eating meat. Meat consumption is a widely unchallenged cultural assumption, so examining it means delving into uncharted territory. Meat-eaters may be quick to defend their right to eat meat without consciously unraveling how this habit and their attitudes about it became ingrained in the first place. They may feel their vegetarian children threaten their own dietary preferences, which might be something they'd rather not probe too deeply. Even if parents are not meat-eaters, it still would be helpful to gain clarity about why other people eat meat (even if most meat-eaters don't clearly understand this themselves) in order to better explain this prevalent phenomenon to their vegetarian children.

It is crucial to avoid showing favoritism toward or snubbing those children who follow or veer away from their parents' eating style. Surely we might feel closer to those who eat as we do, but all our children, vegetarian or not, need to know they are loved equally, irrespective of what they do or do not eat. In two-parent households, it can seem natural for both parents to engage in a conversation with children about their eating choices. If a child decides to become vegetarian even though both parents eat meat, a three-way dialogue will be imbalanced. It is not unusual or unreasonable for children in this situation to feel their parents are ganging up against them. Vegetarian children commonly believe their meat-eating parents will attempt to coerce them into eating meat, and all too often their fears are confirmed.

Being a member of a family doesn't necessitate that everyone practice an identical diet. Nevertheless, sharing the same way of eating can draw families closer, especially if their eating choice is founded on similar values. Regardless of whether you or your children are vegetarians, you each are deserving of respect. Although commonalities can fashion a tighter bond, what we and our children choose to eat should have no bearing on the fundamental building blocks of a sound and loving relationship.

Uprisings

> The function of freedom is to free somebody else.
> —*Toni Morrison*

One of the most disconcerting moments for parents is the discovery that their children do not see the world as they do, that their perspectives and priorities are contrary to theirs, and that what is important to them may be insignificant to their children or vice versa. Choosing vegetarianism for ourselves and our families can be an uplifting, life-affirming milestone for us, one that we hope our young ones will wholeheartedly embrace and pass on to their children and their children's children. But with such high expectations can come deep disappointments. How will we respond to our school-age children or teenagers if they refuse to follow our new direction? What will we do if children who were raised vegetarian from birth decide to jump ship when they are a bit older? Where will we draw the line if our children or their friends want to bring meat into our homes?

Just as it is important for nonvegetarian parents to respect a young person's choice to become vegetarian, we must also recognize older children's autonomy to decide the opposite. Even if we feel strongly that eating animal products will be detrimental to their health or that eating meat is a violation of our moral code, do we have the right to impose our belief system on children who are mature enough to rationally make such determinations for themselves?

When children think their parents will react harshly to their choices or activities, they learn to lie about them. It is a sad state of affairs when young people sneak meat or other animal products behind their vegetarian parents' backs because they are afraid of a stern tongue lashing or worse. Most children don't want to let down their parents, so they master the art of deception in order to participate in diversions of which their parents normally would disapprove. When kids can't trust their parents to treat them with respect and honor their responsible choices, even though they may disagree with them, then both lose. A breach of trust, even if transgressed by only one side, affects both parties equally. If kids can't trust their parents, parents soon will discover that they can't trust their kids. Thus begins the breakdown of the parent-child relationship, because two of the primary ingredients for strong familial ties—mutual respect and parallel trust—will have been violated.

Despite our reservations and displeasure, if we want to keep the channels of communication flowing freely with our children, we must accept that not every choice they make will be agreeable. Most of us prefer that our children feel free to discuss their choices with us, even if their choice isn't ours. Otherwise we may encourage dishonesty because our children fear us. The only way to create and maintain an open verbal exchange is to establish a comfortable, nonjudgmental environment in which children feel safe regardless of what they reveal.

Reprimanding older children for desiring or indulging in foods that are "off-limits" only will serve to make them angry and resentful toward both the "food laws" and the "food police" who attempt to enforce them. While it is logical and appropriate for parents to monitor young children's food choices, we lose some of that control as they grow up and become more independent. We cannot (and should not) insert ourselves into every area of their lives, so we may not always be certain what our children are or aren't eating.

At some point we must come to trust that when given the opportunity, our children will make the right choices for themselves, even if they aren't the choices we feel are best for them. As parents, we only can lay the foundation. If it is solid, there is a good chance that even if our children stray from what we have taught them, they eventually will return to it. This is the primary reason that parents ought to explain to children at an early age precisely why vegetarianism is so important to them and why it is the path they hope their children will follow for a lifetime.

If you have established a vegetarian household and the older children—whether they are your biological offspring, stepchildren, foster children, or older adoptees—do not want to go along with the program, there may not be a lot you can do to compel them. Pressuring children in these predicaments will only stir up resistance and provoke defiance. Because parents and guardians pay for their children's food, it makes sense that they should have authority over how their dollars are spent. However, if children are accustomed to eating meat, a sudden, drastic, and obligatory shift to vegetarianism isn't fair. Vegetarian parents and nonvegetarian children need to figure out a compromise for what will work best given their unique living arrangements, financial situation, relationship history, eating habits, and health needs. Only you can determine what is suitable and practical given the circumstances and requirements of your children and other family members.

Vegetarians may be in a quandary when asked to sponsor a meat meal, whether for children, parents, friends, or strangers. If parents do not want meat to be cooked, served, or eaten in their homes, they definitely have the right to insist that the youngsters in the house comply with their requests. On the other hand, mature children who do not want to be vegetarian should have the option of eating meat when they are away from home. When nonvegetarian children go out to restaurants with their vegetarian families, it is up to the parents to determine whether they are comfortable paying for a meat-based meal or having meat consumed in their presence. Since nonvegetarian diets include peanut butter sandwiches, bean burritos, and pasta with marinara sauce, it's a simple matter for a meat-eater to share some plant-based meals.

Some vegetarian parents do not mind if meat is prepared in their kitchens, or even if the pots and pans they use to cook their vegetarian dishes also are used to cook meat. Others, however, do. Some parents will go out of their way to fix two different meals—one for the vegetarians and one for the meat-eaters. Or they might ask or allow the meat-eaters to prepare a meat dish for themselves. If the nonvegetarian children are old enough, parents might invite them to join them shopping so the children can select the meat they want and the parents do not have to be involved with handling it. Those parents who are opposed to buying meat but do not mind if it is prepared and eaten in the home might ask their nonvegetarian children to use their own money (from allowances or after-school jobs) to pay for it. The same deal could be arranged for eating at restaurants.

The essential considerations to keep in mind as you determine the food parameters for your family are your children's emotional and bodily health, your ethical stance, and finding a solution that does not involve putting either in jeopardy. It can be harmful to use food as punishment or reward. Restricting children's nutritional intake can be devastating to both their physical and psychological health and never is recommended for any reason. Conversely, rewarding children for good behavior with food can trigger an aberrant emotional response whereby children learn to use their favorite foods as a replacement for love or as a salve for unhappiness, potentially leading to obesity, eating disorders, and other health and psychological problems.

It is important that when a food, such as meat, is not permitted in the home, that parents do not use it as a "treat" away from home or as a recompense for "good behavior." Conversely, no foods should be forced upon children. If young people detest particular foods or have made a reasoned or ethical choice to avoid certain ones, as in the case of vegetarianism, their preferences deserve to be respected. Even though children legally are minors, live under our roofs, and are financially dependent on us, their bodies remain their own domain. To constrain children to eat what they vehemently do not want to is a violation of their basic rights as individuals and an abuse of parental power.

Chapter 3

The Beat of a Different Drummer: Family, Friends, and Culture

If our choice to be vegetarian affected just our immediate family, wouldn't life be a piece of cake? After all, which foods we put in our mouths and offer our family members is—or at least ought to be—a personal decision. Still, because we are social beings and do not exist in a vacuum, we can't escape the involvement—and occasional intrusion—of others.

Family, friends, schoolmates, and colleagues may pressure us to conform or grumble that we are "being difficult." Teachers and other parents may not understand or respect our children's diet and its associated lifestyle choices. Interim caregivers may be unaware of what is and isn't appropriate for vegetarian youngsters. Social functions, birthday parties, holiday celebrations, visits with friends and relatives, and even going out to restaurants may develop into perplexing hurdles. Indeed, it can be challenging enough to figure out the basics of vegetarianism for ourselves and our families, let alone explain our decision to others.

This chapter will help you weather some of the sticky predicaments vegetarians occasionally encounter. It will support you in your choices, coach you in the fundamentals of vegetarianism, assist in alleviating the anxiety that can occur when relationships are strained by splintered perspectives, inform you about animal ingredients commonly found in prepared foods, present sage advice for a multitude of circumstances, and provide safety-net strategies you can turn to whenever the need arises.

Preparing ourselves and our children for almost any social situation will help us face the world together with confidence. If we learn to anticipate and plan for the unexpected, life as a vegetarian *can* be a cinch.

Being Different

> It isn't that they can't see the solution. It is that they can't see the problem.
>
> —G. K. Chesterton

In the most fundamental ways, people are the same: we each need food, clothing, and shelter; we crave love and respect; and we want to be safe, happy, healthy, and fulfilled. People who are parents want the best for their children. Regardless of superficial differences, parents everywhere have this in common. In fact, our similarities to people from other countries, cultures, races, ethnicities, and religions—or even those with contrary political views and perspectives on life—far outweigh our distinctions. At the same time, we all are unique. Even identical twins have dissimilar opinions, feelings, aspirations, and experiences.

Many aspects of our lives can make us feel "out of step" with or disconnected from the majority. At times we may feel "left out" because of concerns about our appearance, handicaps, beliefs, or habits. We may be self-conscious or embarrassed about our physical disabilities, skin color, hair, height, weight, family, clothing, car, income, occupation, or even the house or neighborhood where we reside. Many of these matters we cannot alter, regardless of how hard we try or how much we wish that they were different. It seems that the best way to cope with those aspects of ourselves and our lives that we dislike (or think others dislike) and cannot change is to employ tolerance and acceptance. The same is true, of course, for characteristics we find distasteful in others. There is a very real possibility that our feelings about what is offensive stem from our own prejudices and constricted points of view rather than having any basis in fact. To put it another way, what we consider to be irritating or "an issue" just may be a figment of our own narrow attitudes, and if we broadened our perspectives and opened our hearts, the "problem," as we see it, might very well disappear.

It is valuable to investigate our prejudices toward others if we want to better understand how others could have prejudices toward us. Few of us consider ourselves "peculiar," "weird," or "eccentric," though we may jokingly take on these labels. When we are among those of like body, mind, or outlook, we feel "normal" and "natural," and we fit in with everybody else. It's only when we get into "mixed company" that our so-called differences become apparent, unsettling, and potentially problematic—if not for us, then for those who are unlike us. Naturally, those who are unlike us tend to hassle us the most about being ourselves.

In other words, we all are alike, while at the same time we all are unique. What distinguishes us from each other generally is not an impediment unless we or someone else turns it into one. Even so, we have choices about how to respond to such interpretations. Fortunately, we never are obliged to accept someone's negative perspective of us as accurate.

When contemplating conceiving a child, our idiosyncrasies, physical anomalies, or even whether or not we are considered attractive, rarely are afforded much, if any, consideration. Granted, there are some genetic factors that should give us pause when weighing the choice to be biological parents. For instance, knowing with near certainty that a child would inherit a horribly disabling, disfiguring, or deadly condition should make responsible adults think twice before having children. However, is it warranted to ban the procreation of certain people simply because particular physical traits or beliefs they might possess and pass on to their children could result in prejudicial attitudes toward them? If we believed this to be true, none of us would be permitted to have children, since no one fits a cookie-cutter equivalent of "perfection." Besides, whose idea of "perfection" would be taken into consideration to make these decisions: the majority public's, the government's, politicians', teachers', social workers', the medical profession's, judges', the clergy's? As a culture, we treasure variety and diversity, and to suggest that one group should be more highly valued and has the right to procreate because its members harmonize with a random ideal, while another should be prevented from having children because it is not in conformity, would be an affront to our most fundamental concept of freedom.

There are those who would suggest that it is unfair and selfish of parents to raise their children as vegetarians because it would immediately put these children at a disadvantage by virtue of being in a minority, even if no other distinguishing characteristics are taken into account. This is ludicrous! To submit that it is irresponsible to raise children with a healthful, ethical diet solely because it could present a few hurdles in a nonvegetarian society is preposterous. We are not a homogeneous culture, and we should not be expected or encouraged to aspire to the convention of the majority merely because it might be the easiest path to follow. If we extend this type of illogical thinking, we easily could say that people who are extremely short or tall, have red hair, are left-handed, or are atheists should not have children because, being in the minority, our society might have a bias against them and life could be a bit more challenging for their offspring than for others without such social "handicaps."

Vegetarianism is only one attribute that will make our children stand out from the rest. Because the combination of each child's personality and gifts are unmatched, there will be many qualities, both notable and minor, that will set each child apart from his or her peers. We and they should no more be embarrassed about being vegetarian or requesting special food than parents and children with religious-based dietary restrictions, particular health-related needs, or any other distinctions that warrant special acknowledgment and accommodation. Furthermore, being "different" does not imply inadequacy, incompetence, or inferiority. It takes courage to keep our own pace, step to the music we hear, and stand up for what we believe is right, true, and best for ourselves and our loved ones. Vegetarianism is a noble choice about which we and our children have every reason to feel proud.

Dealing with Relatives

> I realized either I was crazy or the world was crazy; and I
> picked on the world. And of course I was right.
>
> —*Jack Kerouac*

Even after we reach adulthood, marry, and have our own homes and families, our parents and other relatives may still treat us as though we have not yet grown up and are incapable of making mature and responsible decisions. As senior family members, they may feel they have the "right" or even the "obligation" to express their views on child rearing and family life and point out what we are doing "wrong." If we select a path for our family that significantly veers away from the manner in which we were raised, our relatives may interpret our move as an affront to their parenting abilities or their effectiveness as role models. In some families, it is presumed that their power structure, mode of interaction, and way of managing children are the only paradigms that are acceptable. Any deviation from these patterns can wreak havoc among the generations or, at the very least, could easily be misunderstood.

Like everything else, families change; that's just a basic fact. If all goes well, they improve as they keep pace with the times and the unfolding saga of the culture that surrounds them. Often it is hard for elders to appreciate the evolution that younger generations experience, and fresh approaches to parenting may be confusing or hard for them to accept. It also could be that the older generations truly believe that their way is the one and only "right" way—after all, it was good enough when their parents raised them and when they raised us, and everyone turned out just fine, right? Jesting aside, the reality is that they might sincerely be concerned that how we have chosen to raise our families is, to their mind, risky and unsound.

If your parents, grandparents, and other relatives are supportive of your choice to raise your children vegetarian, consider yourself fortunate; not all families are similarly blessed. If your parents or other relatives are vegetarian, you are even luckier. For the rest of us, family dealings that revolve around vegetarianism can be extremely trying, particularly when parents or other significant family members "push our buttons" or attempt to instill fear or guilt about our decision. At the heart of their reactions are good intentions—they want the best for our children the same as we do—but their concerns and the expression of them can be painful, even when we realize they are misinformed or misdirected.

Extended family members frequently need reassurance that raising children as vegetarians is safe and healthful. Consequently, we may need to teach our families about the basics of vegetarian nutrition and point out plant-based sources of common nutrients they suspect are lacking in our children's diets. (See Chapter 6.) Sometimes, however, the most heartfelt efforts on our part will not make a dent in stubborn attitudes, and there may be nothing we can do to convince our parents, grandparents, aunts, and uncles that "this vegetarianism" is sensible and nutritionally prudent. It may be necessary simply to agree to disagree and walk gingerly around the topic in the future. Nevertheless, with reinforcement from well-respected health professionals (found in books, newspapers, journal articles, public lectures, and other media), grandparents and extended family members often eventually come to understand our position on vegetarianism, respect it, and, on not-too-rare occasions, explore or even adopt it for themselves.

Perhaps the most vital issue regarding family members who are unsupportive of our resolve to be and raise our children as vegetarians is, at the minimum, that they respect our choice, regardless of whether they oppose or disapprove of it. Respect in this case involves refraining from criticizing our decision, especially in front of our children; honoring our food guidelines when they have charge of our children in our absence; and purchasing gifts of food for our children that are consistent with the vegetarian parameters we have set.

It is customary for grandparents to want to indulge their grandchildren and humor them with homemade or store-bought goodies and treats. Sometimes it's a bid to win their love, but mostly grandparents (and aunts and uncles) just consider it their privilege to spoil the little ones. In these instances, it may be difficult to explain our position and have our relatives actually hear us. They may interpret our restrictions as an attempt to waylay their joys of grandparenting, or they might think we are being mean or cruel because we are "depriving" our offspring of many of the pleasurable foods typically associated with childhood. They might attempt manipulative tactics, making comments such as, "It was good enough for you when you were growing up," or "You always used to like _____ when you were little; why shouldn't your children have the same pleasures?" or "One little bite won't hurt." Try to see these maneuvers for what they are—caring gestures of concern—and look for the hidden kernel of love that motivates them, while acknowledging that these statements also can be irritating and even insulting.

Trouble can brew vigorously, however, when grandparents and other family members sneak "forbidden foods" to our children behind our backs. This undermines our role as parents, sets a precedent for future behavior, and is deceptive and unfair to both us and our children. Furthermore, children develop tenacious food preferences and habits when they are young, and although we don't want them clamoring for items that don't fit into our food parameters, we'll have an uphill battle once they have tried them. With repeated exposure, such as at Grandma's house, a brouhaha is bound to follow, along with an inquisition over why certain foods are acceptable to eat elsewhere but not at home. This can lead parents down a slippery slope of hypocrisy, which children detect like radar. If we don't want to go down this path, we must put a stop to it at the first sign that relatives are attempting to compromise our parental authority around food issues.

As hard as it may be to assert ourselves about child rearing matters with our own parents, know that they will recover. In time, they either will meet our requests or together we can plan gatherings that don't involve food. When relatives realize that despite our love for them we mean business and might even suspend their visits with our children, or at least put an end to unsupervised visits if we cannot have faith in them, they will be more compliant. Rarely do loving relationships necessitate this type of harsh intervention, as it can be distressing for everyone involved, especially the little ones. Nevertheless, if family members resolutely refuse to honor our children's vegetarianism, it may be our only remaining option.

It is crucial that both they and our children know that lying about food is never acceptable. When relatives give our children "off-limits" foods and then encourage them to lie to us about what they've eaten in an effort to prevent an argument, they commit a deep, inexcusable breach of our relationship and shatter the trust that binds it.

Always provide appropriate foods, snacks, and treats anytime your children visit their relatives. Make sure that relatives' pantries are stocked in advance or pack provisions the day of the visit. It is unreasonable to expect extended family members to know which foods to buy or keep on hand, so if we eliminate the guesswork, it will make it easier for them to adhere to our wishes. In addition, we will have the comfort of knowing our children will be properly nourished with the familiar vegetarian foods we endorse and they like. Remember to include a few special items—treats you don't necessarily give your children every day, such as nondairy frozen desserts, carob-coated raisins, or whole-grain cookies—with each visit, as this will help grandparents dote on their grandkids without worry. After all, pampering the little ones is among the greatest delights of grandparenting, and food is a natural point of indulgence.

If you are not vegetarian but your children have chosen to be, the same general approach applies for extended family interactions as with the nuclear family (see Chapter 2, "Team Building," page 38). Don't recruit relatives to tempt your children with nonvegetarian food, even if you would prefer that they eat meat. This will cause a serious rift between you and your children, as well as drive an unnecessary wedge between your children and their relatives. If your relatives strive of their own accord to give your vegetarian children meat, intervene at once and explain to them why this is completely unacceptable. If children are mature enough to make choices about their diet, it is essential that these choices be respected by both their parents and other family members. Young children may be unable to adequately express themselves if relatives pressure them about food, so be alert for clues that your kids feel uncomfortable visiting certain relatives and eating at their homes. Let your children know that you always are in their corner and that they can talk to you openly, safely, and confidentially about any concerns they may have, whether or not they are food related. Loving and accepting our children unconditionally reinforces a trusting relationship, even if our diets and outlooks about food, or life in general for that matter, differ.

Teaching Teacher

> One learns through the heart, not the eyes or the intellect.
> —*Mark Twain*

Unless there is a reason for people to know about vegetarianism—for instance, if they are vegetarian themselves; have a vegetarian partner, friend, or family member; or have studied vegetarian nutrition—they most likely will know very little about it. Therefore, when our children are under adult supervision away from home, it is our responsibility to become vegetarian educators and not presume that others understand what being vegetarian means or entails. This is especially critical when children are in situations where they are in the minority or may be the only vegetarian in the group, as with a school setting, athletic team, youth group, or dance troupe. If there is no support system available on which they can rely, such as vegetarian friends or siblings, vegetarian children can feel segregated and left out. When feelings of isolation proliferate, they can have a negative impact on a child's confidence, self-esteem, academic performance, and general happiness.

Teachers play a pivotal role in ensuring that vegetarian children are comfortable in the school environment, but it is up to parents to inform them of how they can best be of assistance. It isn't necessary for teachers, teachers' aides, the school principal, or the nurse to know the "whys" behind our or our children's vegetarianism.

Focusing on ideology can get in the way of the practical needs of our kids and detract from the more significant day-to-day concerns confronting them. On the other hand, if a teacher or other staff member reveals a desire to understand our (or our children's) reasons for being vegetarian, then by all means we should seize the opportunity to explain and perhaps also offer to provide literature on vegetarian ethics, health benefits, and nutrition.

Nevertheless, in the school setting, gaining respect for our children's vegetarianism and guaranteeing their needs are met are paramount, regardless of how the staff or other students may feel about it. Without a doubt, it will be easier to deal with a teacher who demonstrates curiosity and concern, but even an educator who shows no personal interest in vegetarianism still can follow our instructions and be vigilant on our children's behalf. Here are some simple requests we can present to teachers:

- Shield vegetarian children from teasing, ridicule, or bullying due to their vegetarianism (as for any other reason).
- Supply vegetarian alternatives for all students whenever meals, snacks, or treats are provided for the class.
- Avoid embarrassing vegetarian children by drawing attention to their vegetarianism.
- Abstain from pitying or patronizing vegetarian children because they do not eat the same foods as the rest of the class.
- Realize that vegetarian children do not celebrate personal, national, or religious holidays by eating animal products. Therefore, stories, events, or activities that directly or indirectly encourage meat consumption are inappropriate for them.
- Inform teachers' aides, substitute teachers, and guest instructors in advance about the special dietary requirements of the vegetarian students in your custody and acquaint them with these guidelines.
- The needs of vegetarian children are no less notable and consequential than cultural, ethnic, or religious distinctions, or dietary restrictions associated with religious prohibitions or food allergies, and they deserve similar regard.

Whenever possible, send vegetarian treats with kid appeal to your children's teachers and ask them to share with the whole class. This is a particularly good idea around holidays or other celebrations when nonvegetarian foods are in abundance. When all students can partake of the same food, no one feels "singled out" or is reluctantly put in the spotlight. In addition, delicious vegetarian fare is a marvelous way to introduce others to vegetarianism and tastefully illustrate how enjoyable this healthful food can be.

Depending on the school, the teacher, and our children's ages and willingness to assert themselves, our ongoing involvement may be essential, but it will be primary when the subject of our children's vegetarianism is first broached. Teachers may not appreciate the importance of maintaining and accommodating our children's diets or understand how to help them "fit in" rather than "stand out." They may habitually or absentmindedly overlook what is and isn't acceptable for our children, or they might forget to advise their aides or substitute teachers about it. Unless our young ones are old enough and ably confident to speak up for themselves, an occasional reminder or intervention may be vital to our children's success at vegetarianism and their comfort at school.

Interim Caregivers

> Man is not the creature of circumstances. Circumstances are the creatures of men.
>
> —*Benjamin Disraeli*

Some parents feel strongly that they should be the sole caregivers for their preschool children. Others believe that raising children is a family or community affair. Still others are comfortable sending their young tots to day care centers or, if they can afford it, having a nanny tend to their little ones from infancy onward. No matter how we feel about it, sooner or later someone else will be in charge of watching over our precious children for brief or extended periods, be it Grandma, a teacher, a neighbor, or a baby-sitter. We can save ourselves needless anxiety by accepting the inevitable and planning ahead.

The strategies we use with interim caregivers outside the home can be the same ones we would use with schoolteachers. Likewise, food matters can be handled in a fashion similar to the school setting. One of the chief contrasts between public schools and other arrangements is that with interim caregivers, parents have more direct input regarding appropriate activities for their children and more explicit control over their food options. This is particularly true when the supervision is for hire, as with a child care center, nanny, or baby-sitter. Because these are independent contractors, they essentially are parents' paid employees. Therefore, we have the final say in the care we expect for our children while they are in their custody. If we do not approve of their methods or choices, we have the option to terminate their services and enroll our children in another program or hire a different nanny or sitter.

If, however, the caregiver is an unpaid neighbor or relative, and we cannot afford to compensate a professional or someone who is not a friend or family member, we could be placed in an awkward predicament. It always is more difficult to express complaints to volunteers who are giving of themselves freely out of the goodness of their hearts. Still, as parents it is our responsibility to oversee our children's care and nutrition. If one or both are not up to our standards, it is our obligation to intercede and outline our expectations. Usually, close friends, family members, and neighbors do not go against our wishes intentionally; they simply may not be clear about what we want and need for our children, or they may need support in providing suitable foods.

When a caregiver comes to our home, the terms can vary considerably. At home we have the greatest command over the food and care our children receive, much more so than in a school environment or with an outside caregiver. If we are fortunate to have a home-based business or home office and are accessible during the hours the caregiver is around, we personally can oversee the handling of food and activities and can make ourselves available to address concerns whenever they crop up. For most of us, however, sitters usually will be in our homes while we are out, making it difficult for us to monitor exactly how they are tending to our children. In the home environment, the parameters basically are in place regarding which foods, snacks, beverages, toys, music, and entertainments are available. We know what is there and as long as the caregiver doesn't bring anything into the house that we disapprove of, it will be relatively simple to establish the protocol we want her or him to observe.

With both in-home and outside-the-home interim caregivers, it is helpful to put our specifications on paper so they and we have a printed copy of what we are asking of them, and we each can refer to it any time a question arises. Here are a few suggestions for food-related and other issues that might be included on your guideline sheet:

- Acceptable foods, snacks, and beverages
- Suitable and unsuitable restaurants
- Appropriate and inappropriate toys, games, and activities
- Approved and off-limits television programs, movies, videos, music, computer games, and Web sites
- Unacceptable language and slang words
- Allowable and prohibited forms of discipline

For outside-the-home caregivers, we need to determine whether we or they are responsible for supplying the food and beverages, which one of us will cover food costs, and how we will manage the arrangements. If they will be preparing meals on occasion, it is a good idea to provide quick and easy recipes that we are certain our children will eat. It also is important to stipulate which foods and ingredients are and aren't vegetarian, as nonvegetarian caregivers might presume something is acceptable when it is not. Ask caregivers to alert you in advance about any day trips or outings they have planned so you can offer to provide extra provisions, if necessary, or make informed decisions about your children's participation. The ethics that inspire our dietary choice also may apply to other aspects of our lifestyle. For example, we may prefer that our children go to the water slide or a ball game rather than a rodeo, zoo, or circus. Therefore, we may wish to help plan special activities.

For in-home caregivers, we also need to point out what is unacceptable to bring into our houses in the form of food, drink, toys, videos, reading materials, or games; where appropriate foods are stored and how to prepare them; and what time meals and snacks should be served. Of course, these guidelines are in addition to any standard rules we might have about nannies or sitters entertaining guests while they are on duty, using the telephone or computer, transporting our children to activities, taking them to restaurants or the movies, carrying out bath and bedtime rituals, and so forth. While providing all these directions may seem daunting, a simple written communication can be shared in a caring and friendly way.

Even if we wish we could single-handedly take care of our children twenty-four hours a day, seven days a week, the occasional or even more frequent use of an interim caregiver can be a welcome relief for both parents and children. Spending time with other adults is not only fun for our youngsters; it can be interesting and educational, too. For parents, having time off from the role of parenting is relaxing and restorative. It also can help us gain new perspectives on parenting and see our little ones in a warm, fresh light when we return.

Eating In, Eating Out

> Everybody, soon or late, sits down to a banquet of consequences.
> —*Robert Louis Stevenson*

Eating In

Whether we prefer to cook at home from scratch, use prepared and packaged convenience foods, or eat out at restaurants, vegetarian families are faced with a few minor hurdles. How vigilant we need to be will be based on the type of vegetarian we are: vegan, total vegetarian, ovo, lacto, or ovolacto. Because vegans choose foods solely from the plant kingdom and avoid all animal products—including dairy, eggs, and honey—vegans need to be aware of a few more animal derivatives than do ovo-, lacto-, or ovolactovegetarians. However, if an item is vegan, other types of vegetarians can rest assured that it is suitable for consumption.

It is advantageous to get into the habit of reading food labels so we can identify ingredients that typically are animal derived. Once we are able to recognize "hidden" animal products, we can make intelligent choices about whether or not we want to eat foods that contain them or serve such foods to our families. Here are some of the more common but often overlooked animal-derived ingredients, their customary sources, their function in processed foods, and where they most frequently are used. Read the package label or contact the manufacturer directly if you have questions about a specific product or ingredient source.

Albumen and Albumin

Source: the principal protein in egg white (albumen), though also present in animal milk, animal blood or tissue, and plant tissues and fluids

Function: to bind ingredients

Commonly found in: pastries, baked goods, soups, stews, and meat analogs

Carmine and Cochineal

Source: the dried and ground bodies of female beetles

Function: to color food

Commonly found in: juices, beverages, confections, fruit fillings, puddings, yogurt, ice cream, candies, and baked goods

Casein

Source: the principal protein in animal milk

Function: to whiten, bind, or fluff

Commonly found in: cereals, breads, cheese analogs, ice cream, fruit sherbets, nondairy whipped toppings, coffee whiteners, egg substitutes, and a wide variety of other foods

Gelatin

Source: animal protein derived from cows or pigs

Function: to thicken or gel

Commonly found in: puddings, yogurt, marshmallows, sour cream, frozen desserts, cheese spreads, and the capsules of pills and supplements

Lard

Source: fat from around the internal organs of pigs

Function: to add flavor and enhance texture

Commonly found in: refried beans, chewing gum, baked goods, processed foods (also used in soaps)

Lipase

Source: enzymes usually derived from pigs or cows, though can be from fungus

Function: to break down fats

Commonly found in: cheese and cheese products, cream, margarine, ice cream

Oleic Acid

Source: components of fat from pigs or cows

Function: to flavor or bind ingredients

Commonly found in: baked goods, beverages, ice cream, confections

Palmitic Acid

Source: most is from fat of pigs or cows; some is from soy

Function: to emulsify

Commonly found in: butter, baked goods, cheese flavoring

Pancreatin and Pancreatic Extract

Source: enzymes derived from pigs or cows

Function: to facilitate digestion

Commonly found in: digestive aids

Pepsin

Source: enzymes derived from pigs or cows

Function: to break down proteins

Commonly found in: cheese and cheese products and digestive aids

Rennet

Source: a mixture containing rennin; the lining membrane of the stomachs of unweaned animals, principally young calves

Function: to curdle milk

Commonly found in: cheese and junkets

Rennin

Source: an enzyme principally derived from the mucous membrane of the stomachs of young calves

Function: to coagulate milk

Commonly found in: cheese and junkets

Royal Jelly

Source: a substance produced by the glands of bees

Function: to fortify with B vitamins, minerals, and amino acids

Commonly found in: nutritional supplements

Tallow

Source: fat from sheep or cows

Function: to moisturize, lighten, or fluff

Commonly found in: baked goods, cake mixes, shortening, and cooking oil

Whey

Source: the watery liquid that remains after most of the fat and more valuable proteins have been removed from animal milk

Function: to add protein and improve texture

Commonly found in: baked goods, ice cream, dry mixes, sports supplements, and many processed foods

An easy way to dodge animal products and eliminate the need to read labels is to center the family's diet around whole plant foods—that is, foods that are minimally processed: fresh or frozen vegetables; dried or canned legumes (peas, beans, and lentils); whole or lightly refined grains; fresh and dried fruits; and nuts, seeds, and nut and seed butters. This also will curtail the potential hazards our children might experience from ingesting preservatives, food colorants, and other food additives that many parents prefer they don't have. Look for organically grown produce and products, as this is the most effective means to reduce our families' exposure to agricultural chemicals and avoid genetically modified organisms.

If you keep convenience foods on hand, seek out those that have undergone the least processing and only contain ingredients that are familiar and pronounceable. A lengthy list of chemicals or multisyllabic words is a good indication that an item has been highly processed and overly refined and may not be something we want to give to our families.

It isn't necessary to shop in a natural food store, although most likely we will find the widest selection of whole, unprocessed, organic foods there. Fortunately, many mainstream supermarkets have natural foods sections and small to large offerings of organic produce. Another alternative is to shop online. A number of organic food merchants ship both fresh produce and pantry staples, such as dried beans, grains, pasta, condiments, and more, overnight (to prevent spoilage), direct to your home or office (see the Resources section, page 349).

When we cook with and use the least processed foods, not only are we bypassing substances we don't want our families to ingest, we are saving money, too. Processing, refining, and packaging foods are costly, even though the end product has reduced value in terms of nutrition. Furthermore, it isn't necessary to rely heavily on meat analogs, soy cheese, and other vegetarian specialty items, which often contribute significantly to an inflated grocery bill. Certainly these foods are a boon when schedules are hectic, tots and teens are ravenous or impatient, or we're too pooped to cook, but it is best if the more costly items are used occasionally rather than depended on as everyday fare.

Here is an inventory of pantry staples that you can use to stock your kitchen, along with a roster of possibilities from which you can select. This list is not all-inclusive, so you may want to add to it or pick and choose from what is in season and available in your area. Relying on these basic foods for the majority of your family's diet will safeguard their health as well as your bank account. Whenever anyone suggests that vegetarian food is boring, just let them have a peek at this list!

Fresh Vegetables

Alfalfa sprouts	Butter lettuce	Escarole
Artichokes	Cabbage	Fennel
Arugula	Carrots	Frisée
Asparagus	Cauliflower	Garlic
Avocado	Celery	Kale
Beans, green	Chard	Leaf lettuce
Beans, wax	Collard greens	Leeks
Beets	Corn	Mesclun (mix of
Bell peppers	Cucumbers	baby lettuces)
Bok choy	Dandelion greens	Mushrooms
Broccoli	Eggplant	Mustard greens
Brussels sprouts	Endive	Okra

Fresh Vegetables (continued)

Onions

Peppers

Potatoes

Radicchio

Radishes

Romaine

Rutabagas

Scallions

Snow peas

Spinach

Squash, summer

Squash, winter

Sugar snap peas

Sweet potatoes

Swiss chard

Tomatoes

Turnip greens

Turnips

Watercress

Yams

Fresh and Dried Fruit

Apples

Apricots

Bananas

Blackberries

Blueberries

Cherimoyas

Cherries

Cranberries

Currants

Dates

Figs

Grapefruit

Grapes

Kiwis

Lemons

Limes

Mangoes

Melon

Nectarines

Oranges

Papaya

Passion fruit

Peaches

Pears

Persimmons

Pineapples

Plantains

Plums

Pomegranates

Prunes

Raisins

Rhubarb

Strawberries

Tangelos

Tangerines

Whole Grains

Amaranth

Barley

Buckwheat

Bulgur

Corn

Kamut

Millet

Oats

Pasta (whole wheat, wheat, spelt, rice, quinoa, corn)

Polenta

Quinoa

Rice (arborio, basmati, brown, jasmine, wild)

Rye

Spelt

Teff

Triticale

Wheat

Legumes (Canned and Dried)

Adzuki beans
Anasazi beans
Appaloosa beans
Black beans
Black-eyed peas
Brown beans
Calypso beans
Cannellini beans
Chickpeas (garbanzo beans)
Chili beans
Cranberry beans
Fava beans
Great Northern beans
Green peas
Green split peas
Kidney beans
Lentils (brown, green, red, French)
Lima beans
Mung beans
Navy beans
Pinto beans
Red beans
Soybeans
Sprouts
Yellow split peas

Nuts and Seeds (Raw)

Alfalfa seeds (for sprouting)
Almonds
Brazil nuts
Cashews
Chestnuts
Flaxseeds
Hazelnuts
Hickory nuts
Macadamia nuts
Pecans
Pine nuts (pignolias)
Pistachios
Pumpkin seeds
Sesame seeds
Sunflower seeds
Walnuts

Spices and Fresh or Dried Herbs

Allspice
Basil
Bay leaf
Capers
Caraway seeds
Cardamom
Cayenne
Chili powder
Cilantro
Cinnamon
Coriander
Cumin
Curry powder
Dill weed
Fennel seeds
Fenugreek
Garlic
Ginger
Marjoram
Mint
Mustard powder
Mustard seeds
Nutmeg
Onion
Oregano
Paprika
Parsley
Peppercorns
Rosemary
Saffron
Sage
Star anise
Tarragon
Thyme
Turmeric

Additional Pantry Staples and Condiments

Note: Although many of these products are not essential, they will add fun, flavor, and variety to your family's diet. Several, such as fortified soymilk and flaxseed oil, will be mainstays; others can contribute to a higher grocery bill, so select them with care.

Beverages
Fruit juice, unsweetened (fresh, frozen, bottled, or packaged)
Herbal teas
Milks, fortified (soy or grain)
Vegetable juices

Fruit Products, Prepared
Apple butter
Applesauce
Fruit (frozen or canned in juice)
Fruit leather, unsweetened

Legumes, Prepared
Bean dips
Beans, canned
Hummus
Refried beans (canned)
Tempeh
Tofu (plain or seasoned)

Nut and Seed Butters
Almond butter
Cashew butter
Peanut butter
Soynut butter
Sunflower seed butter
Tahini

Fats and Oils
Canola oil, organic
Flaxseed oil, organic

Fats and Oils (continued)

Nut oils (hazelnut, walnut)

Olive oil, virgin

Safflower oil

Sesame oil, toasted

Sunflower oil, high oleic

Vegetable oil spray, nonstick

Seasonings, Condiments, and More

Bragg's Liquid Aminos

Broth, vegetable (powder, cubes, or canned)

Cheese, vegan (dairy free, soy)

Egg-free mayonnaise

Garlic puree

Ginger puree

Ketchup

Lemon juice, frozen

Miso (fermented bean paste)

Mustard, prepared (yellow, brown, Dijon)

Nutritional yeast (Red Star Vegetarian Support Formula T6635+)

Pepper, ground

Pickles

Salsa

Salt

Sauce, bottled (barbecue, teriyaki, sweet and sour)

Sauerkraut

Sea vegetables (hijiki, nori, wakame, agar)

Tamari (naturally brewed soy sauce)

Vinegar (balsamic, cider, rice, wine)

Yogurt, vegan (dairy free, soy)

Whole-Grain Products

Bagels

Bread

Cereal (dry)

Whole-Grain Products (continued)

Cornmeal

Crackers

Flour (whole wheat, barley, rye, buckwheat, spelt, rice, etc.)

Pita bread

Popcorn

Porridge blends

Pretzels

Rice cakes

Tortillas (flour, corn)

Sweeteners

Agave nectar

Barley malt

Blackstrap molasses

Jams and preserves

Maple syrup, pure

Rice syrup

Sugar (unbleached, dried cane juice)

Miscellaneous

Baking chocolate squares (dairy free, semisweet, and unsweetened)

Cocoa or carob powder (dairy free and unsweetened)

Meat analogs (veggie burgers, wieners, slices, "ground round," or sausages)

Soup (canned, boxed, or instant)

Tomatoes, canned

Tomato paste

Tomato sauce

Vegetables, frozen

When shopping in natural food stores, select items primarily from these five whole-food categories:

✓ Vegetables

✓ Fruits

✓ Whole grains
✓ Legumes
✓ Nuts, seeds, and their butters

Look for variety in foods and select vibrantly colored produce so you can plan meals that are both healthful and appetizing. Sidestep the snack food aisle, as these items tend to be as unhealthful and devoid of nutrition as comparable products found in ordinary supermarkets. Furthermore, those sold in natural food stores generally cost a lot more.

The cardinal rule for reining in the family food tab is to seek the greatest nutritional value for the least expensive price. One way this can be accomplished is by organizing a food buying club with other vegetarian families, so the group can purchase foods in bulk at a discount. Another route is to buy as much as possible from the bulk food section at your local retail food cooperative or natural food store. Contrary to popular myth, vegetarianism can be an extremely frugal way to feed a family, especially if an emphasis is placed on fresh, whole, unprocessed foods. Although cooking from scratch may require a bit more planning and time in the kitchen than serving prepared convenience foods, the health, nutrition, appeal, versatility, and financial benefits to families are unquestionably worth it. And once you get the hang of it, most homemade meals come together very quickly.

Eating Out

Eating out as a vegetarian family comes with another set of small challenges. Fortunately, many restaurants these days are familiar with vegetarianism or at least have a vague understanding of what it means. Some are well versed in the various kinds of vegetarianism and immediately can grasp our needs. Nevertheless, to prevent any confusion or mistakes with our orders, it is important to detail exactly what we do and do not want in our food. Depending on the establishment, the waitstaff may or may not be knowledgeable about how dishes are prepared, so we will need to know what questions to ask. Here are a few that might work for your situation:

- Is there chicken broth in the rice?
- Is there beef stock in the soup (or marinara sauce)?
- Is there butter on the potatoes (or vegetables)?
- Is there lard in the refried beans (or tortillas)?

- Are there eggs in the pasta?
- Is there gelatin (or cheese) in the salad dressing?
- Are the French fries cooked in pure vegetable oil or in the same oil in which animal products are fried?
- Are there egg products in the veggie burgers and are they cooked on the same griddle as the hamburgers?
- Are there eggs, butter, milk, or cheese in (or on) the bread, rolls, buns, or pizza crust?
- Is there fish sauce (or chicken broth) in the stir-fried vegetables?
- Is there pork (or eggs) in the spring rolls?

When taking part in a planned event at a nonvegetarian restaurant, it makes life a lot easier if you phone ahead and determine which menu items are suitable for you and your family. Chefs often are pleased to do something special when they have a little advance notice.

Many family-style and chain restaurants do not make all their food (or sometimes any of it) on the premises. It is not uncommon for bread, sauces, dressings, pasta, cakes, pies, and other items to be made elsewhere and delivered, so it can be difficult if not impossible for waitstaff to determine all the ingredients in the items the restaurant serves. When in doubt, it is smart to either do without or go elsewhere.

When eating out, some vegetarians prefer to carry a printed card with them that details the foods they want to avoid. They then can simply hand the card to the waitstaff and skirt any lengthy or embarrassing discussions. A sample card might read:

I am a vegetarian and do not eat the following:

- meat, fish, or fowl (including lard and chicken or beef broth)
- eggs
- dairy products (including butter, cheese, yogurt, milk, and cream)
- gelatin
- honey

Are there any dishes on your standard menu that do not contain these ingredients and, if not, can the chef prepare something special that would be suitable?

You can tailor the wording and the food and ingredients list to your own requirements. For many waitstaff and chefs, having something in writing makes it easier for them to remember what to look for or leave out of a dish.

Ethnic restaurants frequently have a fair selection of traditional vegetarian dishes, so they normally are a good choice, especially if you have adventuresome youngsters. The following are just a few of the possibilities you might want to investigate in your area: Ethiopian, Middle Eastern, South Indian, North Indian, Greek, Italian, Mexican, Chinese, Japanese, and Thai.

Of course, other than home, the safest place for vegetarians to eat is at a vegan or vegetarian restaurant. Generally these establishments are well acquainted with the needs of all types of vegetarians, so it should be painless to get a meal there that suits your family's specific needs. It's a positive sign that more and more vegetarian eateries are springing up, and all sizes and kinds of restaurants are beginning to realize that they must cater to the vegetarian population if they want to continue to grow their businesses.

Celebrations and Holidays

Joy is not in things; it is in us.

—*Charles Wagner*

Most of us look forward to celebrations, those few days in the year when we come together with friends and family to commemorate a special occasion. Birthdays, national or religious holidays, weddings, anniversaries, graduations, and reunions are considered happy events or milestones in our lives that are worthy of the extraordinary. Food tends to be a central feature of such festivities. People enjoy gathering in the kitchen or around the buffet or dinner table to talk, nibble, and refill their plates and glasses. Sharing food and drink inspires camaraderie and conviviality. Memories are forged at these times and their potency continues to influence young people long after they leave home and start families of their own.

Although food can be an impetus for sharing and bonding, it also can be a source of contention, creating a barrier between family members and friends when they cannot agree or respect each other's choices. This can be especially tough to deal with when ethics and health issues are drawn into the fray. No one likes to be publicly challenged about their parenting skills, even when they are confident they are doing right by their children. Arguments over food pit family members against each other and easily can get out of hand and become divisive. Discussions about food are best held long before the gathering takes place so preparations can be made for vegetarians (and others with special dietary needs) who will be attending, and hostile or conflicting views can be aired in private. Talking about the health hazards or moral sedation of meat eating while Grandpa or Uncle Bill is gorging himself is embarrassing and unfair to everyone present. Likewise, it is discourteous and insensitive for anyone to incite a debate with a vegetarian parent or child during what is intended to be a joyful occasion, and it is especially thoughtless if other children are present.

Customarily, feasts for holidays and celebrations are not overly compatible with vegetarianism, so they may not be how we wish to observe events with our families. Some vegetarian parents do not want to expose their children to the site of an animal's carcass as the emblem and focal point of a holiday or want the image of relatives picking at its bones to be seared into their children's minds. If we want our little ones to remain sensitive to the pain and suffering of all life and to acknowledge that the word *meat* is merely a euphemism for an animal's flesh, then we might want to consider starting alternative customs where there is no likelihood of this occurring.

Often, nonvegetarian family members balk at the idea of a meat-free celebration or holiday meal. They may have the idea that a festive event must always include particular foods or a roasted whole animal or carveable animal parts. It can be hard for them to adapt to the prospect of altering traditions they may have followed since childhood, practices that their parents, grandparents, and even great-grandparents might have ritualized. In a way, such a change could feel like a betrayal to their ancestors and a disloyalty to the precious memories of their own childhoods. They might think the rest of the family and our children are being "deprived" if no meat is served. They also might associate meat with affluence, as this has been its role historically. With this belief intact, family members may regard a feast without animal products as "shabby," "cheap," "mediocre," and "shameful." They may be embarrassed to invite friends or colleagues to such a gathering lest it be viewed as chintzy and they as miserly. Therefore, as much as we need our nonvegetarian loved ones to be mindful of our wishes, we also must be considerate of theirs and concede the emotional attachments they have to the foods and customs that steer their behavior and beliefs.

When we cannot see eye-to-eye on food at family get-togethers and the issue has become a topic of conflict, it is time to contemplate some options. If we cannot tolerate a celebration replete with meat and animal products, and our push for a totally vegetarian feast is squelched or ignored, we have no choice but to fashion an alternative. Here are a few suggestions:

- Go to the get-together with enough vegetarian dishes for you, your partner, and children to have a complete and satisfying meal, but tote along sufficient extra food so the nonvegetarians can sample what you brought.
- Invite family and friends to a strictly vegetarian banquet at your home, and let them know you'll be providing *all* the food.
- Suggest going out to a vegetarian restaurant.
- Resolve to visit *after* the meal.
- Plan gatherings that don't involve food.
- Create events centered around activities (a skating party, a walk through country lanes, or a forest hike), followed by vegetarian snacks and beverages.

Some families are open to change and are very willing to explore new ways. Others may be fearful of or angry toward anyone who wants to tinker with their time-honored traditions. If senior family members are not familiar with vegetarianism, they may hold stereotypes and myths about what we eat. They might believe that vegetarian food is bland, tasteless, hard to digest, paltry, boring, and certainly not satisfying or elegant enough for a party. They may be under the false impression that vegetarians subsist on a meager diet of granola and "rabbit food," such as carrots, celery, and lettuce—hardly festive fare. Hence, it might prove worthwhile to introduce wary family members and other doubting Thomases to hearty or gourmet vegetarian foods that will surprise and delight them. A simple vegetarian dinner party, buffet, luncheon, brunch, or similar affair could easily win over skeptics if the food is delicious and impressive. What is served doesn't need to be fancy or complex as long as it is appetizing and tastefully presented. The item most likely to bring a smile of understanding is a good vegetarian signature dish that knocks their socks off.

For vegetarian families who long for a Norman Rockwellesque holiday table, there are plenty of pure vegetarian choices from which to select. A seitan or lentil roast, tofu "turkey," or luscious winter squash (recipe on page 331) can be stuffed, "carved," and served with a delectable gravy (recipe on page 332) and a wreath of delicious greens (recipe on page 327). All of these make a spectacular centerpiece, too. Traditional side dishes, breads, salads, and desserts are easily made totally vegetarian with just a few minor substitutions. Consequently, no one needs to miss out on his or her favorite specialties, because the fun, flavor, variety, and merriment are equally plentiful and accessible at a meal without meat.

Of course, the Normal Rockwell fantasy of the perfect holiday table is not the only approach we can take. Although it might seem strange to those raised with a more conservative outlook, it is possible to devise an exquisite vegetarian repast that in no way resembles traditional holiday fare. This is where creativity and imagination converge to spark fresh ways to observe life's happy moments while establishing modern customs that match our ethics and style and that we are proud to pass on to our children.

Events such as family picnics, ball games, and reunions that typically include an outdoor barbecue still can be enjoyed by vegetarians. With the ease and convenience of veggie burgers and veggie dogs, vegetarian baked beans, kabobs (recipe on page 318), and even vegan mayonnaise for potato and pasta salad, no vegetarian family needs to go without the food and fixings that are picnic standards.

Birthdays can present a few obstacles, too, but none that cannot easily be overcome. When children are younger, it is important to communicate with other parents to ensure that when our children visit their homes or are invited to birthday parties and other celebrations that vegetarian food and snacks are available for them. We may teach receptive parents about vegetarianism and its significance to us and our children so that they understand which foods are and are not appropriate. If they are interested, we might distribute vegetarian recipes that have been successful in our own homes for their families to enjoy. If they are not especially supportive, we can pack a lunch or snack for our little ones, or we might suggest ideas for simple, common, vegetarian foods (such as peanut butter and jelly sandwiches, pasta with tomato sauce, cheeseless pizza, hummus with pita bread, or vegetables with dip) that parents can prepare so that their children and ours can share the same foods when they visit. For birthday parties, we can offer to supply our children with vegetarian items (such as vegan cake and nondairy frozen desserts) with plenty to share so that no one feels left out and no other parents need to take responsibility for providing something special for our children. Another possibility is to make vegetarian snacks for all the children and bring them to the party so everyone can partake of at least a few of the same foods.

It always is considerate to remind parents ahead of time about our children's needs and to let them know about any foods we will be bringing to their party. This way they can make preparations for serving the additional items and can adjust the menu, if necessary. We also can ask about what they will be providing, as oftentimes birthday parties revolve around a special theme that incorporates the food. We might want to explore ideas with them so that the foods we send along are compatible with what they have planned.

The more open, honest, and direct we are about our children's diet and the accommodations they require, the more likely it is that other parents and our own extended families will be willing to meet us partway. It might take patience and perseverance, but with time and tolerance we can take satisfaction and pride in the knowledge that our children are being respected and provided for when they are in the company of others, and that they can be happy, comfortable, and welcome in any social setting.

Chapter 4

Returning Home: Nourishing Spirit

Once we and our children feel secure in our own vegetarianism, it's time to figure out how the pieces fit together within the puzzle of our unique family system. This chapter centers on the home and community experiences and how we can build inviting, trusting, and nurturing environments.

First we take a look at the often unspoken "house rules" we have about food and the eating rituals and precedents we have deliberately or unwittingly put into place. Next we appraise our communication style and determine its effects on our children's esteem. Most notably, we examine the power of parental example and the vital part our own choices play in shaping our children's sense of belonging and broader worldview. After that we discuss the importance of creating a comfortable and relaxed living space where our children feel welcome and safe and we both are refreshed and revitalized. Then we explore the role compassion plays in vegetarianism and how we can use it as a valuable and practical teacher. Finally, we cover the significance of actively participating in the wider vegetarian community, where we draw from the acceptance, encouragement, and wisdom of others, allowing support and friendships to flourish.

Establishing House Rules

Question assumptions.

—*Anonymous*

In every home there are countless unspoken "rules," guidelines with which all who reside there are expected to comply. There are rules for children about trust and honesty and rules for what is considered acceptable and appropriate behavior. There also are rules about food, such as established mealtimes, which meals will be shared at the table with the rest of the family, who is in charge of cooking and cleanup, who does the grocery shopping, and in which rooms it is okay to eat. Often these rules are so ingrained that they aren't questioned or discussed; we simply know what is and isn't permissible.

The same is true, of course, in vegetarian households—the adults set the "food rules" and everyone is expected to follow them. When the entire family is vegetarian and the children are very young, it is easy to stick to the "food rules" because parents or guardians are doing the shopping, cooking, serving, feeding, and cleanup, so they oversee everything in the house that is food related. Clashes are more likely to arise when children are older and able to make contrary food decisions on their own, when children are the only vegetarians in the family, when one parent is vegetarian and the other is not, or when children eat outside of the home (for example, at a friend's or relative's house, with another custodial parent, or with a noncustodial guardian). It is these times that the "food rules" become paramount and occasionally controversial. Therefore, to keep kitchen skirmishes to a minimum, it is helpful to evaluate the "food rules" in our homes to ensure they satisfy the needs of others while meeting our own requirements.

Let's begin with the foods that are permitted in the house, as this is perhaps the most critical food parameter for vegetarian families. Here are a few questions to consider when shaping the "food rules" for your household.

In your home, is it acceptable . . .
- for anyone—such as nonvegetarian friends and family—to bring meat or other animal products into the house?

- for nonvegetarian friends and family to store meat or other animal products in the refrigerator or freezer?
- for animal products to be cooked in the same pots and pans used to cook vegetarian foods?
- for nonvegetarians to eat meat at the table when a vegetarian meal is being served?
- for nonvegetarians to use the same sponges and dish mops to clean their soiled dishware as those used to wash the vegetarians' pots, pans, and plates?

The "food rules" also extend outside the home, so here are some additional questions that may be relevant to your circumstances.

As a parent, is it acceptable . . .
- for your children to eat meat or other animal products at their nonvegetarian friends' homes?
- for your children to eat meat or other animal products at their noncustodial parent's home?
- for grandparents or extended family members to offer your children meat or other animal products?
- for your children to order meat or other animal products at restaurants?
- for your children to make their own decisions about what they will or won't eat when they are away from home?

Depending on the ages of the children, it can be helpful and insightful to solicit their views in devising the "food rules," so invite them to be a part of the process. As with all parameters, especially those around food, it is important that parents explain why they have instituted certain policies. When children participate in the decision-making, understand their parents' motives, and realize that the house rules aren't in place just to torment them, they generally are more willing to abide by them of their own accord rather than cave in due to parental pressure.

A vegetarian family's house rules regarding food may, of course, deal with more than just meat and animal products. Some parents do not want their children to consume empty-calorie, high-sugar, high-fat, carbonated, or caffeine-laden products, so these, too, may be considered contraband. We also may have many implied expectations of our children with regard to food. Although we might be aware of some of these assumptions, there are others we may impose reflexively, without giving them much thought. Here are a few more "food rules" to contemplate.

In your home, do you . . .
- require your children to clean their plates at every meal?
- insist that your children eat the same foods you are eating?
- use dessert as a reward?
- use foods the children dislike as a punishment?
- force your children to eat foods they cannot stand?
- oblige your children to try at least a bite of unfamiliar foods?
- succumb to the pressure of your children's food demands?

Children's appetites wax and wane, the same as adults'. They are not always hungry when the dinner bell rings, or they may be ravenous between scheduled mealtimes. It can be tough for parents to sort out their children's food needs day-to-day. Insisting that children clean their plates may be an unfair demand that discounts their innate ability to monitor their appetites and know when they are hungry or full. (Some overweight adults trace their habit of overeating back to forced plate-cleaning.) In addition, young children's small stomachs become full much more quickly than older children's or adults', so they may need to eat smaller but more frequent meals instead of three large ones. Start with small portions at mealtime and be ready to provide seconds (or thirds) if children want more. It will be easier for them to eat all or most of what is on their plates if they aren't overloaded with more food than they can reasonably consume.

Adults' tastes and children's tastes are not the same. Some children enjoy complex or sophisticated flavors at an early age and then turn up their noses at them when we least expect it. Other children prefer mild, simple, naturally sweet and tender foods and those that don't require much chewing. Still others like certain foods one day and not the next, or they go on stubborn food jags when just a single food or two is tolerable. There's only one thing we can be certain of when it comes to children and food: their tastes will change—it's merely a matter of when.

Although it can be a valuable bonding tool for families to share the same foods, occasionally some compromises need to be made. Our spicy vegetable chili might be better enjoyed by the little ones if there isn't much (or any) garlic, onions, and hot seasonings. An easy solution is to set aside a portion for the children and spice up a separate quantity for those who appreciate strong flavors and a little "heat." The marinara sauce with broccoli might be more acceptable to the tots if the sauce is blended so the broccoli isn't visible. A sprinkling of bread crumbs, a creamy nut-based sauce, or a yummy dip can spark children's interest and make plain vegetables much more appealing and palatable. Finger foods are terrific, especially for young children, even though the adults may prefer to use utensils. Most children are enamored with baby vegetables, such as baby zucchini, baby corn, or baby carrots. Some foods will be more fun and enticing for children if we (or they) arrange them into animal shapes or funny faces. With a little imagination, moderate adjustments, and gentle coaxing, we often can persuade children to try new foods or eat what's being served without making a big production or preparing separate dishes to appease each member of the family.

If children are extremely picky eaters, it is best to provide a single alternative to what is being served and give them a choice of either item A or item B. If they refuse both, they can be excused from the table or remain seated until everyone else has finished eating. Missing one meal on occasion will not damage children's health. When they are hungry enough, they will be more eager to eat the regular family meal or more inclined to accept the alternative food that is offered. If parents regularly succumb to their children's mandates for an exceedingly limited range of foods, the children will have no impetus for trying new foods and parents will be held hostage by their children's demands.

Food should never be used as a reward or punishment. Food is nourishment, not a device for behavior modification. If children become accustomed to food as compensation for good behavior, they will learn to overindulge and comfort themselves with it whenever they are feeling blue or out of sorts. Contrarily, if food is used as a punishment—either by regularly forcing children to eat foods they dislike or by depriving them of nourishment as a reproach—children will become resentful and perhaps in time could acquire serious disorders such as phobias about food or a habit of overeating caused by the fear of never getting enough.

There is a balance between putting too much emphasis on food and too little. Each family must work with each child to discover how to comfortably accent the positive aspects of eating without overemphasizing negatives, instilling "food fears," or forcing children to eat foods they truly find distasteful. Encouragement and praise go a long way in promoting healthful eating habits and prompting children to try new foods. All the same, children never should be required to eat foods they absolutely cannot stand, and at no time should adults force unwanted food into youngsters' mouths.

There will be times when our children will be bowled over or sucked in by advertisements for meat and animal products and other foods we do not want them to have. Impressionable young people can be powerfully influenced by such promotions or by what they see other (nonvegetarian) children eating. Our kids might clamor for these items when we are in the supermarket or car and might even pitch a public fit over them, depending on their ages and personalities. As long as our children are eating well and are healthy, there is no good reason to give in to these tantrums and manipulations. There is nothing that can justify the "need" for fast food or junk food, and compromising our beliefs to pacify our children sets an unnecessary and dangerous precedent.

In exploring our "food rules," we need to take a serious look at the unspoken suppositions we have about food and eating. How our children come to regard food will depend largely on how we view it and how we transmit these views to them. Are the "food rules" we impose on them ones that we are willing to follow ourselves? Are our "food rules" fair, just, loving, and respectful? Do our opinions about food simply reflect the views of our parents, our culture, or advertising messages? Have we sufficiently challenged and updated our assumptions before we influence our children?

Communication and Respect

> We don't see things as they are, we see things as we are.
>
> —*Anaïs Nin*

Our communication with others always conveys far more than information. Indeed, *how* we speak to our friends, acquaintances, colleagues, partners, and children reveals a great deal about our character and our relationships beyond the content of what we say. When we talk to our children (or anyone else, for that matter), we can better understand their responses to us if we remain aware of *how* we are expressing ourselves and are alert to the *purpose* behind our communication. Whatever rolls off our tongues becomes an appreciable reflection of our values, beliefs, and emotions, as well as an honest representation of how we truly feel about our kids.

Every interaction with others is unique, so with each conversation we need to explore and consider our motives. Here are some points to reflect on whenever we are speaking with our children.

Is our intent to:

- inform
- advise
- instruct
- guide

- encourage
- support
- show affection
- express concern

Or is it to:

- reprimand
- hurt
- belittle
- insult

- shame
- reject
- minimize
- negate

We teach our children many lessons when we talk with them, but not all are beneficial or what we truly want to impart. As parents, it perhaps is far preferable to refrain from speaking until we are clear about the point of our message and have considered the permanent impact our words will have on our children. Once something is spoken, it cannot be retracted. Children long remember and suffer from parents' damaging remarks that either seemed insignificant at the time they were spoken or were thoughtlessly uttered in a moment of distress or heated anger. What we consider to be "harmless," "mild," or "petty" may be devastating to a child's dignity and sense of self-worth. Thus we must ask ourselves: Is this what I intend?

Even when children seem to be ignoring us, they hang on our every word, absorb what we are saying, and hunger for our approval and encouragement. A parent's disparaging comments can strike a painful chord deep within a child's heart, leaving an indelible wound. Although as adults we may be better at shrugging off hurtful remarks, children have not yet acquired the seasoned ability to be objective and detached. When stinging assertions come from those they trust and rely on most—their parents—the hurt can be immeasurable.

Young people often demonstrate considerable interest in sharing with us their views about life, their feelings, their ideas, and their dreams. Even if what they have to say is not earth-shattering, it is of tremendous significance to *them*. When our children talk to us, do we actually listen? Do we hear the emotion that they are not yet able to put into words? Do we acknowledge their opinions and recognize them as equally valid as our own, even if we disagree with or don't completely understand them? Can we honor their choices, tastes, and perspectives nonjudgmentally?

If we don't pay attention or we show disinterest when our children speak, eventually they will stop talking to us—perhaps not completely, but certainly about those subjects that are most dear to them and, therefore, ought to be most dear to us. Regardless of our age, when we expose our deepest feelings, we want to know that someone is listening and cares. Otherwise, what is the point of baring our souls? Children cannot turn themselves on and off, as if they were a light switch, based on whether or not we are prepared to sit still and hear them. Consequently, it is up to us as adults to adjust our schedules and activities so we can be there when our children are eager and ready to share.

Vegetarianism can draw families together or pull them apart, depending upon the bridges we build to span the distance between our perspectives. If your children are vegetarian and you are not, know that they are part of a growing group of independent young thinkers who are making a viable, intelligent choice to end the senseless deaths of billions of animals that are killed each year for food, to create an environmentally sustainable culture, to strive for a peaceful world, and to safeguard their own health. To have raised children who are capable of coming to such insightful, ethical conclusions says a lot about your skillfulness as a parent. With this awareness, vegetarianism is something about which you and your children can feel extremely proud—even if you don't see eye to eye about it.

The wisdom of children can be exasperating and even intimidating at times—especially when they come to profound realizations long before we do. It can be tempting to minimize the importance of vegetarianism when our children choose it and we do not. Yet dismissing what they deem important, because it seems frivolous to us, can cause them to be resentful and rebellious. If our children want to be vegetarians but we do not wish to join them, we owe it to them to learn all we can about it, support them in their choice, hear their concerns, and give them encouragement and practical advice that will help them be healthy, strong, and confident about their decision.

We all have deep-seated feelings about food, even though we may not consciously acknowledge them. We may be daring, territorial, open-minded, fearful, playful, obsessive, nonchalant, finicky, sentimental, or regimented about what and how we eat. Some children do not like to be teased at mealtime, while others don't mind one bit. Some children like to eat their food in a particular order, or don't want the foods on their plate to touch, or they loathe certain textures, or they are skeptical of anything green. These kinds of "quirks" are perfectly normal. As parents, we must be sensitive to our children's likes and dislikes and respectful of their individual preferences, which will transform and evolve over time. It is reassuring to know that without any intervention, our children's eating habits will mature and their repertoires will broaden. However, admonishing children for the various food stages they go through may very well cause them to be stuck there even longer.

How we approach the topic of vegetarianism with our children can inspire them to pride and confidence or disempower them with anxiety and self-consciousness. Whether we lead with our own vegetarianism or they guide us with theirs, or we share the journey together, we have endless opportunities to learn, teach, and practice acceptance, tolerance, and respect. Although these qualities are valuable in all areas of life, vegetarianism is an ideal vantage point from which to comprehend and appreciate them.

Setting the Example

> Children have never been good at listening to their elders, but they have never failed to imitate them.
>
> —*James Baldwin*

We don't need a formal classroom in order to teach our children. In all honesty, they are learning from us constantly, beginning the moment they are born. Because our lessons can be either constructive or destructive, it is important to remember that whenever children are around they are soaking up everything they see and hear, whether it is deliberate or inadvertent on our part. Therefore, if we want our "instructions" to be beneficial, we need to pay attention to all that we think, say, and do.

When we shop for food, plan menus, prepare meals, eat out or at home, pack lunches, or even talk about food we are modeling our vegetarianism. If we give them the impression it is a struggle and a chore to maintain, this is how our children will view it. On the other hand, if we present vegetarianism as a joyful, loving, life-affirming experience, our children will see it this way instead.

Food is a central point of interest for all people—regardless of age, ethnicity, gender, race, or culture—because it is crucial to our very existence. Consequently, the subject of food makes an excellent tool for teaching children about responsibility, diversity, tolerance, acceptance, and other valuable issues and concerns.

Nearly all of the world's cuisines feature meatless dishes both for daily staples and special celebrations. Exploring various cultures through their indigenous foods presents a delicious and exciting forum for children to learn about geography, sociology, history, economics, agriculture, and environmental sustainability. Hence, meals centered around ethnic cuisines and themes can be turned into fun and fascinating learning opportunities while providing quality time with family. Whenever feasible, we can delve more deeply into various cultures and, along with food, we can study their languages, dress, and social customs. Then, with a little ingenuity, we can incorporate what we discover into special meals that blend these various elements and produce a hands-on experience that brings multicultural awareness and appreciation down to earth.

How we approach our own eating is a template for how our children should approach food. It would be unrealistic as well as unfair to ask our children to eat foods we shun or insist that they have balanced meals when we do not. In order for our children to learn good eating habits, we must practice what we preach. We also must explore our own attitudes and "hang-ups" about food to gain awareness about what we unintentionally might be teaching our little ones through our behavior, remarks, and demeanor. If we are hooked on sweets, it should not be surprising that our children find them irresistible, too. If we generally eat on the run or overindulge in coffee, soda pop, cookies, cakes, chips, fries, or other less-than-healthful foods, we can better understand why our offspring are following these same patterns.

Many childhood health problems, including childhood obesity, are associated as much or more with environmental influences as with genetics and other uncontrollable factors. What, when, and how we eat, as well as whether our lifestyle is sedentary or active, strongly affect our children's views and behavior. Our body image—positive or negative—exercise habits, and comfort level with food are inescapably connected to our children's perceptions about their own bodies and attitudes toward food and health. Our likes, dislikes, fears, preferences, cravings, and addictions are readily apparent to our children and present an open invitation for them to imitate us.

Certainly, we cannot and should not aim for personal perfection in our diet or lifestyle, as this is unattainable and establishes an impossible standard for our children to achieve. Nevertheless, we steadfastly can bear in mind the impact of our choices on impressionable minds, and advocate and strive for consistency between our ethics and our actions. At the same time, it is important to acknowledge our shortcomings without shame or embarrassment. Recognizing that parents are fallible—the same as anyone else—helps children become more accepting of their own foibles, encourages them to be more flexible, and allows them to see their parents as sincere and honest people whose minor flaws merely contribute to making them more lovable, real, and human.

Creating a Nurturing Environment

Assume the best.

—*Anonymous*

Home is the one place where we ought to be able to relax, not worry what others think about us, and feel comfortable kicking back and simply being ourselves. Sadly, many young people feel that home is where they are judged most harshly, where no matter how hard they try they can never succeed or meet their parents' expectations, and where being themselves is met with ridicule, scorn, or suspicion rather than acceptance. Under such conditions, what reasonable person would want to spend time there? When children feel that home is a prison and their parents are the wardens, it is nearly impossible to maintain a close family relationship.

Ideally, trust and respect will be cultivated when children are very young, but parents still can nurture these qualities effectively with older children, including those who are adopted, those for whom we are providing foster care, those living with us part-time as with custody arrangements, or those who are part of a blended family. However, if young people have been neglected or mistreated during their early years, there is much healing to be done before rebuilding can begin and trust can bloom.

Sometimes, especially if children are very angry or hostile or parents are dealing with their own issues from childhood or beyond, counseling or therapy with a trained mental health professional is a necessity. In fact, in certain instances it may be the only practical solution for restoring family harmony and finding inner peace. Nevertheless, many family crises can be averted through good old-fashioned face-to-face communication—talking and listening, nonjudgmentally and respectfully, while maintaining an open heart and mind. In this age of instant messaging, ordinary conversations often seem slow paced and dragged out. Yet it is the simple act of being patient, giving young people time to gather their thoughts and find the right words, and letting them speak without interruption that can let them know how deeply we care about their experiences and feelings.

When we are rushed and harried we are incapable of nurturing ourselves, let alone our children. Forging a caring environment requires us to slow down and carve out space for those we love. Many parents try to shield or conceal their inadequacies or fear of a close relationship by overscheduling commitments and activities for both themselves and their children. With so much to do, we end up being too busy to be bothered by demanding, time-consuming matters that call for patience and composure, such as honest conversation—there simply are too few hours in the day. Being overworked or overburdened, trying to fill every moment of every hour with "productive diversions," and being stressed to the max make for an odd but prevalent badge of courage in our modern society, for both adults and children.

Good parenting takes effort, but it also requires time and presence; we actually have to *be* there if we truly want to participate in and be a part of our children's lives. Tangible involvement is the only way to provide the loving guidance that is needed to steer our children in the directions we want them to go. This entails slowing down, relaxing, and carefully choosing and pacing our own and our children's undertakings.

If we are frazzled and stressed, our children likely will be as well. No matter how enlightened we may think we are, it is tough to stay centered and calm in the midst of a maelstrom. It is even more difficult for children, who are easily swept up by the currents of their parents' frantic emotions or behavior. Creating a peaceful home begins with nourishing our own inner calm and spaciousness. Only when we are relaxed and open will we be capable of providing the nonjudgmental, accepting atmosphere that is essential for children to feel safe, nurtured, and loved.

Expanding Compassion

> Teaching a child not to step on a caterpillar is as valuable to the child as it is to the caterpillar.
>
> —*Bradley Miller*

There perhaps is no more practical route for teaching children about compassion than starting with what is on our plates. Because eating is central to our lives and something we all do several times a day, vegetarianism provides an ideal example of compassion in action. Indeed, it certainly seems disingenuous for people to broach matters of peace when they consume products of violence and death at mealtime.

Many people come to vegetarianism because of a desire for better health. For others, it is a last resort for recovering from severe illness. Still others believe that a plant-only diet is the best protection from disease for both themselves and their children. There also are people who gravitate toward this way of eating out of concern and respect for animals, or the damage that animal-based food production causes to the environment, or the pitiful wages and horrifying accidents that are commonplace among workers in slaughterhouses and meatpacking plants. Regardless of our initial standpoint, we can deepen our understanding by launching an investigation of additional rationales for being vegetarian.

These days, people seem to be more impassioned by discussions of financial gain and material wealth than by ethics and their practical application to daily living. We are hesitant to speak out on ethical issues because so often people who have differing points of view respond defensively or even angrily. Nevertheless, living our ethics and imparting them to our children are essential aspects of child rearing, and if we overlook or minimize the significance of this, we will miss opportunities to instill in our children the values we cherish.

It is admirable to acknowledge the endless and needless suffering involved with the production of meat and other animal products. Speaking out on behalf of those who cannot speak for themselves is something about which we can and should feel good and about which our children can feel righteous. As noble as it is to safeguard the health of our bodies and to encourage our children to do the same, the act of being a vegetarian for humane reasons teaches children about compassion in a personal, direct, and tangible way. Fortunately, in a free society our diets are something over which we have control, and helping our children choose humanely imparts the wisdom of caring and kindness at an early age.

Of course, teaching children about humane eating will undoubtedly spark discussions about why so many other people—including friends, classmates, and relatives—eat meat. Our children are bound to ask, "Don't other people know that meat is made from animals? Don't they care?" These are tough questions for parents to answer, because we don't want to condemn the nonvegetarians who are an important part of our children's lives. So what should parents say?

The best approach, as always, is the honest one. At some point we will need to explain, but exactly how we respond will be unique to each of us and will depend on our personal beliefs, our individual style, and the ages of our children. However, fluffing over the truth will only leave young people with more questions and doubts. Therefore, we need to determine how to address their inquiries with openness, candor, and tact. What makes this dilemma especially difficult is that if we teach our children that vegetarianism is "right," they will automatically conclude that people who eat animals are "wrong." Surely we might agree with this sentiment, but the challenge lies in teaching our little ones that those who eat meat are not necessarily "bad people"; they just may be unaware, uninformed, or unable to change. Moreover, while some people express their compassion primarily through dietary choices, others might do so by being an inspiring Scout leader, providing relief for world hunger, or simply performing kind, neighborly acts.

When we open the door to altruism through our food choices, we lay the groundwork for our children to explore and act upon all forms of compassion:

- compassion for themselves, including their physical, emotional, and spiritual health
- compassion for other people
- compassion for other animals and life forms
- compassion for the earth and the ecosystems that sustain all living beings

These four realms present a lifetime of learning for children, parents, and families. They can be the impetus for countless activities and excursions, such as community involvement, charitable work, adopting animal companions in need of homes, planting gardens, learning sustainable crafts, practicing responsible hiking and camping, and so much more. When our ethics encompass all areas of life, including what we eat and don't eat, we discover that everything is relevant and interconnected. Our lifestyle choices truly do matter, and what we choose to do with our limited time on this earth can make an enormous, positive difference to so many.

Vegetarianism can be significantly more than a diet. It has the potential to provide lifelong good health, inner peace, and moral congruity. What an incredible bequest to offer our children and future generations—the gift of life and compassion for all.

Building Community

> Friendship is born at that moment when one person says to another: What! You, too? Thought I was the only one.
> —*Clive Staples Lewis, author of the* Narnia *series*

No matter how certain we are that the path of vegetarianism is the right one for us and our children, we are, at least for the time being, outnumbered. Being in the minority can make vegetarians feel isolated, both as individuals and as families. Furthermore, without support it can be tempting to acquiesce to the pressure of an unsympathetic society to conform or to the urge to be anonymous and blend in with the crowd. Of course, doing so would compromise our beliefs, our ethics, and our health, and leave us in a moral quandary.

Vegetarians don't have to live on the cultural fringe, succumb to coercion, or pander to the masses. We can build our own community and network of support through relationships near and far. The majority of vegetarian parents simply are ordinary people with children who don't feel, look, or behave much differently than any other kids their age. But because we are vegetarians, we have something unique in common that can create a bond between us even before we know much else about each other.

Nearly all cities and a large number of midsize towns have vegetarian societies that can provide information, fellowship, and a sense of belonging. Often they sponsor regularly scheduled share-a-dish (potluck) meetings that frequently include a guest speaker. Some groups plan outings to restaurants and movies, have recipe swaps, or present children's programs. Joining and participating in our local vegetarian society can provide a boost to our morale as well as be an opportunity to solicit tips from other parents or a chance for us to extend guidance to them based on the wisdom we've gained from our own experiences. It also can be an opening for our children to forge friendships and realize they are not the only vegetarian youngsters in the world, even though at times it might feel that way.

If there is no vegetarian association in your area, you can start one. (See the Resources section for information on contacting EarthSave International, the International Vegetarian Union, or the North American Vegetarian Society.) If one already exists, you might want to initiate a special-interest group for vegetarian parents, nonvegetarian parents of vegetarian children, vegetarian families, or vegetarian youth. If there is only a small group of interested people where you live, you could host weekly or monthly dinner parties or organize share-a-dish meals that alternate among your homes. With sufficient members, you could bring in national presenters or host vegetarian education programs for local schools, the PTA, faith-based associations, or the community at large. You could organize a vegetarian sports team, Scouting or hiking association, book club, or cooking classes. With a little imagination, the possibilities for developing our local vegetarian communities and supporting our children and each other are endless.

To find like-minded parents, try posting flyers at your food cooperative, natural food stores, vegetarian restaurants, community youth clubs, or houses of worship. Place an ad in your local newspapers and on store bulletin boards. Go to your neighborhood council meetings and make an announcement. Reach out in whatever way you can and when you find interested parties, ask them to continue the outreach as well. Getting groups off the ground can have a domino effect, but often it takes a little nudging to get them going. If there are no other vegetarians or interested people where you live, try the next closest town or city. If it is larger than yours, there might already be a group up and running in which you could participate.

Another great way to meet like-minded vegetarians is to attend local or national vegetarian conferences and festivals. These often are promoted in vegetarian magazines and newspapers (see the Resources section), so be on the lookout for them. Vegetarian families frequently plan their vacations around these events, as they typically are child and family friendly. Some even provide special children's activities or child care services. Getaways like these can be wonderful for children, particularly if they have no vegetarian buddies in their hometown. Young people may, for the first time, discover that they are not alone and can make friends with kids just like them in other cities, states, or countries. Parents have a chance to gain support as well, share tips, and know that there are many other families who share similar joys and challenges.

With the ease of the Internet, vegetarian children and parents can quickly find online friendships and pen pals, so even if there are no "real-life" peers with whom we can communicate, it is comforting to have this resource. Occasionally, online relationships develop into "real-life" ones where families meet at conferences, resorts, or retreats, talk on the telephone, or travel to each other's homes.

Sometimes our success with being a vegetarian family hinges on the support and encouragement we receive from others. If we reach out, we'll find many arms just waiting to reach back.

Chapter 5

An Ounce of Prevention: Food Safety for Vegetarians

Sharing Responsibility

> In uplifting, get underneath.
>
> —*George Ade*

Children develop greater respect for food, menu planning, meal preparation, and cleanup when they are actively involved. It's hard to teach children these skills, however, unless we know them ourselves through firsthand experience. To engender enthusiasm for healthful eating, we need to educate ourselves not only about proper nutrition but about basic cooking techniques, food safety, and kitchen sanitation, too.

Even fairly young children can participate in food preparation and be taught good habits and hygiene through discussion, example, and practical training. Using clean hands, a youngster can learn to gently toss a salad (be sure to use a very large bowl!), shape cookie dough, break the ends off string beans, soak alfalfa seeds for sprouting, tear fresh lettuce leaves or kale into pieces, help set the table or clear away dishes, separate items for recycling or composting, and so forth. These simple tasks not only are educational, children enjoy them, and they foster a sense of purpose, responsibility, and belonging. At first it might seem that involving young children in kitchen chores is an imposition that requires too much adult supervision and extra time. It's true that initially we might need to divide our attention between doing our own necessary tasks and assisting the little ones with learning theirs, and this can slow us down a bit. Fortunately, children tend to learn quickly, especially if we don't demand perfection and breakneck speed, or expect them to have an adult's level of dexterity.

Children who are involved with food- and kitchen-related chores—from seeing how food is grown to shopping, storing, menu planning, meal preparation, cooking, and cleanup—develop a healthy relationship with food and feelings of independence and self-sufficiency that will lead them into adulthood. Of course, common sense asserts that young children should not handle or use kitchen knives or other potentially dangerous equipment—such as food processors, blenders, or pressure cookers—and older children should not use these tools without direct adult supervision. It also is important for children to be kept away from open flames and for parents to discourage children from cooking and stirring hot foods until they are tall enough to comfortably reach and see into pots and pans on the stovetop.

Keeping It Clean

> You've got to think about big things while you're doing small
> things, so that all the small things go in the right direction.
> —*Alvin Toffler*

Personal Hygiene

A budding cook's first lesson should begin with learning good personal hygiene, and an update is important for chefs of any age. Many diseases are transmitted to and from us—through human contact, air, and food—simply because we don't spend the minimal time and effort necessary to prevent spreading potentially harmful bacteria. Hygiene is one of the most important keys in preventing foodborne illness, which can be devastating, particularly for children. Youngsters with colds, runny noses, coughs, ear infections, and open cuts or wounds on their hands should not be involved with food preparation until they are better. Parents with young children in diapers and those not fully toilet trained should be fastidious with their hygiene at all times, especially when they work in the kitchen. *The most effective means of inhibiting the transmission of infectious bacteria is to wash hands thoroughly and frequently.*

To wash hands thoroughly means to:
- Use running water and lather with soap.
- Scrub under nails, between fingers, backs of hands, and up wrists.
- Count to twenty slowly or sing your favorite song ("Happy Birthday" is one possibility).
- Rinse completely.
- Dry hands with a paper towel.
- Turn off faucet using a paper towel.

The reason it is important to use a paper towel to dry hands when working in the kitchen is that cloth towels, particularly those that are reused, are teeming with bacteria and only will serve to spread more. Turning off the faucet with a paper towel is another critical step, because we contaminate sink handles with our dirty hands when we turn on the water. If we touch the handles again with our clean hands, we undermine the point of having washed them.

To wash hands frequently means:
- before working in the kitchen
- after using the bathroom, changing diapers, or assisting children in the bathroom
- after coughing, sneezing, blowing the nose, or wiping children's noses
- after touching the head, hair, open wounds or sores, nose, ears, eyes, or other parts of the body
- after touching dirty surfaces
- after chewing gum, using toothpicks, or smoking
- after touching or using chemicals
- after feeding, petting, playing with, or cleaning up after pets
- after taking out the trash, handling compost, sweeping, or mopping the floor
- during food preparation, as needed

The First Line of Defense

> Vision is the art of seeing the invisible.
>
> —*Jonathan Swift*

It is estimated that there are seventy-six million cases of foodborne illness annually in the United States, resulting in approximately 325,000 hospitalizations and 5,000 deaths. We primarily are aware of food poisoning that occurs outside the home at clubs, catered events, hotels, fast-food eateries, and full-service restaurants, but home cooks frequently spread dangerous foodborne bacteria, too. We don't hear much about it because it rarely is reported. In fact, most home cooks aren't aware that essentially all "twenty-four-hour bugs" experienced by both children and adults are caused by foodborne pathogens, not flu viruses. Those most susceptible to food poisoning and most likely to be severely incapacitated by it are children, elders, people with chronic illness or compromised immune systems, and pregnant women. Nevertheless, the good news is that most foodborne illnesses are short term and minor and all are preventable.

Factors in Foodborne Illness

The following are the most crucial contributors to food poisoning:

- infected food handlers (especially those with symptoms of nausea, diarrhea, or vomiting)
- food handlers who practice poor personal hygiene
- inadequate cooking of food
- improper cooling of food
- improper reheating and use of leftovers
- ingesting raw, contaminated foods
- cross contamination
- improper cleaning of equipment
- poor food storage and holding practices (hot and cold)
- improper thawing of frozen foods
- toxins

The following factors contribute to the multiplication or reduction of foodborne bacteria:

- food type
- acidity

- temperature
- time
- oxygen
- moisture

Food Type. The public perception is that food poisoning is predominantly caused by improperly cooked or contaminated meats (including poultry and fish), making it strictly a concern for meat-eaters. To a large extent this is true; however, vegetarians, especially those who consume dairy products and eggs, also are at high risk. Although the risk of contracting food poisoning is lessened somewhat for vegans and total vegetarians, they, too, must be careful and take precautions. The most common foods and food ingredients that are potentially hazardous—that is, those that are capable of supporting rapid-growth microorganisms—include the following:

- foods of animal origin, such as meat, milk, fish, shellfish, edible crustacea, and poultry
- foods of plant origin that have been heat treated
- raw seed and bean sprouts

Of course, there are countless other foods that provide excellent breeding grounds for dangerous foodborne bacteria. The following list contains just a few of the many vegetarian and vegan foods that often are overlooked as potentially hazardous:

- *beans:* all types of cooked beans
- *whipped butter:* whipping introduces bacteria
- *cheese:* soft, unripened cheese such as cottage cheese, ricotta, brie, and cream cheese are more hazardous than hard cheese, although all cheeses should be refrigerated
- *coffee creaming agents:* all nondairy coffee creaming agents in liquid form
- *eggs:* fresh shell eggs, fresh eggs with the outer shell removed, and hard-boiled eggs
- *garlic:* when stored in oil and garlic-in-oil products
- *mayonnaise or other acidified salad dressings (including tofu-based mayonnaise and salad dressings):* if the pH is above 4.6 and/or it is combined with other food products
- *melons:* cut up
- *onions:* cooked or dehydrated (if reconstituted) when in oil

- *pasta:* cooked
- *pastries:* cheese and cream filled
- *pies:* dairy cream, synthetic cream, custard, pumpkin, tofu based, and those covered with toppings that support microbial growth (such as whipped soy-based toppings, whipped cream, or meringue)
- *raw seed and bean sprouts:* all types
- *potatoes:* baked, boiled, broiled, mashed, or fried
- *porridge:* oatmeal and other cooked hot cereals
- *refried beans:* all varieties
- *rice and other cooked grains:* boiled, steamed, fried, pilafs, Spanish rice, and cooked rice used in nori rolls and vegetable sushi
- *sauces:* Hollandaise, cream sauces, and other sauces that contain potentially hazardous ingredients
- *sour cream:* if the pH is above 4.6 and/or it is combined with other food products
- *soy protein:* tofu, tempeh, reconstituted TVP, and other moist soy protein products
- *vegetables:* cooked

Acidity. Most bacteria cannot survive in foods high in acid. High-acid foods include most fruits and other foods to which an acidic ingredient has been added. Meats and vegetables are considered low acid. The term *pH* is used to define how acid or basic (alkaline) foods are. A scale from 0 to 14 is used. The lower the pH, the more acid the food; the higher the pH, the more alkaline the food. A pH of 7 is considered neutral—that is, neither acid nor base. Most bacteria cannot grow if the pH of a food is 4.6 or less. The pH of meat, fish, poultry, and eggs ranges from 5.1 to 8.0. See Tables 5.1, 5.2, and 5.3 for approximate pH levels of various foods.

Temperature. The ideal temperature at which food pathogens grow varies depending on the bacteria. Some bacteria, such as *Listeria*, are cold loving and prefer temperatures between 38°F and 60°F. Others love the midrange and like temperatures between 70°F and 120°F. Nevertheless, most food safety experts agree: *Temperatures between 41°F and 140°F, known as the "danger zone," are highly conducive for the proliferation of the majority of bacteria that cause foodborne illness.* As temperatures approach

TABLE 5.1

The Approximate pH Levels of Dairy Products and Mayonnaise

pH −4.6 (acidic range)	pH near 4.6 (midrange)	pH +4.6 (alkaline range)
mayonnaise	buttermilk	butter
yogurt		cheese
		cream
		milk

TABLE 5.2

The Approximate pH Levels of Vegetables

pH −4.6 (acidic range)	pH near 4.6 (midrange)	pH +4.6 (alkaline range)
beets	eggplant	asparagus
dill pickles		beans
olives		broccoli
rhubarb		Brussels sprouts
sauerkraut		cabbage
tomatoes		carrots
		cauliflower
		celery
		corn
		green peas
		lettuce
		onions
		parsley
		parsnips
		potatoes (tubers)
		potatoes (sweet)
		pumpkin
		spinach
		squash
		turnips

TABLE 5.3

The Approximate pH Levels of Fruits

pH −4.6 (acidic range)	pH near 4.6 (midrange)	pH +4.6 (alkaline range)
apples	bananas	melon
grapefruit	figs	
lemons	grapes	
limes		
orange juice		
pears		
plums		

either end of the danger zone, bacterial growth slows and eventually stops. At temperatures at or near 140°F, bacteria begin to die. Refrigeration slows growth rate, but it does not kill bacteria. For this reason, liquids need to be reheated to boiling temperatures, and solid foods should be reheated to 165°F.

Time. When conditions are ideal, bacteria double every fifteen to twenty minutes. This means that a single bacterium can multiply to numbers that can make us sick within just a few hours. Unfortunately, all foods contain bacteria, and much more than one. Therefore, cooling and heating food quickly is one key to food safety. *Food should never be kept in the "danger zone" of between 41°F and 140°F for more than two hours, and perishable foods should never be held at room temperature for more than two hours.*

Oxygen. Bacteria vary in their requirements for oxygen. Some bacteria will grow only when supplied with oxygen (i.e., aerobic bacteria). Other bacteria grow only when oxygen is excluded or absent (i.e., anaerobic bacteria). These are the bacteria that can grow in a vacuum-sealed jar or can, such as the pathogen *Clostridium botulinum*, which causes botulism. Most of the bacteria that cause foodborne illness can grow either with or without the presence of free oxygen (i.e., facultative bacteria).

Moisture. All foods contain water. However, water in some foods is "suspended" or "tied up," making it unavailable to bacteria. Jams and jellies are examples of suspended water activity. Although there is water in jam and jelly, the sugar in them binds with the water, making the water unavailable. Salt also ties up water. *Water activity* is the name for the measure of the available water in a food. The higher the number for a food's water activity, the more water is available. The number 1.0 represents 100 percent available water; 0.85 means the food contains 85 percent available water. Foods with a water activity of 0.85 or less are considered safe from foodborne pathogens because most bacteria need more water than this to survive. Most vegetables have a water activity level of 0.85 or greater, and most fruits have a water activity level of 0.90.

Preventing Cross Contamination

There are many different types of foodborne diseases caused by various pathogens. Although some of these diseases typically are associated with meat and fish—such as *E. coli 0157:H7 enteritis* and scombroid poisoning—the pathogens that cause these diseases can be transferred to plant foods through *cross contamination.* Cross contamination means introducing bacteria from one food source into another or through human stool due to inadequate hygiene. Cross contamination occurs most often when raw meat, fish, poultry, or eggs are handled. If the utensils, cutting surfaces, and even the hands that touched these raw animal foods are not properly sanitized before they touch other foods, cross contamination takes place. If these other foods receive no further cooking, the cross contamination creates a hazardous condition. This can be especially critical in households where some family members are vegetarian and some eat meat or other animal products. But even in vegetarian homes, vegans and total vegetarians may be put at risk of cross contamination if some family members are ovo-, lacto-, or ovolactovegetarians. Beyond aesthetics, there are critical health reasons for keeping plant-based foods, utensils, and cutting boards separate from those that are used to prepare meat, dairy, and eggs. In "mixed" households of vegetarians and meat-eaters or those with vegans and vegetarians who eat dairy products and/or eggs, you can prevent cross contamination by doing the following:

- Use separate cutting surfaces and knives for animal products and plant-based foods.
- Sanitize all cutting surfaces and utensils after cutting animal products. Wash your cutting boards with soap and *hot* water after each use (or put them in the

dishwasher). Plastic cutting boards are most easily sanitized. If animal products of any kind come in contact with your cutting boards, wash them in a bleach solution to prevent bacteria from remaining on them. For hard, non-porous surfaces, use ¼ teaspoon liquid chlorine bleach to 2 cups warm water (between 75°F and 120°F). Keep the surface wet for ten seconds. Do not rinse. Allow to air dry. For porous surfaces, such as wooden cutting boards, keep the surface wet for ten seconds, rinse, and allow to air dry. You may want to keep a ready supply of the bleach solution in a labeled spray bottle near the sink, but change the solution often as its potency will diminish over time. (Note: Chlorine bleach is a hazardous substance and a corrosive. Use only as directed on the package label and follow all warnings as instructed.)

- Have family members wash their hands thoroughly after handling animal products and before touching other foods.
- Thaw meat in the refrigerator *below* plant-based foods so meat drippings do not come in contact with the plant foods.

Cross contamination also can occur by introducing bacteria from one contaminated plant-based food to another. You can reduce the risk of cross contaminating food by practicing the following safety procedures:

- Use a separate spoon for tasting and stirring.
- Use a tasting spoon only once (i.e., do not put the tasting spoon back into food).
- Use a separate cooking utensil for each dish being prepared.
- Keep utensils clean.
- Wash hands between preparing different recipes.

Under the Microscope

> It's what you learn after you know it all that counts.
> —*John Wooden*

There are two types of foodborne diseases: *bacterial infection* and *bacterial intoxication*. With bacterial infection, large numbers of bacteria cause the illness, and there can be a relatively long incubation time before symptoms appear, with diarrhea being the most common one. Infectious foodborne bacteria usually are heat sensitive and will be destroyed with cooking. However, those that form spores—including the pathogens associated with the diseases *Bacillus cereus* (which causes both infection and bacterial intoxication) and *Clostridium perfringens enteritis*—are not destroyed by heat. Bacterial intoxication is caused by poisonous waste from bacteria. This disease is very fast acting, and vomiting typically occurs shortly after the contaminated food is ingested. Many of these toxins are heat resistant and can be lethal to children and others in high-risk categories.

The bacteria that cause food poisoning cannot be detected by sight (i.e., the appearance of food) or smell (i.e., the aroma of food). *The only way to avoid contracting foodborne illness is through prevention.* (See Table 5.4.)

Learning Good Habits

> Things do not get better by being left alone.
> —*Winston Churchill*

How can we tell when food has become contaminated with bacteria? We can't. A food item may appear to be safe and wholesome and yet be rife with dangerous pathogens. Therefore, it is necessary to observe good food protection and sanitation practices in the purchase, storage, and handling of foods at home.

Food safety begins with safe food purchases. As a rule, look for foods that are in sound condition; free of insects, dirt, and debris; and stored at the proper temperature.

Canned and Packaged Foods

Do *not* purchase or use if:
- top or bottom is swollen
- is rusting or leaking
- has dents along rim or seam
- has flawed seal (on baby food or other food in jars)
- has off odor
- has foam on top of can when opened
- juice is milky
- "sell by" date has passed

Major Foodborne Diseases

Illness or Pathogen	Time to Develop	Symptoms and Duration	Source	Foods Involved	Prevention
Bacillus cereus	1½ to 5 hours	Nausea; vomiting; diarrhea; lasts 6–24 hours	Soil; dust	Cooked rice and other grains; cooked pasta; cooked oatmeal and other cooked cereals; vegetable dishes	Cook foods to proper temperatures; cool foods safely; reheat food to 165°F or above
Botulism	12–36 hours	Vertigo; visual disturbances; inability to swallow; respiratory paralysis; lasts several days to a year	Soil; water	Improperly processed low-acid canned food; garlic-in-oil products; grilled onions; leftover stews; potatoes; vacuum-packaged foods	Avoid improperly canned products; do not use home-canned products; use careful time and temperature controls; use proper cooling techniques
Campylobacter	2–5 days	Fever; cramping; abdominal pain; nausea; vomiting; diarrhea (may be bloody); lasts 3–6 days (postinfection complications	Birds; water; animal feces (including domestic cats and dogs); food production animals; wild animals;	Raw and undercooked poultry and other meat products; raw or unpasteurized animal milk; contaminated water or ice	Avoid cross contamination; use careful time and temperature controls in cooling and reheating; avoid untreated water; avoid ice unless certain it is made from safe

Illness or Pathogen	Time to Develop	Symptoms and Duration	Source	Foods Involved	Prevention
Campylobacter (continued)		may include reactive arthritis and neurological disorders)	infected human beings		water; use good hygiene; wash fruits and vegetables carefully, especially if eaten raw; peel fruits and vegetables if possible
Clostridium perfringens	8–22 hours	Abdominal pain; diarrhea; dehydration; lasts 24 hours	Human beings (intestinal tract); animals; soil	Cooked meats; poultry; gravy; beans that have been cooled slowly	Avoid cross contamination; use careful time and temperature controls in cooling and reheating; always reheat to 165°F
E. coli 0157:H7	3–9 hours	Vomiting; diarrhea (could be bloody); fever; kidney failure; hemolytic uremic syndrome (HUS); lasts 8 days	Human beings (intestinal tract); animals (particularly cattle)	Beef and other red meats (especially ground beef); cheeses; raw milk; water contaminated by farming operations; plant foods contaminated by tainted water (lettuce, raw vegetables, raw fruits); unpasteurized apple cider and juice	Avoid cross contamination

(continued)

TABLE 5.4 (CONTINUED)

Illness or Pathogen	Time to Develop	Symptoms and Duration	Source	Foods Involved	Prevention
Hepatitis A (viral agent)	15–50 days	Fever; jaundice; enlarged liver; lasts indefinitely (could be weeks to months)	Water; infected human beings	Raw oysters; clams; ready-to-eat foods	Avoid cross contamination; good personal hygiene; minimize hand contact
Listeriosis	3 days to several weeks	Nausea; vomiting; headache; fever; chills; backache; meningitis; spontaneous abortion; lasts indefinitely, depends on treatment; has high fatality rate in the immune-compromised	Soil; water; mud; human beings; domestic and wild animals; fowl	Unpasteurized milk and cheese; vegetables; poultry and meats; seafood; prepared and chilled ready-to-eat foods	If lactovegetarian, use only pasteurized milk and dairy products; cook foods to proper temperatures; avoid cross contamination; clean and disinfect surfaces; avoid pooling of water; observe "use by" dates
Norwalk virus	24–48 hours	Nausea; vomiting; diarrhea; abdominal pain; headache; low-grade fever; lasts 24–48 hours	Human beings (intestinal tract)	Raw shellfish; raw vegetables; salads; prepared salads; water contaminated from human feces	Avoid fecal contamination from cooks by practicing good personal hygiene; thoroughly cook foods; use chlorinated water

Illness or Pathogen	Time to Develop	Symptoms and Duration	Source	Foods Involved	Prevention
Salmonella	6–72 hours	Nausea; vomiting; fever; diarrhea; cramps; headache; lasts 2 days	Domestic and wild animals; humans	Poultry; eggs; meat; milk; high-protein foods (including beans and soy products)	Avoid cross contamination; refrigerate foods; good hygiene; proper cooling; if using eggs in baking, do not taste raw cookie dough or cake batter; do not make or drink homemade eggnog; avoid homemade mayonnaise and homemade ice cream containing raw eggs
Scombroid poisoning	Few minutes to 1 hour	Nausea; vomiting; peppery taste in mouth; facial swelling; flushing; short duration, usually lasts a few hours	Tuna, mackerel, bluefish	Poorly cleaned, inadequately cooled, and improperly refrigerated fish	Avoid cross contamination
Shigella	12–96 hours	Fever; diarrhea (could be bloody); chills; cramps; dehydration; lasts 1–2 weeks	Human beings (intestinal tract); flies	Potato salad; pasta salad; raw vegetables; dairy products	Avoid cross contamination; avoid fecal contamination; control flies; good hygiene

(continued)

TABLE 5·4 (CONTINUED)

Illness or Pathogen	Time to Develop	Symptoms and Duration	Source	Foods Involved	Prevention
Staphylococcal intoxication	1–6 hours	Nausea; vomiting; diarrhea; dehydration; lasts 12–24 hours	Human beings (skin, nose, throat, infected sores); animals	Ham and other meats; cooked foods; custards; potato salads	Avoid contamination with hands; good hygiene; exclude cooks with skin infections; proper refrigeration and cooling
Yersinia	3–7 days	Fever; abdominal pain; vomiting; diarrhea; arthritis; septicemia; lasts 1–3 days	Animal feces; birds; lakes and streams; soil	Raw vegetables; milk and other dairy products; ice cream; salad; seafood	Thoroughly cook foods; prevent cross contamination; wash hands; wash all foods eaten raw; do not allow animals in the kitchen

Frozen Foods

Do *not* purchase or use if:

- food is thawed
- large ice crystals are in or on food or there are other signs of thawing and refreezing

Dry Foods (i.e., cereals, rice, grains, flour, pasta, crackers, etc.)

Do *not* purchase or use if:

- packaging is not intact
- signs of rodents (i.e., gnawed package, holes in package, rodent droppings)
- evidence of insect infestations (i.e., grain beetles, flies, cockroaches)

After foods are purchased or prepared they must be safely stored. All potentially hazardous foods—such as tofu and tempeh; soyfoods; seitan; other high protein items; cooked beans; cooked potatoes, rice, and other cooked grains and pasta; cooked vegetables; cut melon; dairy and egg products—must be stored at the appropriate temperature (40°F or below) or frozen (0°F or below). There are several ways to properly thaw frozen food:

- in the refrigerator
- under cold, running water
- in the microwave with immediate cooking afterward
- as part of the cooking process

Ready-to-eat potentially hazardous food that will be refrigerated for more than twenty-four hours should be marked with a date by which the food should be consumed (begin with the day of preparation). Most foods held at 40°F or below can be stored safely for two to four days.

After foods are cooked, they should be served at once. If cooked food must be held for a while, it should be kept at 140°F or above. If you have leftovers, cool them rapidly. Nearly half of all cases of food poisoning are caused by improper cooling. The longer food is in the "danger zone" (41°F to 140°F), the more bacteria will be multiplying to dangerous levels. Here is the safest method to cool food at home:

Step 1:   Clear the top shelf of the refrigerator. If the shelf is not a metal rack, place a metal cooling rack on it so air can circulate under the container holding the food to be cooled. Make sure there is sufficient space above the container holding the food so air can circulate all around it.

Step 2: Place the food to be cooled in a *shallow* metal (the best choice), glass, or lead-free ceramic pan. Do *not* use a plastic container to cool food. (Plastic retains heat and does not allow food to cool quickly.) Fill the pans to 2 inches for thick foods (such as pureed vegetables, mashed potatoes, chili, stew, thick soups, beans, grains, pasta) and 4 inches or less for clear liquids (such as vegetable broth and thin soup). If chilling tofu slices, place them in a single layer.

Step 3: Do not cover the pan. This allows heat to escape more quickly.

Step 4: Stir the food frequently, about every twenty to thirty minutes, drawing the colder outer edges of the food toward the middle of the pan to blend with the hotter contents from the center, and move the hotter center contents toward the outer edges.

Step 5: To ensure safety, cooked food should reach 70°F within two hours and 41°F in four more hours, for a total cooling time of *no more* than six hours. If it appears that the cooldown will not be fast enough, take steps to quicken cooling such as using an ice bath (setting the pan directly in ice or ice water) or place the pan in the freezer. The safest way to check food temperatures is by using a kitchen thermometer that registers 0°F to 220°F.

Step 6: Cover food only after it has completely cooled. Refrigerators should be kept at around 35° to 37°F in order to store food at or colder than 40°F. Date leftovers so they can be used within two to four days. *When in doubt, throw it out.*

Proper reheating of leftovers is just as critical as proper cooking and cooling. Foods that cool down through the "danger zone" and are reheated through the "danger zone" require an "extra jolt" to ensure their safety. Foods should always be reheated to a minimum internal temperature of 165°F, and liquid foods must be reheated to boiling. If foods are reheated in the microwave, they should be reheated to 190°F to eliminate "cold spots," or reheated to 165°F in all parts of the food. Slow cookers (i.e., crockpots) do not heat foods hot enough or quickly enough to prevent foodborne illness and therefore should never be used to reheat leftovers.

Young children often enjoy eating unseasoned tofu, even though most adults find it too bland to be palatable. It's convenient to give youngsters a piece of tofu straight from the package, so many parents get into the habit of doing this. Tofu that is cooked or baked and vacuum sealed, or made and sold in aseptic boxes, is safe for immediate consumption. However, tofu that is packed in water and sold in tubs is a prime medium for breeding foodborne pathogens, especially if temperatures have been less than ideal during transport from the manufacturer to warehouse to store to home. Therefore, this kind of tofu should *never* be used "raw" in recipes (such as tofu salad, spreads, dips, or smoothies) or fed directly to children. Water-packed tofu must be boiled in water or steamed for five to ten minutes prior to using in order to destroy any potentially dangerous bacteria that might be on it. If the tofu comes in a thick block, cut it into thinner slabs so the internal temperature can more quickly reach 165°F. Then use the proper techniques for rapidly cooling the tofu before proceeding with a recipe or giving it to children to eat plain. This step may be omitted if the tofu will be cooked (as with tofu scramble), baked, or used in recipes with other ingredients that will be cooked together. Some children and adults develop "tofu tummy"— gas, bloating, cramps, nausea, vomiting, fever, headache, or diarrhea—after eating "raw," water-packed tofu and come to the conclusion that they must be allergic to soy products or tofu. This is not necessarily the case. "Tofu tummy" can mimic some of the symptoms of a food allergy, but it usually is attributable to mild to severe food poisoning caused by foodborne pathogens. With proper care, this easily can be averted.

In addition to managing the critical control points for preventing foodborne illness—proper cooking; rapid cooling; avoiding cross contamination; and storing, holding, and reheating food at safe temperatures—*fresh produce should always be washed thoroughly before eating or cooking.* This is best done simply by scrubbing it with your hands under plain potable water. Still, washing will not remove agricultural chemicals that have been absorbed into the vegetable or fruit. The only way to avoid ingesting these chemicals is to purchase organic foods. If you do not have access to fresh organic produce, always remove the outer leaves of lettuce, cabbage, and other leafy greens, and peel root vegetables and fruits when appropriate and possible.

When hand-washing dishes, wash them all within two hours, before bacteria can begin to form. Allow dishes and utensils to air-dry in order to eliminate recontamination from hands or towels.

Keep sponges and dishcloths clean because, when wet, these materials harbor bacteria and encourage their growth. Home cooks commonly use dishcloths or sponges to mop up areas where they have worked and then reuse the cloth or sponge in other kitchen areas after minimal rinsing. The odor in smelly dishcloths and sponges is caused by bacterial growth. A contaminated dishcloth can house millions of bacteria after just a few hours. Instead of cloth towels, consider using paper towels to clean up and then throw them away immediately. If you use cloth towels, wash them often in the hot cycle of your washing machine.

Brown-Bagging It

> Tell me, I'll forget. Show me, I may remember. Involve me, and I'll understand.
>
> *—Chinese proverb*

Packing Safe Lunches

If we could send a refrigerator to school with our children, there wouldn't be a problem with packed lunches, because the best way to prevent foodborne illness is to keep perishable foods cold. It's risky to leave tofu sandwiches, hummus, or pasta or potato salads in a warm locker until lunchtime. If you know your children's food can't be kept cold, choose only foods that are safe to eat even if they haven't been refrigerated.

Safety-Smart, Nutritious, Take-Along Foods

- *Protein foods:* Nuts, seeds, and nut and seed butters (including peanut butter), trail mix, snack-type soy and rice puddings, soymilk and fortified soy shakes in shelf-stable boxes.
- *Fresh fruits and vegetables:* Apples, bananas, oranges, peaches, plums, grapes, grapefruit, carrot and celery sticks, green pepper strips, green salad with cucumber and tomato. Whole fruits and vegetables are good "travelers"; just be sure to wash them thoroughly before packing in order to remove the soil you can see as well as some of the bacteria and residues you can't see.
- *Dried fruit:* Raisins, apricots, apples, bananas, pineapple, prunes.
- *Juices:* 100 percent vegetable or fruit juice in shelf-stable boxes, cans, or bottles. Chill or freeze them the night before.

- *Other beverages:* Fortified soymilk, rice milk, amazake (a naturally sweet, fermented, rice-based beverage), and soy shakes in shelf-stable boxes are good lunchbox additions. Chill or freeze them the night before.
- *Unopened canned foods:* Canned fruit, canned bean dips, and other canned items with safe, easy-open lids are ideal for lunch boxes. Chill them the night before so they can help keep other foods in the lunch box cold.
- *Instant dry mixes:* Individual serving cups of dry soup, oatmeal, rice pudding, and seasoned mashed potatoes can be part of a safe, quick, and nutritious lunch if children have ready access to hot water or a microwave oven.
- *Bread and crackers:* Bread, bagels, rolls, English muffins, breadsticks, soft and hard pretzels, whole-grain crackers, potato and tortilla chips, rice cakes, lavash, pita bread, muffins, granola, dry cereal, popcorn, cookies.
- *Others:* Jams and jellies, mustard, ketchup, pickles, pickle relish.

Potentially Hazardous Foods

Note: These foods *must* be kept at the proper temperatures (40°F or below for cold foods; 140°F or higher internal temperature for hot foods) during the entire time they are stored; otherwise they will become unsafe to eat. Most freeze packs and thermoses keep foods at safe temperatures for only two to four hours. If you have any misgivings about the temperature of your children's packed lunches (from the time they leave home to the time the lunch is eaten), leave out these items.

High-protein foods (raw and cooked):
- dairy
- eggs and egg products
- tofu
- tempeh
- seitan
- beans and bean dips

High-carbohydrate foods (cooked):
- pasta
- potatoes
- rice
- soups, sauces, gravies
- food mixtures that contain any of the above items

Others:
- warm iced tea (bacteria is naturally found in tea leaves)
- sprouts (all kinds)
- any food marked "keep under refrigeration"

Which Foods Are Not Potentially Hazardous?

Low-protein, dry high-carbohydrate, and high-acidity foods are not potentially haz-ardous. However, cross contamination still can occur. Therefore, be sure to follow appropriate food safety and sanitation measures to avoid transferring disease-causing organisms from a contaminated food or surface to a safe one.

Lunch Box Food Safety Tips

Step 1: Keep everything that touches food clean. Wash your hands with hot, soapy water before preparing food, and wash all surfaces that touch food, such as utensils, bowls, and countertops. Use a fork or spoon rather than your hands to mix or prepare foods.

Step 2: Wash fruits and vegetables. Washing them removes visible dirt as well as the bacteria, viruses, and insecticide sprays that you can't see.

Step 3: Refrigerate any lunch items prepared the night before. Perishables—such as tofu, tempeh, meat analogs, beans, soy yogurt, tofu-based sauces or salad dressings, rice salad, cold pasta, potato salad, etc.—must be kept cold (40°F or colder). Snacks, cookies, granola, and other nonperishables that go limp in the fridge should be added to the lunch box the next day.

Step 4: Keep cold foods cold and hot foods hot. Use an insulated lunch bag or box along with freeze packs to keep cold foods cold. Frozen juice boxes and frozen soy yogurt cups also can help keep lunches chilled; by lunchtime they will be thawed and ready to eat. An insulated bottle or thermos can be used to keep hot foods hot.

Step 5: Make sandwiches with cold ingredients—chill both the bread and sandwich filling before assembling. Room-temperature bread can act as an insulator, warming up cold fillings and preventing room-temperature fillings from cool-ing down, even in an insulated tote equipped with a freeze pack. Whenever pos-sible, freeze sandwiches the night before. They will be thawed in time for lunch.

Step 6: Children should be instructed to wash their hands before eating lunch. This will reduce the risk of contamination by harmful bacteria. Remind them that caution should be used when sharing lunches with other children; allergic reactions to food items or ingredients are possible, and they cannot be certain what their friends' lunches contain.

Step 7: Throw away leftovers. Insulated lunch bags and boxes, even with a freeze pack, keep food safe only until lunchtime and generally don't work for all-day storage. Any perishable leftovers should be discarded and not brought home.

Step 8: Clean lunch bags and boxes every night. This keeps bacteria from growing inside. A weekly cleaning with baking soda and water will help eliminate any unpleasant odors.

Kid-Approved Packed Lunches

Here are a few suggestions to make packed lunches fun and tasty so your children will eat nutritiously:

- Plan the lunch menu with your children.
- Have your children help prepare the lunch.
- Children enjoy foods that are easy to eat. Make portion sizes small and convenient.
- Make fruit and vegetables easy to eat. For instance, slice carrots into sticks and pack a separate container of dip, or peel an orange and pack the separated segments.
- Be creative; make lunches fun. For example, use a cookie cutter to cut out sandwich shapes.
- Take the children shopping with you, and teach them how to read food labels and buy nutritious items for their lunches.

Picnic and Potluck Protocol

Practice is the best of all instructions.

—*Aristotle*

Planning Safe Picnics

Children love picnics, but food spoils quickly in the summer heat. In hot weather, it is especially important to pack food carefully to prevent foodborne illness.

How to prepare safe and tasty picnic food:

- Use an insulated cooler with sufficient ice or ice packs to keep the food at 40°F or lower. Pack the food directly from the refrigerator into your cooler.
- Use commercial ice packs or make your own. To make your own ice pack, take some ice cubes and place them in a heavy plastic freezer bag. Wrap the bag with foil and place this "ice pack" or a commercial freeze pack inside your insulated cooler to keep food cold.
- Don't put the cooler in the trunk; carry it inside the air-conditioned car.
- Use a separate cooler for drinks so the one containing perishable food won't be constantly opened and closed at the picnic site.
- Plan just the right amount of food to take so that you won't have to worry about the storage or safety of leftovers.
- Make several sandwiches one at a time. Wrap each sandwich by itself and freeze it separately. After the sandwiches are frozen, put them together in a big plastic bag and keep them in the freezer until you're ready to leave. Simple sandwiches, such as peanut butter and jelly, seitan slices, or vegan deli "meats" freeze best.
- When you leave the house, place the frozen sandwiches in your cooler. They will thaw by lunchtime. Put lettuce, tomato, and vegan mayonnaise in separate containers in the cooler and add them to the sandwiches just before they are to be eaten.
- Freeze small cans or boxes of juice or small containers of soy yogurt or applesauce, and place them in your cooler. The frozen food will thaw by lunchtime and will help keep other foods cold.
- Serve safe, warm-weather lunch foods such as fresh or canned fruit, raw vegetables, raisins, trail mix, crackers, cookies, pretzels, or popcorn.
- Pack all food in clean plastic wrap or sandwich bags.

Tips for serving safe food at the picnic site:

- Keep the cooler in the shade. Don't leave it in direct sunlight or in the trunk of the car.
- Keep the lid on the cooler, and avoid opening the cooler frequently.
- Add more ice if the ice begins to melt.

- Do not leave food out for more than two hours. If the air temperature is 85°F or hotter, keep food out less than one hour.
- Serve food from the cooler quickly.
- Serve small portions so the food doesn't stay out of the cooler too long.
- Be sure to take plenty of clean serving spoons and forks so each dish has its own. If one dish spoils, the bacteria won't be moved to another dish through a contaminated utensil.
- Pack clean, soapy sponges, cloths, and wet towelettes for cleaning surfaces and hands.

General rules for food prepared at the picnic site:
- Keep veggie burgers and dogs cold until you're ready to grill them.
- Cook food completely at the picnic site; avoid partial cooking ahead of time.
- Cook food thoroughly until it is hot in the center.
- Use a clean plate to serve cooked food.

Share-a-Dish Meals and Parties

Share-a-dish gatherings and parties are lots of fun and a great opportunity to taste new recipes. Unfortunately, they also can be a perfect breeding ground for foodborne pathogens. Soups, casseroles, spreads, dips, pasta and potato salads, and more typically sit on buffet tables at room temperature for hours on end. Because share-a-dish meals often are considered "pot luck"—that is, the host doesn't have control over what dishes guests bring—there is little control over how foods are handled, stored, or served.

If you are the host of a share-a-dish gathering, here are some recommendations to keep you, your children, and your guests safe from foodborne illness. If you are not the host but are attending a share-a-dish event, pass on these suggestions to the appropriate person in charge.

> ### Keep hot foods hot. Keep cold foods cold.

1. Food display and service should be *well planned* in advance so that potentially hazardous foods are handled, stored, and served properly and at the correct temperatures.

2. Hot foods must maintain an internal temperature of 140°F or higher (preferably between 140°F and 160°F).

3. Reheated foods must reach 165°F or higher and then be reduced to 140°F or higher for holding or serving. Soups should be heated to boiling; they then can be transferred to a covered electric crockpot for serving. Casseroles must be reheated to an internal temperature of 165°F and can be kept hot (140°F or higher) on the buffet table with warming trays, chafing dishes, or slow cookers.

4. Cold foods must be maintained at 40°F or colder during service or storage. Keep foods cold by nesting dishes in bowls of ice.

5. Use a "stab thermometer" for checking the internal temperature of food and disposable gloves to cover cut or scraped hands (or long or painted fingernails).

6. Maintain a list of the names, addresses, and phone numbers of everyone who brought an item to the event, including what they prepared. Foods should be transported to the event in a clean vehicle with proper temperature control.

7. Food handlers cannot be ill, have an "asymptomatic" illness, or open cuts or wounds. Handlers should not be permitted to use tobacco or eat or drink while handling foods. Proper hand washing should be strictly enforced after restroom use, smoking, drinking, eating, or handling garbage or dirty dishes.

8. Have only one person designated to serve. Do not permit self-service for adults or children. Do not allow children to handle or serve food.

Don't Pass the Food Poisoning, Please

Share-a-dish meals are an easy way to entertain or be entertained. The planning and expenses for the host are minimized, and everybody shares in the work. Here are some pointers to keep in mind when selecting your own offering of a dish to share.

1. Don't assume there will be time or room in the host's kitchen for final preparations when you arrive. Plan to bring an item that is "ready to go" unless you have checked with your host first.

2. Can your dish be served safely at room temperature? If not, how will you keep it hot or cold?

3. Is your food easy to serve and eat?

4. Will your dish travel well, or does it require extra care to arrive in good shape?

5. Bring all the necessary containers and utensils for serving and eating. Your host may have other plans, but if you arrive "well tooled," there won't be any surprises.

6. Thermal containers, ice chests, and insulated coolers will keep hot foods hot and cold foods cold. Pack food and nonfood items separately, and thoroughly heated or chilled foods in separate containers.

7. Remember that food spoilage in progress is almost impossible to detect. It takes only an hour for bacteria to grow to dangerous proportions in warm, moist conditions. This growth does not alter the taste, odor, or appearance of most foods at the time they are being served. Take extra precautions with high-protein and moist high-carbohydrate foods.

When we practice safe food habits through wise purchasing, appropriate storage, and proper cooking and cooling, our children will learn from both our instruction and our example. In addition, we will maximize the benefits of the wholesome foods we serve our families while protecting them from one of the most prevalent but preventable human health hazards—foodborne illness.

Now that we understand the basics of food safety, we can implement these valuable techniques in our home kitchens; when we pack lunches, travel, and go on picnics; and when we plan share-a-dish gatherings and parties. In the next section we will cover the essentials of vegetarian nutrition from birth through adolescence.

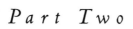

Part Two

Nourishing Our Children

Chapter 6

Vegetarian Nutrition 101

This section of the book provides a practical plan for healthful eating from birth through adolescence. Teaching our children to enjoy good nutrition from the start presents an incredible opportunity to chart their course for a lifetime of health. The food habits and attitudes our youngsters learn will be reflected throughout their lives in reduced risk of cancer, heart disease, weight problems, and allergies, as well as fewer ailments during childhood. Being well nourished gives children a tremendous advantage in providing the raw materials to grow, thrive, learn, and play well.

We begin with a simple yet comprehensive food guide and the nutritional strategies to implement it. In the next chapter, we cover infant feeding, including the requirements of lactating women. Then we outline nutrition information for children and teens. Finally, we help you and your little ones navigate through the potential hazards of restaurant eating, celebration meals, school lunch programs, and media messages about food and body image. Following this section, you'll find a treasury of easy-to-prepare, delicious recipes that support the menus and nutrition guidelines covered in this book.

> The attitudes towards vegetarian diets have progressed through the years—from onetime ridicule and skepticism through condescending tolerance, gradual and sometimes grudging acceptance, and finally, to acclaim.
> —*Mervyn Hardinge, M.D., Dr.P.H., Ph.D.,*
> *Professor Emeritus, School of Public Health,*
> *Loma Linda University*

Are Vegetarian Diets Nutritionally Adequate?

Well-meaning friends, acquaintances, or relatives may express concern that your children won't get all the nutrients they need on a vegetarian diet (particularly if they haven't kept up-to-date with the scientific research on nutrition and health). You, too, may have heard rumors that plant-based diets are inevitably low in protein or lack certain nutrients.

It is true that children on overly restrictive diets, such as those limited to vegetables or fruits, tend to grow poorly. Eating plans that provide insufficient calories, are deficient in minerals over long periods of time, and prohibit the use of the supplementary vitamin B_{12} and fortified foods where needed will retard children's growth and lead to health problems. The trouble isn't that these youngsters are on vegetarian diets but that their diets are very poorly planned. *Any* sort of eating pattern that is not well designed can lack nutrients. The general meat- and dairy-consuming population provides plenty of examples of children who are anemic, fail to thrive, and are malnourished in a variety of ways (including being overweight).

> Appropriately planned vegan and lactoovovegetarian diets satisfy nutrient needs of infants, children, and adolescents and promote normal growth.
> —*Position of the American Dietetic Association:*
> *Vegetarian Diets*

Studies clearly have shown the growth of vegetarian infants, children, and teens to be similar to the growth of nonvegetarians. Simple and sound guidelines for planning balanced diets are the focus of this section.

Are Vegetarian Diets Risky? Am I Depriving My Child?

Forty years ago, the major theme of the research on vegetarian nutrition was dietary adequacy and answering questions such as, "Can vegetarians get enough protein?" The focus and capabilities of researchers have changed considerably in four decades. Now we see immense studies following the disease and mortality trends among hundreds of thousands of people practicing various types of eating patterns. Today scientists typically ask, "To what extent do vegetarian diets improve our ability to stay healthy?" Instead of being viewed as "risky," vegetarian diets are linked with *less* risk of chronic disease. Protection against heart disease? Less likelihood of obesity, several types of cancer, and diabetes? A diet packed with antioxidants and protective nutrients? This isn't deprivation. This sort of start for a child can be viewed as a gift!

Here's another advantage: vegetarians tend to take more interest in nutrition. Rather than being complacent, vegetarians are likely to seek out accurate information on dietary sources of vitamins and minerals. When we recognize the importance of good nutrition and healthful eating, the children in our lives benefit enormously. This is a legacy that will serve them their entire lives.

Granted, not *all* vegetarians have health in mind when they adopt this way of eating. Young people as well as adults often are drawn to meatless diets for entirely different reasons, such as a deep concern about animals or the environment. For them, the benefits they reap in improved health are a bonus. Still, a sensible dietary plan is vital for all vegetarians, regardless of their motivations.

Total Vegetarian Food Guide

The Total Vegetarian Food Guide (see Figure 6.1) provides a practical model for balanced nutrition that can be used by everyone four years of age and older. This guide is patterned after the U.S. Food Guide Pyramid with three significant improvements:

FIGURE 6.1

Total Vegetarian Food Guide

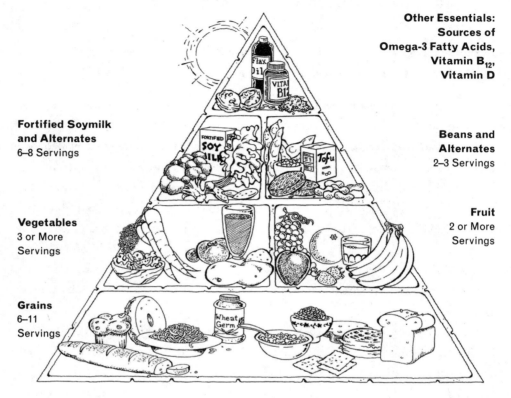

Other Essentials:
Sources of
Omega-3 Fatty Acids,
Vitamin B$_{12}$,
Vitamin D

Fortified Soymilk
and Alternates
6–8 Servings

Beans and
Alternates
2–3 Servings

Fruit
2 or More
Servings

Vegetables
3 or More
Servings

Grains
6–11
Servings

Artwork by Dave Brousseau

Reprinted with permission from *Becoming Vegan*, Book Publishing Co., Summertown, Tenn. © 2000 by Vesanto Melina, Brenda Davis, and Davd Brousseau.

1. *Foods of animal origin have been replaced by plant foods that contain similar amounts of key nutrients.* The group that is particularly high in protein, iron, and zinc is called Beans and Alternates. High-calcium foods form the Fortified Soymilk and Alternates group.

2. *The recommended intake of Fortified Soymilk and Alternates is six to eight servings.* This is more than double the number of servings from the Milk and Alternates group in the U.S. Food Guide Pyramid, for two reasons. First, this allows a variety of calcium-rich plant foods to be included in reasonable serving sizes. In the U.S. Food Guide Pyramid, one serving equals 1 cup of milk, while

in the Total Vegetarian Food Guide, one serving equals ½ cup of fortified soymilk, 1 cup of steamed broccoli or kale, 1 tablespoon of blackstrap molasses, and so on. (See Table 6.1.) Second, the number of servings of calcium-rich foods reflects the Dietary Reference Intakes (DRI) for calcium, which have increased since the U.S. Food Guide Pyramid was designed.

3. *The Other Essentials group points out sources of omega-3 fatty acids, vitamin B_{12}, and vitamin D.*

A food guide is a framework to help us select different kinds and amounts of foods. Ideally its purpose is to educate consumers about food choices most likely to promote physical well-being and to prevent or postpone the onset of diet-related chronic diseases. However, national guides, such as the U.S. Food Guide Pyramid and Canada's Guide to Healthy Eating, are the product of other pressures, too. For example, meat and dairy marketing boards primarily are concerned with creating consumer markets for their products when they exert their influences on national nutrition policies.

The Total Vegetarian Food Guide was designed with the health of you and your family in mind. It includes the best features of the U.S. Food Guide Pyramid in presenting a balance of food groups that provide key nutrients. For example, while many plant foods contribute to the total protein intake for a day, those in the Beans and Alternates group are particularly strong overall in the amount of protein they provide, along with supplying the minerals iron and zinc. Foods in the Fortified Soymilk and Alternates group are rich in calcium. At the same time, foods in both of these groups are cholesterol free and low in saturated fat. Over the next pages, we will go through each food group in the guide, showing the nutritional contribution made by each and giving tips for its use in children's diets.[*]

Beans and Alternates

Protein Power

The protein requirements of children are easily met by vegetarian diets. Which foods are the protein providers? This question can be answered simply: *all* plant foods. Protein is an essential part of every plant cell. Breakfast cereals, peanut butter, bread, veggie

---

[*]Note for ovolactovegetarians: An egg can be counted as a half serving from the Beans and Alternates group. A half cup of cow's milk or yogurt or 1 ounce of cheese can be counted as a serving in the Fortified Soymilk and Alternates group.

TABLE 6.1

The Total Vegetarian Food Guide

A Guide to Daily Food Choices for Ages Four Years and Older

The ranges in servings allow for differences in body size, activity level, and age. For example, smaller, less active people need fewer servings; larger, more active people need more. Small children may need smaller servings. *Also see the Plant-Based Food Guide for Toddlers (one to three years of age) on page 188.*

Food Group *servings per day*	What Counts As a Serving?	Important Comments
Beans and Alternates (beans, tofu, nuts, and seeds) *2–3 servings*	1 cup cooked legumes (beans, lentils, dried peas) ½ cup firm tofu or tempeh 1 serving veggie "meat" (1 burger or wiener, or 2–3 lunch slices) 3 tbsp. nut or seed butter ¼ cup nuts and seeds 2 cups soymilk	Eat a wide range of these protein-rich foods. When eaten together with foods in this group, vitamin C–rich vegetables or fruits will boost iron absorption. Nuts and seeds provide vitamin E and minerals.
Fortified Soymilk and Alternates *6–8 servings*	½ cup fortified soymilk ¼ cup calcium-set tofu ½ cup calcium-fortified orange/fruit juice ¼ cup almonds 3 tbsp. almond butter 1 cup cooked (or 2 cups raw) high-calcium greens: kale, collards, Chinese greens, broccoli, okra 1 cup high-calcium beans: soy, white, navy, Great Northern, black turtle beans ¼ cup dry hijiki seaweed 1 tbsp. blackstrap molasses 5 figs	Get to know your calcium sources! Many of these double as servings from the Vegetables and the Beans groups. Include calcium-rich foods with every meal. To count as a serving in this group, foods should provide at least 15% of the Daily Value (DV). Check labels.

Food Group servings per day	What Counts As a Serving?	Important Comments
Grains (bread, cereal, whole grains, and pasta) *6–11 servings*	1 slice of bread 1 oz. ready-to-eat cereal ½ cup cooked grains, cereal, or pasta ½ large roll or bagel 2 tbsp. wheat germ 1 oz. other grain products	Choose mainly whole grains. Good examples are brown rice, barley, quinoa, millet, oats, wheat, and kamut berries, as well as whole-grain breads and cereals.
Vegetables *3 or more servings*	½ cup vegetables 1 cup raw leafy vegetables ¾ cup vegetable juice	Eat a variety of colorful vegetables. Include raw vegetables each day. Many green vegetables are rich in calcium.
Fruits *2 or more servings*	1 medium apple, banana, orange, pear ½ cup fruit ¾ cup fruit juice ¼ cup dried fruit	Select an assortment of fruits. Vitamin C–rich choices are citrus fruits, kiwi, strawberries, guava, papaya, cantaloupe, and mangos.
Other Essentials: Vitamin B_{12} to meet recommended intakes	Fortified foods or supplements supplying: 0.9–1.8 micrograms/day for children 2.4 micrograms/day for adults 2.6–2.8 micrograms/day during pregnancy and lactation	Pay attention to these important nutrients. Look for foods fortified with vitamin B_{12}.

(continued)

TABLE 6.1 (CONTINUED)

Food Group serving per day	What Counts As a Serving?	Important Comments
Vitamin D to meet recommended intakes	Fortified foods or supplement with 5 micrograms/day (10–15 micrograms for those over 50 years of age) or sunshine	It just takes a little sunshine on the face and hands to make vitamin D; otherwise use fortified foods or supplements.
Omega-3 fatty acids 1–2 servings	1 tsp. flaxseed oil 4 tsp. canola oil 1 tbsp. ground flaxseeds 3 tbsp. walnuts	Flax oil is an easy-to-use source of omega-3s: use it in dressings for salads and on baked potatoes, vegetables, and grains.

Extra pointers:

- Drink six to eight glasses of water and other fluids each day.
- Limit intake of fats, oils, and added sugars, if used.
- Get at least thirty minutes of physical activity each day.
- Eat a wide variety of foods from each food group.

burgers, soymilk, soup, broccoli—in fact, almost every food eaten during the day contributes protein for body functions and the growth, maintenance, and repair of cells.

Children need about 0.5 to 0.7 grams of protein for each pound of body weight. Soyfoods (tofu, soymilk, tempeh, veggie "meats") are particularly good protein sources; these generally are well digested and easily utilized by the body. When soyfoods are used regularly (in addition to other foods, such as grains and vegetables), protein requirements are at the low end of the range: about 0.5 to 0.6 grams per pound.

When we rely on a "whole-foods" diet in which much of the protein comes from beans, peas, lentils, and whole grains, and little from soyfoods, the recommended protein intake for children is at the higher end of the range: about 0.6 to 0.7 grams per pound. The higher requirements are due to differences in digestibility.

As teens reach adulthood and complete their growth spurt, the amount of protein needed per pound of body weight gradually decreases to about 0.4 grams per pound. Recommended intakes for athletes are a little more; however, these still can be met with no problem on vegetarian diets (see page 229). It's important for athletes to know that the amount of protein per calorie is higher in many plant foods (such as lentil soup) than, say, in a cheeseburger. Plant protein easily supports muscle development, strength training, and endurance activities.

Foods in the Beans and Alternates group are considered key protein providers because on average they provide about 12 to 15 grams of protein per serving. They have approximately twice the protein content of grains. For details on the amount of protein in various foods, see the six menus in Tables 9.2 (page 208) and 10.1, (page 219). These menus easily meet and even exceed recommended protein intakes.

The column headed "Important Comments" in Table 6.1 advises us to "Eat a wide range of these protein-rich foods." Lentils, split peas, and beans are high in protein yet generally very low in fat (as little as 1 to 3 percent of the calories come from fat). Soybeans are unusual because they contain relatively high amounts of healthful polyunsaturated oils. This is one of the qualities that makes soy so versatile. Nuts and seeds are somewhat lower in protein. At the same time, they are higher in fat, making them an important component in the diets of energetic children and active teens.

If you are a little intimidated by the thought of introducing beans, peas, and lentils to your family's diet or don't know good ways to prepare the foods in this group, you're in for some treats. Learning to use these foods has elements of a world food tour. Whether we prefer European pea or lentil soup; African stew; Mexican chili, fajitas, and burritos; Italian pizza and pasta; Middle Eastern hummus; Asian-inspired stir-fry; or good old American veggie burgers, each part of the world has contributed savory ways to use these highly nutritious foods. Furthermore, these excellent protein providers offer several major advantages over meat. (See Table 6.2.)

If you have regarded nuts as salty, high-fat snack foods, here's a chance for an update. When we eliminate animal products from our meals, our intake of fats (especially saturated fats and cholesterol) drops substantially. Nuts and seeds provide valuable plant oils and many important nutrients. For example, walnuts contribute essential omega-3 fatty acids; almonds are rich in calcium; cashews provide zinc; and Brazil nuts (which are actually big seeds!) are concentrated sources of the antioxidant selenium.

Nuts and even nut butters are not given to infants and young toddlers because of possible choking hazards (and in families with food allergies, introducing peanut butter should be delayed). However, nut butters can be thinned with soymilk or juice or put into shakes and smoothies, thus allowing youngsters to partake of these valuable foods.

For growing children, teens, and vegetarians with high energy needs, nuts and seeds balance the very low fat levels of most other plant foods and assume a place of importance in the diet. In addition, they provide protective phytochemicals (plant chemicals) and help with mineral absorption.

TABLE 6.2

Comparisons Between High-Protein Plant Foods and Meats

High-Protein Plant Foods	Meats
Are high in fiber.	Are fiber free.
Are generally low in fat; fat is primarily unsaturated.	Are high in total fat and saturated fat.
Are cholesterol free.	Are high in cholesterol.
Lower cholesterol.	Raise cholesterol.
Contain many protective phytochemicals.	Contain no phytochemicals.
Many provide calcium.	Lack calcium.

Tahini (a paste made from ground sesame seeds) or almond butter may replace the butter or margarine on morning toast or other breads. Tahini and ground sunflower seeds (or sunflower seed butter) can form a flavorful base for salad dressings. For some new and novel ways to add nuts and seeds to your diet, explore the breakfast recipes (pages 250 to 264), try African Stew (page 308), sample the sandwich spreads (pages 269 to 282), and feast on a variety of sumptuous desserts (pages 338 to 347).

Can Vegetarian Diets Be Too Low in Protein?

There are two situations in which the protein intake of children and teens may be insufficient. The first occurs if the overall diet is too low in calories, as in anorexia nervosa. The second happens if foods in the Beans and Alternates group are left out of the diet. For example, protein intake could be too low if the majority of food is from "empty calorie" items (i.e., those that are high in sugar and fat) or if the diet is built around salads and fruit. If a youngster tries to live on toast and jam for breakfast, chips or a snack bar plus juice for lunch, and the nonmeat parts of the family's evening meal, the diet will be short of protein along with zinc, calcium, iron, and vitamins. If we aim for a balance of foods, as in the Total Vegetarian Food Guide, protein needs will be met—and then some.

If your child has an allergy or intolerance to beans, soyfoods, peanuts, or nuts, it still is possible to be a vegetarian. It just takes a little extra planning and perhaps the help of a dietitian who specializes in vegetarian nutrition. (See the Resources section and www.andrews.edu/NUFS/vndpg.html.)

Fortified rice milk is fine as a source of dietary calcium; however, it is significantly lower in protein than soymilk (0.5 grams per cup for rice milk compared to 7 to 8 grams per cup for soymilk) and has negligible amounts of iron. So if rice milk is used, make sure that protein and iron needs are met in other ways. (In Tables 7.3 on page 169, 9.2 on page 208, and 10.1 on page 219, the nutritional analysis of the menus on the left has been done using fortified rice milk.)

Protein Quality

In the past, plant proteins were considered to be of lower quality than animal proteins because they have a slightly different combination of the same amino-acid building blocks. This concept arose in an era when scientists were feeding "mono diets" to baby rats during a stage of growth when they tripled their weight in a few weeks and grew fur on their bodies. Later it was determined that humans at any stage have protein requirements that are quite different than those of rats. Another difference is that after the first six months on breast milk or formula infant diets include variety.

Nutrition experts now recognize that the typical vegetarian diet is a mixture of plant foods with assorted combinations of amino acids (the building blocks of proteins). We do not have to carefully combine proteins at each meal (as was suggested in the first edition of the book *Diet for a Small Planet* by Frances Moor Lappé, which was published in the 1970s). All we need to do is follow the Total Vegetarian Food Guide. Over the course of a day, our diets will provide all the amino acids we need.

> Plant sources of protein alone can provide adequate amounts of essential amino acids if a variety of plant foods are consumed and energy needs are met.
> —*Position of the American Dietetic Association: Vegetarian Diets*

Pumping Iron

In addition to being protein providers, the Beans and Alternates are key sources of iron and zinc. Nonvegetarians and vegetarians alike can find it a challenge to get enough of these minerals during the growth years, infancy through adolescence. Women's diets often fall a little short, too, when it comes to these minerals. In fact, our need for these minerals provides one of the best reasons to make sure we eat two servings a day from this group: beans, split peas, lentils, soyfoods, veggie "meats," and nuts and seeds.

Iron in plant foods is absorbed at a slightly lower rate than iron in meats. This is counterbalanced by two essential facts. First, plant foods contain plenty of iron. For example, soybeans, lentils, tofu, pumpkin seeds, green beans, broccoli, cauliflower, mushrooms, kale, and blackstrap molasses all contain triple the amount of iron per calorie compared with ground beef. If we build our diets on plant foods, and include choices from the Beans and Alternates, we're not likely to run short of iron. See the menus on pages 169, 208, and 219 for examples that meet and exceed recommended iron intake.

Second, the typically high intake of vitamin C in vegetarian diets boosts iron absorption significantly. Fruits that are particularly high in vitamin C are listed in Table 6.1. Vegetables with plenty of this vitamin are bell peppers, broccoli, Brussels sprouts, cauliflower, collards, and snow peas. It turns out that there is no greater incidence of iron-deficiency anemia among vegetarians than among meat-eaters.

To avoid iron deficiency, we must ensure intake of iron-rich foods. In addition to those just mentioned, we get iron from a wide variety of beans, nuts and seeds, many vegetables, whole and enriched grains, and dried fruit (apricots, currants, figs, prunes, and raisins).

A medium-size baked potato provides 1.7 milligrams of iron; a half-cup of the grain quinoa supplies 2.2 milligrams of iron; and a cup of soymilk, 1 milligram. Iron-fortified veggie "meats," breakfast cereals, and Cream of Wheat can make a big difference in the iron intake of some children.

Recent nutrition recommendations have advised vegetarians to aim for 1.8 times the iron intake that is recommended for nonvegetarians. (These are the amounts given in Table 6.3.) This is both intelligent and achievable, since there are so many ways to get iron in plant-based diets. (See also Table 6.4.)

Think About Zinc

Where there's protein and iron, zinc tends to turn up, too. This mineral is crucial for immune system support, cell division, growth, wound healing, and our sense of taste.

TABLE 6.3

Recommended Intakes for Selected Minerals and Vitamins, Ages One to Eighteen

Recommended Intake per Day	1 to 3 Years	4 to 8 Years	Girl 9 to 13 Years	Boy 9 to 13 Years	Girl 14 to 18 Years	Boy 14 to 18 Years
Iron, mg	12	18	14	14	27	20
Zinc, mg	3	5	8	8	9	11
Calcium, mg	500	800	1,300	1,300	1,300	1,300
Vitamin B$_{12}$, mcg	0.9	1.2	1.8	2.4	1.8	2.4
Vitamin D, mcg	5	5	5	5	5	5

Minerals: What They Do and Good Dietary Sources

Mineral	What It Does	Food Sources	Special Tips
Calcium	Builds bones and teeth (along with protein and other minerals); helps pass nerve impulses, relax muscles, and clot blood.	Fortified soymilk, calcium-set tofu, calcium-fortified orange juice, almonds, almond butter, high-calcium greens (kale, collards, Chinese greens, broccoli, okra), high-calcium beans (soy, navy, Great Northern, black turtle beans), blackstrap molasses, figs, hijiki seaweed	45% of bone growth occurs during ages birth–8; 45% from ages 8–16; then the final 10% until about age 30.
Chromium	Helps us use carbohydrates properly and supports the action of insulin.	Whole grains, pecans and other nuts, mushrooms, asparagus, prunes, spices	Refined grains have lost chromium. Cooking acidic foods (such as pasta sauce) in stainless steel may add chromium to sauce.
Copper	Helps us to use protein properly and is a part of certain enzymes and hormones.	Legumes, seeds, nuts, millet, barley and other whole grains, avocados, mushrooms, peas, potatoes, sweet potatoes, tomato juice	Too much zinc (from supplements) can create imbalance and copper deficiency.

Mineral	What It Does	Food Sources	Special Tips
Fluoride	Helps harden bones and teeth.	Seaweeds, teas, beverages, vegetables (amounts vary considerably)	Fluoridated water and fluoride drops deliver known amounts; fluoride dental treatments are also a source.
Iodine	Is an essential part of hormones produced by the thyroid gland that control the body's use of energy. Intake is crucial during pregnancy.	Iodized salt, seaweeds, breads that use iodine-containing dough stabilizer	For adequate intake, rely on ½ tsp. iodized salt.
Iron	Helps carry oxygen to cells throughout the body and get rid of waste; is a part of the energy and immune systems; assists mental processes of learning.	Legumes (beans, peas, lentils, soyfoods), whole and enriched cereals, seeds, nuts, figs, dried apricots, prunes, raisins, fortified meat analogs, blackstrap molasses	Eating vitamin C–rich foods at the same time helps the body absorb iron. Cast-iron and stainless steel cookware add iron to foods.
Magnesium	Is part of teeth and bones; helps change food into usable energy and pass nerve impulses.	Greens and other vegetables, whole grains, nuts, seeds, beans (including the cocoa bean), fruit	Magnesium is part of the chlorophyll molecule that makes greens green.

(continued)

TABLE 6.4 (CONTINUED)

Mineral	What It Does	Food Sources	Special Tips
Selenium	Is a powerful antioxidant that protects cells from damage and possible disease.	Brazil nuts and other nuts, whole grains, lentils, beans, seeds (one Brazil nut provides the day's supply!)	Intakes of North American vegans generally are more than adequate.
Zinc	Supports growth, the immune system, wound healing, reproduction, and our ability to taste.	Legumes (beans, peas, lentils, soyfoods), whole (but *not* enriched) cereals, seeds, wheat germ, cashews, almonds, pecans, pine nuts, fortified meat analogs, mushrooms	Zinc (and iron) availability increases with sprouting (lentils, mung beans), soaking (beans, grains), yeasting (whole-grain bread), roasting (nuts), and use of fermented foods (sourdough bread, tempeh).

Undoubtedly, it's important in the lives of our little ones! Concentrated sources of zinc are seeds (pumpkin, sunflower), sesame tahini, nuts (especially cashews and pine nuts), beans of all types, and tofu. Zinc also is abundant in quinoa, millet and other whole (but not refined) grains, wheat germ, and mushrooms.

Here are some tips to help meet recommended intakes:

1. Make sure overall caloric intake is adequate.

2. Start the day with zinc-rich foods. Try tahini on toast, Vegetable Tofu Scramble, Granny's Grand Granola, Swiss-Style Muesli, Oatmeal Flax Porridge, Apples and Tahini, and Creamy Multigrain Porridge (see Recipes section). Another option is to purchase fortified breakfast cereals.

3. We absorb zinc better from soaked and sprouted foods. Get a few jars and sprout lids and start sprouting lentils (page 307). They're great on salads, sandwiches, burgers, burritos, and roll-ups.

4. Zinc is well absorbed from fermented soyfoods: tempeh, miso, and natto.

5. Add a little bag of trail mix with nuts and seeds to children's lunch boxes and backpacks.

6. Some veggie "meats" (such as Yves products) are fortified with zinc. Choose these for extra zinc.

Fortified Soymilk and Alternates

The Calcium Crew

In the Total Vegetarian Food Guide, the calcium-rich foods form the Fortified Soymilk and Alternates. This group includes a rather diverse assortment, with some foods doing "double duty" as Beans and Alternates (such as calcium-set tofu, fortified soymilk, almonds, and sesame tahini), as Vegetables (such as broccoli, kale, collards, Napa cabbage, bok choy, Chinese greens, and okra), or as Fruit (figs and calcium-fortified orange/fruit juice).

In this book, we concentrate on plant sources of calcium. We recognize that the reasons that inspire people to give up meat—whether they are health, environmental, animal rights, or ethical concerns—also apply to the milk produced by animals. As a bonus, plant foods are free of some of the disadvantages of dairy products, and they are rich in nutritional benefits that dairy products lack, such as fiber and the wealth of protective phytochemicals.

Calcium Through the Day

It is believed that before the dawn of agriculture, which occurred about ten thousand years ago, our ancestors' diets provided an estimated 1,400 to 2,000 milligrams of calcium per day without a single drop of cow's milk. This is about twice as much calcium as we take in today. Their diets included a variety of calcium-rich plant foods, eaten over the course of a day. This works very well, because we absorb calcium most efficiently when we eat calcium-rich foods at different times throughout the day, rather than having a big dose of calcium all at once. For example, we absorb much more calcium when we drink 6-ounce servings of fortified soymilk at three meals and one snack, rather than downing the total 3 cups all at once.

We help our children absorb calcium when we provide one or two calcium-rich items at each meal, and as snacks. Table 6.5 offers a few ideas.

A simple way to get enough calcium is to rely on fortified soymilk. Fortified beverages (soy, rice, and juices) generally are fortified with the same amount of calcium that cow's milk contains—about 300 milligrams per cup, or 150 milligrams per half cup (check labels).

The "alternates" in this food group provide approximately 125 to175 milligrams of calcium per serving. See sample menus in Chapters 7 (page 169), 9 (page 208), and 10 (page 219) for combinations that meet or exceed the recommended intake for different ages, as shown in Table 6.3.

What if you can't imagine your child drinking 2 cups of fortified soymilk, let alone eating a bowl of kale? When making porridge, use fortified soymilk or rice milk instead of water. Add these milks to pancakes, muffins, cream soups, mashed potatoes, smoothies, and puddings. Blend fortified soymilk with frozen bananas and berries to make "ice cream." Add calcium-set tofu to shakes and casseroles, and blend it into pasta sauce. Offer chunks of marinated tofu as part of a raw vegetable platter, for nibbles.

Calcium Absorption

We don't absorb all of the calcium in our diets. Absorption rates are highest with juice that is fortified with calcium citrate malate (about 50 percent) and with the

TABLE 6.5

Boosting Calcium from Dawn to Dusk

	Calcium-Rich Foods
Breakfast	Almond butter on a bagel, tahini on toast, blackstrap molasses as sweetener on porridge, Vegetable Tofu Scramble (page 261), Apples and Tahini (page 264), Orange Banana Whirl (page 242), Sneaky Dad's Power Punch Smoothie (page 244) made with calcium-fortified orange juice
Lunch or Supper	Raw broccoli florets, marinated tofu sandwich, hummus, Tofu-Vegetable Spread (page 277), Gee Whiz Spread (page 273), Cheeze Please Soup (page 286), Bean Burrito (page 282), Build-Your-Bones Salad with Sesame Tahini Salad Dressing (pages 297 and 289), Protein-Rich Stir-Fry (page 314), African Stew (page 308), Crispy Tofu Fingers (page 315), Cheez-a-Roni (page 310), Colorful Kabobs (page 318), Great Greens (page 327), Whipped Potatoes (page 328), Sensational Stuffed Squash (page 331)
Desserts	Rice and Raisin Pudding (page 340), Muscle Muffins (page 265), Fudgesoycles (page 346)
Beverages (with any meal or as snack)	Calcium-fortified soymilk, rice milk, or juice; Warm Spiced Milk or Warm Cocoa (pages 248 and 249); shake or smoothie with fortified beverage (pages 241 to 245)
Snacks	Figs, almonds, Muscle Muffins (page 265), toast with tahini and a little blackstrap molasses, bagel or bread with almond butter, soy nuts

green vegetables broccoli, kale, collards, Napa cabbage, bok choy, Chinese greens, and okra (about 40 to 60 percent). Calcium-set tofu has an absorption rate that is comparable with cow's milk, in the range of 31 to 32 percent. The proportion absorbed from soymilk, white beans, pinto beans, and sweet potatoes is a little lower, about 22 to 27 percent. Around 20 percent of the calcium in almonds and sesame tahini is absorbed. Thus, of the foods we list as calcium sources, some have absorption rates higher than the calcium in cow's milk, some a little lower.

The Fortified Soymilk and Alternates group does not include foods with low rates of calcium absorption. Although spinach, Swiss chard, beet greens, and rhubarb contain calcium, we absorb only about 5 percent of the calcium in these foods due to the presence of oxalates that bind much of the mineral.

Though it takes a fair amount of kale (1 cup cooked) to count as a serving in this group, note that kale contains more calcium per calorie than 2 percent milk; plus, the calcium in kale is about twice as well absorbed. The calcium-rich greens shouldn't be discounted as important parts of the day's intake.

Childhood Is Bone-Building Time

Our maximum bone mass is attained when we are about thirty years old. Of the grand total bone weight that we reach at age thirty, we gain about 45 percent before the age of eight, another 45 percent between the ages of eight and sixteen, and the last 10 percent between ages sixteen and thirty. (In the decades that follow, there's a gradual decline in bone mass.) We want our children to develop good, solid bones during the bone-building years. If they do, they're more likely to end up with a fair amount of bone remaining at age eighty. Calcium is a key component of strong bones, along with a balanced diet that supplies other bone-building nutrients, and exercise.

Does this mean we must provide our children with cow's milk? Certainly not. Yet so much dairy advertising is done in the media and as nutrition education in schools that the public and most health professionals know more about milk than about other calcium sources.

Is Cow's Milk Essential to Humans?

Educational efforts of the dairy industry, targeted to children across the land, are motivated by a basic drive to sell cow's milk. In the 1940s and 1950s, the National Dairy Council produced its *Guide to Good Eating,* depicting dairy products as one of the four cornerstones of a healthy diet. This industry lobbies to maintain its products as an essential food group in national food guides in the United States, Canada, and other countries.

National food guides are beginning to make slight adjustments that better reflect current scientific research regarding dietary sources of calcium, though change is slow. In presenting cow's milk as indispensable, food guides have ignored the eating patterns of millions of North Americans who, by reason of culture, tradition, preference, ethics, or health choose to use few or no dairy products. In fact, there are many ways to meet our need for the nutrients often contributed by dairy products. The notion that milk and its products are essential foods is outdated and incorrect.

Though several generations of national food guides have presented cow's milk as essential, the most recent U.S. Dietary Guidelines recognized fortified soymilk as an important dietary source of calcium. The *Manual of Clinical Dietetics,* published by the American Dietetic Association and Dietitians of Canada in 2000, acknowledges many alternative calcium sources. While it is true that dairy products are high in calcium, this does not mean that they are our only sources of calcium, nor are they necessarily our best sources.

All mammals other than human beings, including those with enormous bone mass, such as elephants and rhinoceroses, obtain calcium from plant sources after they are weaned. We can build bone the same natural way. It is groundless and illogical to assume that the milk of another species is essential for bone growth and human health.

Potential Problems with Milk

The Type of Fats: Saturated, Trans-Fatty Acids, and Cholesterol.
The fat in dairy products is 66 percent saturated and contains up to 9 percent transfatty acids. Both types of fat are associated with increased risk of heart disease.

Lactose Intolerance.
Lactose is a sugar in dairy products. In 2 percent milk, for example, one-third of the calories come from lactose, one-third from fat, and one-third from protein. It is well known that after the age of four, most people lose, to some extent, their ability to digest lactose. Lactose also is present in human milk. The intestinal change in young children that diminishes their ability to digest lactose appears to be a normal part of maturation that occurs by the age at which weaning would be complete.

This change in the ability to digest milk sugar occurs in 90 to 100 percent of Asians, 80 percent of American Indians, 75 percent of African Americans, 50 to 60 percent of Hispanics, and 20 percent of North American Caucasians. When lactose isn't digested, it reaches our intestines and is consumed by bacteria that produce acid and gas. Symptoms of lactose intolerance can be mild or severe and include stomachaches, gas, bloating, and diarrhea.

Cow's Milk Protein Allergy and Intolerance. Cow's milk contains more than one protein that can trigger an allergic response in children. The result may be inflammation in the gastrointestinal tract. In this situation, whole proteins and large segments of proteins can be absorbed into the bloodstream instead of being broken down and properly digested. Cow's milk allergy has been linked to skin rashes, infant colic, respiratory difficulties, and digestive problems. Research currently is underway to investigate possible links between cow's milk consumption and certain neurological problems as well.

Potential Link to Juvenile Diabetes. In the case of genetically susceptible children, drinking cow's milk may be linked to Type I diabetes, also known as juvenile onset diabetes. According to the American Academy of Pediatrics, more than ninety research studies suggest that when some children consume cow's milk protein, their immune systems can react by making antibodies. Though the antibodies are created to fight against portions of the milk protein, it seems that they also may go to the pancreas and destroy cells that produce insulin. This sequence of events could lead to Type I diabetes.

Contribution to Iron Deficiency. Intake of cow's milk is an important cause of iron-deficiency anemia in infants and children. Dairy products are very low in iron and also interfere with iron absorption.

Possible Link to Crohn's Disease. It is estimated that 20 to 50 percent of U.S. dairy herds are infected with a microorganism the short name of which is MAP. (The long name is *mycobacterium avium subspecies paratuberculosis.*) Evidence suggests that MAP may cause a substantial proportion of cases of Crohn's disease in people who consume dairy products that harbor the MAP organism. MAP is not fully destroyed by normal milk pasteurization methods, and it is present in people with Crohn's disease.

Great Grains

Solar Power
What's great about grains? First, they provide the body's ideal energy source. Through the process of photosynthesis, plants convert and package the sun's

energy into sugars. Long chains of sugar molecules known as complex carbohydrates are present in grains, vegetables (especially root vegetables), and legumes. These are perfect "time release" bundles of calories.

Grains, which are the seeds of cereal grasses, bring a great deal to the human diet. Worldwide, they provide 51 percent of our calories and 47 percent of our protein. They have an excellent balance of calories from protein, fat, and complex carbohydrate. In addition, whole grains contain iron, zinc, selenium, magnesium, other trace minerals, phytochemicals, all of the B vitamins except B_{12}, and dietary fiber.

Selenium, Other Trace Minerals, and Phytochemicals in Grains

Minerals, their functions in the body, and our best food sources are listed in Table 6.4. As you can see, whole grains are featured repeatedly because they contain chromium, copper, magnesium, selenium, and zinc. Zinc is present in whole-grain flour, and the yeasting process that occurs when flour is made into bread helps us to absorb this mineral. The phytochemicals (plant chemicals) in whole grains, plus vitamin E and other antioxidants protect our cells against cancer and a number of chronic diseases.

When wheat is refined, and the bran and germ are removed to produce white flour, about 75 percent of the vitamins and minerals are lost, 90 percent of the fiber, and 95 percent of the phytochemicals. Three or four of these B vitamins—thiamin, riboflavin, niacin, and folic acid—plus iron are added back. The rest of the vitamins, minerals, and fiber are missing from the white bread bun, bagel, or baguette.

Dietary Fiber

Some of the long chains of sugar molecules that plants build are not easily digested in our intestines and pass through us without being absorbed. These chains are known as dietary fiber, and there are many types found in whole grains and other plant foods. On its journey through our intestines, fiber confers great blessings. It soaks up water, makes stools soft, and generally keeps everything moving along smoothly. It helps protect us against colorectal cancer by carrying out toxic substances and supporting the health of the cells that line our intestines. It also promotes a healthy body weight by helping us feel full and satisfied.

On average, North Americans get about one-third of the fiber needed for optimal health. Our bodies do best when we get about 15 to 22 grams of fiber per 1,000 calories. The menus on pages 169, 208, and 219 are in this range. The children's menus (page 208) and those of Eric and Sarah (page 219) provide 20 to 40 grams of fiber. The higher-calorie menus for lactating mothers (page 169) and Fit Freddie (page 219) provide 50 to 60 grams of fiber.

Can Diets Be Too High in Fiber?

Yes, and this is particularly true for children with tiny appetites. Diets composed entirely of fiber-rich whole grains, beans, and raw fruits and vegetables can be bulky, making it hard for children, whose appetites and stomachs are small, to get enough calories. Make these wonderful whole foods the mainstays of the diet, but also provide some refined breads, cereals, and pasta to help your little ones get enough calories. With a bit less fiber in the diet, little tummies don't get filled up so fast. Tofu has about half as much fiber as a similar volume of soybeans. (To pack in more calories, include avocados and nut butters and use oil in baking.)

Should We Avoid Carbohydrates?

The answer depends upon which carbohydrates we're talking about. The complex carbohydrates in whole grains, legumes, and root vegetables are prime energy sources and a great benefit to health. There's no question about it—we need these carbohydrates! Yet when plant foods are refined—as when whole wheat is turned into white flour, and beets and green sugar cane stalks are made into sugar—a lot is left behind: vitamins, minerals, protein, essential fatty acids, protective phytochemicals, and fiber.

Excessive amounts of refined carbohydrates and sugar can damage the health of our children and ourselves. For many of us, cutting back on *refined* carbohydrates helps us to maintain a healthy weight, allows us to get off the blood sugar roller coaster, and improves our intestinal health. We also can reduce our incidence of dental caries. Replacing these highly refined items with nutrition-packed whole foods does us a world of good.

There is a strong and consistent pattern showing that diets high in vegetables and fruits decrease the risk of many cancers, and perhaps cancer in general.

—Food, Nutrition, and the Prevention of Cancer: A Global Perspective, *World Cancer Research Foundation and the American Institute for Cancer Research*

Fabulous Fruit

For a sweet treat, fruit is an excellent choice. Think of papaya, bananas, strawberries, and others that may be your favorites. Blueberries may be one of the most protective of foods, based on the antioxidants they contain. The particular antioxidants in blueberries, known as *anthocyanins*, are what make the berries blue. The colorful components in fruits and vegetables are those very substances that keep us well. When our children eat a colorful spectrum of these foods over the course of a week, a veritable army of disease fighters goes to every cell in their bodies and promotes health. The vitamin C in fruit and pure fruit juice bolsters the immune system, as does beta-carotene (found in apricots, cantaloupe, mango, pumpkin, and vegetables with similar hues). Both vitamins help our children fight infection. Eating antioxidant-rich fruits and vegetables may help prevent asthma or reduce its severity.

A nationwide survey found that more than one-third of high school students had eaten no fruit on the day preceding the survey, instead of the two servings per day that is recommended. Teenagers are notorious for diets that are too high in fat and sugar and low in fiber and complex carbohydrates. Yet a study of the diets of teenaged girls who are vegetarians showed them to consume 20 percent more vitamin C and 40 percent more fiber than nonvegetarian girls of the same age. Our vegetarian youngsters may be doing much better than average.

We can increase the amount of fruit our families eat by:

- giving fresh and dried fruit in packed lunches and as snacks
- making fruit smoothies and shakes
- having a big fruit salad as a weekend brunch treat
- trying Fruit Butter Bars (page 343), Popsoycles (page 346), and Sneaky Dad's Pudding (page 338)

The Incredible Vegetable

> Your mother was right: eat your vegetables.
> —*Dr. John Potter, cancer epidemiologist, Fred
> Hutchinson Cancer Research Center, Seattle*

Even more than fruits, vegetables are strong allies in helping us remain robust. Yet for
many people, the word *vegetable* doesn't bring to mind vibrant color, enticing aroma,
delicious flavor, or bountiful health. If this rings true for you, it's time to update your
attitude about these amazing foods. When children reject vegetables, often they're mir-
roring a lack of enthusiasm demonstrated by adults. Perhaps our childhood memories
are of soggy, overcooked vegetables that were boring, bland, and unappetizing. Luckily,
our children give us the chance to revisit our childhood and this time do it right!

Food Puzzles

We can have fun with our children discussing the parts of a plant we are eating (or
growing): stem (asparagus, celery), roots (beet, carrot), flower (broccoli, cauliflower),
leaf (spinach, kale, lettuce), bulbs (garlic), or tubers that grow underground (potato,
sweet potato, yam).

Fruits contain seeds, and from these new plants will grow. You can find the seeds
in pumpkins, berries, oranges, and pears.

Older children may be interested in this question: "Some people say a tomato is
a vegetable. Others call it a fruit. Who's right?" Also ask about avocados, cucumbers,
eggplants, peppers, squash, and zucchini. Although in our kitchens we use all these

as vegetables, to a botanist all are fruits. A fruit is the part of a plant involved in its reproduction. Other plant parts are vegetables.

Stay-at-Home Travelers

We can try a new vegetable or fruit each week or month and take an interest in the part of the planet it comes from, how it grows, and how it usually is prepared. Even if our opportunities to visit different countries may be limited, we can explore the world from our own kitchens.

Vegetable Variations

The Total Vegetarian Food Guide on page 126 advises us to "Eat a variety of colorful vegetables." Variety helps to ensure that we receive the full range of phytochemicals and fiber. It also makes meals a lot more interesting!

We start infants on well-cooked, mashed vegetables. However, when they're a little older and can manage raw foods without choking, children often prefer uncooked vegetables that they can recognize, rather than something in a casserole, no matter how elegant. This can simplify our lives because all we need to do is scrub the dirt off the carrot and it's ready. Though it may not be gourmet dining, it's high in beta-carotene, other protective antioxidants, and fiber.

When our children's diets contain the minimum five-a-day fruits and vegetables recommended by health experts and by the Total Vegetarian Food Guide, they receive vitamins in abundance, particularly the antioxidants beta-carotene and vitamins C and E. Other food groups contribute B vitamins. Vitamins B_{12} and D require special attention and are discussed in the following section. See also Table 6.6.

Vitamin B_{12}

B_{12} Alert

As our children grow, they need tiny amounts of vitamin B_{12}, gradually increasing from 0.9 to 2.4 micrograms per day, as shown in Table 6.3. Vitamin B_{12} is not made from plants or animals; it comes from bacteria and other one-celled organisms. Bacteria in animals' stomachs result in its presence in meats and other animal products.[*] Plant

*Ovolactovegetarians get some vitamin B_{12} from eggs (0.5 micrograms per egg) and from cow's milk (0.9 micrograms per cup).

TABLE 6.6

Vitamins: What They Do and Good Dietary Sources

Vitamin	What It Does	Food Sources	Special Tips
Folate (folic acid)	Helps build new cells and the genetic material DNA (together with vitamin B_{12}); prevents neural tube defects in the fetus during early stages of pregnancy.	Leafy greens, legumes, oranges, asparagus, avocados, broccoli, Brussels sprouts, cauliflower, beets, parsnips, squash, sweet potatoes, tomato and orange juices, grapefruit, bananas, cantaloupe, strawberries, peanuts, sunflower seeds, sesame tahini, nutritional yeast, whole and enriched grains.	Since the word *folic* comes from the Latin word *folium*, meaning leaf, guess which veggies are excellent sources of this yellow-orange vitamin!
Niacin	Helps convert food to energy; is needed for healthy skin, nervous system, and digestive system.	Whole and enriched grains, legumes, nuts, nutritional yeast. Niacin also can be made from the amino acid tryptophan, which is present in all plant protein.	In making corn tortillas, the traditional Indian and Latin American practice of soaking corn in lime-treated water makes this vitamin more available for absorption. This lime treatment also adds plenty of calcium to the tortillas.

Vitamin	What It Does	Food Sources	Special Tips
Pantothenic acid	Helps release energy from carbohydrates and fat.	All plant foods. Bacteria that live in our intestines and synthesize this vitamin may further contribute to our intake.	This vitamin is widely distributed in plant foods, reflected in its name from the Greek word *panto*, meaning "all" and "every."
Pyridoxine (vitamin B_6)	Has many roles related to our use of protein and amino acids and some roles in use of fatty acids; helps build heme (the protein of hemoglobin) for red blood cells.	Nutritional yeast, brewer's yeast, whole grains, legumes, soyfoods, soymilk, seeds, peas, potatoes, squash, leafy greens, asparagus, avocados, okra, nori (sea vegetable), plantains, bananas, figs, raisins, watermelons, elderberries, and tomato, orange, and prune juices.	Vitamin B_6 is present in whole grains, but it's not added to enriched grains. For a time, B_6 supplements were considered as a treatment for PMS; however, high doses easily can lead to toxicity and side effects. The best choice is to get it from the foods listed—without side effects!
Riboflavin (vitamin B_2)	Helps convert carbohydrates to energy; is needed for healthy skin and normal vision.	Leafy green vegetables, sea vegetables, green vegetables such as asparagus, mushrooms, sweet potatoes, legumes, peas, almonds, peanuts, bananas, whole and enriched grains, fortified nondairy milks. Enriched flour and cereals contain riboflavin; however, enriched white rice does not. (The reason is to avoid the slight yellow color riboflavin would impart.)	This bright yellow vitamin gives color to nutritional yeast and vitamin supplements. 1½ tsp. of nutritional yeast provides the recommended intake for the day. Ultraviolet light destroys riboflavin, so store nutritional yeast in an opaque container or in a cupboard. Many soymilks and cereals are fortified with riboflavin, so a bowl of cereal with soymilk can provide 33% to 150% of the recommended intake for riboflavin.

(continued)

TABLE 6.6 (CONTINUED)

Vitamin	What It Does	Food Sources	Special Tips
Thiamin (vitamin B$_1$)	Helps convert carbohydrates to energy and use amino acids (protein); is essential for nervous system.	Whole and enriched grains and whole-grain products, legumes, nuts, and nutritional yeast.	The B vitamins work as a team to help our energy production system.
Biotin	Acts in production of glucose, fats, and genetic material.	Cauliflower, peanut butter, grains, vegetables, soybeans and other legumes, nuts, seeds, nutritional and brewer's yeasts.	Intestinal bacteria can synthesize this vitamin and further contribute to our intake.
Vitamin A (the plant form is beta-carotene)	Is needed for growth of bones and teeth, for reproduction, and to keep mucous membranes and skin healthy; supports the immune system; may act as an antioxidant and protect against cancer and heart disease.	Deep orange vegetables (carrots, peppers, pumpkin, squash, sweet potatoes, turnips, tomatoes and tomato products, yams), broccoli, green leafy vegetables, nori (sea vegetable), deep orange fruits (apricots, cantaloupe, mango, nectarine, papaya), persimmon, plantain, prunes.	Beta-carotene and other carotenoids provide much of the beautiful orange, red, and yellow color in vegetables and fruits. In green vegetables the color of carotenoids is overlaid by the green of magnesium-rich chlorophyll.

Vitamin	What It Does	Food Sources	Special Tips
Vitamin C (ascorbic acid)	Helps us absorb iron from plant foods and resist infection; may shorten and lessen severity of common cold; is needed to build collagen protein for blood vessel walls, scar tissue, and bone; is an antioxidant; helps make thyroid hormone.	Citrus fruits, strawberries, kiwi, guava, papaya, cantaloupe, mangos; potatoes, bell peppers (especially red), broccoli; vegetables in the cabbage family, leafy greens, tomatoes.	Rely on plant food for your vitamins and you'll get plenty of protective phytochemicals as well. Excess vitamin C can cause diarrhea, nausea, cramps, headaches, and fatigue.
Vitamin E (d-alpha tocopherol)	Is an antioxidant, protects vitamin A and essential fatty acids from destruction, has roles in prevention of many diseases, stabilizes cell membranes and prevents their breakage.	Nuts, seeds, whole grains, wheat germ, leafy green vegetables, hijiki (sea vegetable). Unrefined vegetable oils contain vitamin E, especially olive and sunflower oils. Heat in the oil-refining process destroys vitamin E.	Use the natural form of vitamin E (d-alpha-tocopherol). This is the form in plant foods. Vitamin E protects plant oils from oxidation.
Vitamin B$_{12}$	Helps build our genetic material (DNA) and red blood cells; maintains the protective sheath around nerve fibers.	Fortified nondairy milks, meat analogs, and breakfast cereals. (Read the label to be certain.) Red Star Vegetarian Support Formula nutritional yeast.	Check ingredient list on labels for the words *vitamin B$_{12}$* or *cyanocobalamin* (its other name). Algae, spirulina, sea vegetables, and fermented foods are *not* reliable sources.

(continued)

TABLE 6.6 (CONTINUED)

Vitamin	What It Does	Food Sources	Special Tips
Vitamin D	Helps us absorb and use calcium, aids in bone mineralization; assists the immune system and maintenance of health.	Fortified nondairy milks and breakfast cereals. (Margarines have vitamin D added, but it's generally the form from animals, vitamin D_3.)	Look for vitamin D_2, (ergocalciferol), the vegan form of vitamin D. Vitamin D_3 is from animal skins, sheep's wool, and fish oils.

foods cannot be counted on as reliable sources of this vitamin unless they are fortified with it. Amounts present in a variety of fortified foods are shown in Table 6.7
on page 154. *Vitamin B$_{12}$ must be supplied in our children's diets by fortified foods or supplements.*

Is It Safe to Feed Nutritional Yeast to Young Children?

It is safe to feed nutritional yeast to toddlers, following the same precautions that
should be used when first introducing any new food. Give about ¼ teaspoon of the
yeast mixed with a food that already is part of your baby's diet. Wait for three to
four days to see if any symptoms of allergy appear. Take particular care with youngsters who have a family history of food allergy.

Vitamin D

Vitamin D from Fortified Foods or Supplements

Our children can get vitamin D from supplements, fortified foods, or sunlight. If
supplements are used, we must provide 5.0 micrograms daily, as shown in Table 6.3
on page 133. If we rely on fortified foods, we must aim for 50 percent of the Dietary
Value (DV) in order to get 5.0 micrograms of vitamin D. This is because the DV
is set at 10 micrograms. Most fortified beverages provide 1 to 2.5 micrograms per
cup (10 to 25 percent of the DV).

Vitamin D from Sunlight

Vitamin D is synthesized in our bodies when our skin is exposed to the ultraviolet
light in sunlight. For those with light skin, it takes about ten to fifteen minutes of sunlight on the face and forearms for sufficient vitamin D production. People with dark
skin require from three to six times longer sun exposure or greater skin exposure. This
is because skin pigments, which protect us from sunburn in warm climates, also limit
vitamin D production. Vitamin D synthesis is greatly reduced by the use of sunscreen.

It generally is recommended that infants be protected from direct sunlight with
clothing and/or sunscreen; supplements therefore are preferred over sun exposure.
While it is possible for children to get enough vitamin D from sunshine alone, the
amount of ultraviolet light in winter sunlight is not sufficient in northern states and
Canada during the winter months; thus, a supplement is necessary during this time
of year. (The "Vitamin D Winter" lasts longer the farther north one lives.)

TABLE 6.7

Food Sources of Vitamin B$_{12}$

Amounts can vary between brands and from one time to another, so check labels.

	Vitamin B$_{12}$,mcg
Fortified Meat Substitutes	
Veggie "meat" slices, 1 serving (4 slices)	1.2–1.5
Veggie "ground beef" or burger, 1 serving	1.4
Veggie wiener, 1	0.7–1.5
Red Star Vegetarian Support Formula Nutritional Yeast (T6635+)	
Nutritional yeast powder, 1 tbsp. (8 grams)	4
Nutritional yeast flakes, 1 tbsp. (4 grams)	2
Fortified Soy and Grain Milks	
Edensoy Extra, Enriched Silk, and Soy Dream, 1 cup	3
Rice Dream Enriched, 1 cup	1.5
So Nice and Vitasoy Enriched, 1 cup	0.9
Fortified Breakfast Cereals	
Optimum, 1 cup	6
Fortified Raisin Bran or Kellogg's Cornflakes, ¾ cup	1.5
Product 19, ¾ cup	6
Fortified Grapenuts, ¼ cup	1.5
Nutrigrain, ⅔ cup	1.5
Total, 1 cup	6.2

Supplements: Yes or No?

While it is not necessary to give vegetarian children and teens multivitamins, it definitely is worth considering. If fortified foods are not used, supplements of vitamin B$_{12}$ are essential. If you choose a multivitamin-mineral supplement, make sure that it includes reasonable supplies of vitamin B$_{12}$, vitamin D, iron, and zinc by comparing the amounts with Table 6.3. Generally, vitamin B$_{12}$ is present in higher amounts; if so, the supplement can be given every two or three days. *Don't forget!*

Vitamin D may be provided by a combination of supplement and sunlight.

Multivitamins provide only a fraction of the recommended intake of calcium; otherwise it would make the pill too large to swallow comfortably. Remember that supplements cannot make up for a bad diet, nor can they provide all the beneficial nutrients, phytochemicals, and fiber that are present in foods.

Take care not to leave vitamin-mineral supplements where children can help themselves. Sometimes they think these are treats. Overdosing with supplements can be toxic and even fatal. Excess vitamin D and iron are particularly dangerous. Megadoses of vitamin C can cause diarrhea, nausea, abdominal cramps, headache, and fatigue, and large doses of vitamin A can result in nosebleeds and breakage of blood cells.

The Essential Omega-3 Fatty Acid: Alpha-Linolenic Acid

Two fatty substances are essential to life. One is linolenic acid (LA); the other is alpha-linolenic acid (ALA). LA is called a "parent" in a family of fats known as omega-6 fatty acids, because our bodies can make related compounds in this family from LA. ALA is a parent in the omega-3 fatty acid family.

Vegetarians get enough LA very easily. It is abundant in seeds, nuts, soyfoods, and vegetable oils, and is present in grains, legumes, and vegetables. People who use plenty of vegetable oils—sunflower, safflower, corn, sesame, and cottonseed oils—get much more LA than they need.

With ALA, the story is different. ALA is in very few foods: flaxseed, hempseed, canola oil, walnuts, and butternuts. There also is a little in soybeans, tofu, and greens. As a result, intakes tend to be low. Flaxseed oil and ground flaxseeds are particularly good ways to obtain this essential nutrient because they are highly concentrated sources.

There are not yet firm recommendations for how much ALA we need daily, but a good guess for children older than three years, teens, and adults is at least 2.2 grams. Table 6.8 on page 156 shows us several ways to get our day's supply. Toddlers up to three years of age need about half this much.

Flaxseed oil must be stored in the refrigerator or freezer. Never cook with this oil (nor with hempseed oil or walnut oil), as heat damages the ALA present. Use

TABLE 6.8

Foods to Provide 2.2 Grams of Alpha-Linolenic Acid

Food	Amount
flaxseed oil	1 tsp.
hempseed oil	1 tbsp.
walnut oil	1½ tbsp.
canola oil*	2 tbsp.
ground flaxseeds	1 tbsp.
walnuts	¼ cup (1 oz.)
butternuts	¼ cup (1 oz.)

* To avoid getting canola oil that is genetically modified and contains a reduced amount of ALA, choose organic canola oil.

a little for salad dressings, such as the Liquid Gold Dressing or Nippy Flax Dressing on pages 290 and 296. Flaxseed oil dressings are great on baked potatoes, rice, and steamed greens, too.

Flaxseeds must be ground; whole flaxseeds will pass right through our digestive system without being absorbed. Grind about ¼ cup or more of the seeds in a spice or coffee grinder. A dry blender may be used, but this will provide a coarser grind. The ground seeds will keep for a few weeks without refrigeration, though you may want to put them in the refrigerator or freezer for longer storage. A spoonful of ground flaxseeds can be added to a smoothie or hummus or sprinkled on breakfast cereal, a baked potato, a salad, or other dishes. Ground flaxseeds make an excellent egg replacer in pancakes and cornbread recipes. (See pages 236, 257 and 268.) Take care not to give the ground seeds by the spoonful to little ones, as they could choke on them.

LA and its family members (known as EPA and DHA) play many important roles in our immune systems, in mental and visual development, and as a part of our cell membranes. EPA and DHA are found in fish, though the fish actually get these omega-3 fatty acids from microalgae. For more on these compounds see page 164, and for vegetarian sources of DHA, see the Resources section.

Balancing Protein, Fat, and Carbohydrate

You probably have heard that not more than 30 percent of the calories in the diets of adults should come from fat. Many national and international health organizations make this recommendation to help us reduce risk of heart disease, cancer, and other chronic diseases. We are advised to get 15 to 30 percent of our calories from fat, 10 to 15 percent from protein, and 55 to 75 percent from carbohydrate.

Yet if the fat in vegetarians' diets is composed of whole foods that are good sources of unsaturated fats (nuts, seeds, olives, avocados, and soyfoods) plus small amounts of oils that are rich in monounsaturated fats (olive and canola oil) plus sources of omega-3 fatty acids (flaxseed and its oil, hemp, canola oil, and walnuts), experts suggest that as much as 35 percent of calories from fat can be healthful for adults, teens, and children.

Avoid foods that are rich in trans-fatty acids such as margarine, vegetable shortening, and processed foods (chips, cookies, and pastry). Dairy products contain trans-fatty acids, too.

In breast milk, 54 percent of the calories are derived from healthful fats. Infants thrive on this. During the transition from breast milk or formula to the foods eaten by older children, it works well to have a diet that is fairly high in healthful fats to start with and then gradually decrease the amount of dietary fat over time. Growing children need a somewhat higher proportion of their calories to be derived from dietary fat than do adults. Don't make the mistake of thinking that a good diet for an adult who wants to lose weight or reverse heart disease is the right choice for a child.

Water and Fluids

Drink six to eight glasses of water or other fluids each day. Suitable fluids include water and vegetable or fruit juices, including juices that are diluted 1:1 with water. Many of these beverages provide additional phytochemicals, vitamins, and minerals. Avoid offering your child caffeinated or carbonated beverages.

This applies even more in warm weather, and it is particularly important for athletes. A child quickly can become dehydrated on a hot day, playing in the sun. The symptoms can be cramps, a dry mouth, headache, dizziness, confusion, loss of energy, and nausea.

Jump for Joy

Our primary focus in this section is nutrition; however, no chapter on nutrition and health would be complete without a strong and clear message about the importance of physical exercise. Our children need a minimum of thirty minutes of physical activity each day. So do we. Physical activity, while not a component of "diet" per se, is central to energy balance, building and maintaining strong bones, and overall health.

Chapter 7

Getting a Great Start: Nutrition During Infancy

Before you were conceived, I wanted you.
Before you were born, I loved you.
Before you were here an hour, I would die for you.
This is the miracle of life.

—*Maureen Hawkins*

The first years of a child's life are packed with challenges and rich rewards, for our little ones and for us as parents. A partnership and bond are forming that will last a lifetime. With a good beginning, we lay the foundation for lifelong health.

At first, infants depend on us for every drop of fluid and for all the protein, essential fats, vitamins, minerals, and other protective substances they need. What will give the best possible start? How do needs change over the first few years?

Nature's Formula for Success

Nature has done a *superb* job of designing human breast milk. The balance of protein, fat, and carbohydrate is ideal for infants. The composition of the milk adjusts automatically to meet changing infant requirements over time. Vitamins, minerals, and protective compounds abound. Scientists continue to study this amazing fluid, but have yet to duplicate it exactly. For this reason, it is our first choice as baby's exclusive food for the first four to six months, a mainstay of the diet for the first year, and may well continue for two years or longer. The natural age of weaning is between two and four years of age. This is the age at which lactase, the enzyme that breaks down the milk sugar lactose, naturally declines. Vegetarian women tend to breast-feed for a longer period of time than do nonvegetarians, and this is an excellent trend.

Soy-based and other commercial infant formulas are available, and children can thrive on these; however, they do not contain the substances found in breast milk that boost baby's immune system. There are good reasons for choosing soy formula over cow's milk formula. For more information on these topics, see page 176.

How Breastfeeding Helps Baby

Among its many advantages, breastfeeding:

- provides immune protection through many substances not present in formula
- decreases the likelihood of both viral and bacterial infections and respiratory illness
- protects against gastrointestinal illness and supports maturation of the intestine
- reduces the likelihood of allergies
- helps oral development and reduces the likelihood of speech impediments
- provides easily digested nutrients
- permits excellent mineral absorption
- has the ideal proportions of protein and sodium for the infant's kidneys
- provides the fatty acid called DHA for building brain and eye tissues
- may reduce later risk of heart disease by its effect on cholesterol metabolism
- gives instant satisfaction
- is always at the perfect temperature
- is "food safe"
- helps create a bond with the mother

Breastfeeding may also help infants avoid excess weight gain, because babies nurse until satisfied, but there's not that push to finish off the last half ounce in a bottle.

Research has shown that having been breastfed for at least seven months may reduce the risk of being overweight during the teen years.

Vegan and vegetarian mothers who are able to breast-feed offer their infants a further advantage: studies have shown that their milk contains fewer contaminants compared with milk from nonvegetarian women. Mothers' diets that include meat, fish, and dairy products have a great influence on milk levels of dieldrin and polychlorinated biphenyls (PCBs). Studies of vegetarians show lower levels of pesticides such as DDT, chlordane, and heptachlor, and industrial by-products such as PCBs in milk. In most cases, vegan levels are just 1 to 2 percent of those in milk from nonvegetarians. Naturally, a plant-based diet composed of organic foods is an excellent choice.

How Breastfeeding Helps Mom

Breastfeeding does a great deal to protect the mother as well as her infant, especially when prolonged. Breastfeeding:

- can help mom gradually lose excess fat and weight
- is available at a moment's notice, anytime, anywhere
- requires no bottles to warm and sterilize, even at 2 A.M. (and again at 4 A.M.)
- may reduce the risk of breast and ovarian cancers
- functions as a natural tranquilizer
- can save money on physician visits, antibiotics, and hospitalization
- costs 20 to 40 percent less than infant formula (the savings can be put toward extra food for mom)
- for moms working outside the home, creates less absenteeism due to infant illness
- helps create a bond with the child

As babies become older, after satiating their initial hunger they often suck in bursts and then take little breaks, during which the mother usually responds by talking, cuddling, rocking, and touching. From observation, it appears that babies desire this interaction and emotional nurturing as much as food.

Nutrition for Nursing Moms

It is well documented that vegan and ovolactovegetarian diets can support mothers and infants in excellent health. Milk from well-nourished vegetarians and vegans is similar in composition to milk from well-nourished nonvegetarians. Sample menus that meet (and exceed) our nutrient needs during lactation are shown in Table 7.3, page 169. Naturally, a woman who is larger or more active may have higher requirements, whereas one who is smaller or more sedentary needs less, but these menus give a general idea of what most lactating women need.

To a certain extent, our breast milk reflects our diets, particularly when it comes to vitamins and essential fats. On the other hand, levels of minerals (calcium, magnesium, iron, zinc, and others) in breast milk tend to remain fairly constant, almost regardless of diet. During times of need, our bodies have a remarkable ability to adjust by absorbing minerals with greater efficiency. Yet if we produce milk while eating poorly, we also may rob our bones and other mineral stores. Thus adequate diet is still important, for our own health.

The previous chapter and the food guide on page 126 provide basic nutrition information. Here are some additional points that apply specifically during lactation.

Calories. While breast-feeding, we need about 500 more calories each day than we did before pregnancy, a 20 percent increase. Our requirements are about 200 calories greater than during pregnancy. Each of the following provides about 200 calories: a slice of toast with almond butter, an apple and a glass of soymilk, or a small muffin.

While caloric needs are 20 percent higher than before we were pregnant, our requirement for several vitamins (beta-carotene, vitamin C) and minerals (chromium, zinc, selenium) have shot up much more than 20 percent, as shown in Table 7.1. This means the foods that provide us with calories must be packed with minerals, vitamins, and protective substances. Food choices should be made with special care, focusing on items such as whole grains, legumes, vegetables, fruits, and nut butters.

With plenty of other responsibilities to occupy our attention, we need simple, tasty recipes. Good choices are the Chocolate or Carob Shake, page 242; Sneaky Dad's Pudding (not just for youngsters), page 338; Tricolor Quinoa-Corn Salad, page 301; Raw-Raw Vegetable Platter, page 302, served with a zippy dip or dressing; and African Stew, page 308. The Recipe section of this book, beginning on page 231, offers highly nutritious dishes that can be made quickly. Hummus, for instance, can be a mainstay. Another good idea is to keep marinated tofu in the fridge.

TABLE 7.1

Increased Vitamin and Mineral Requirements During Lactation Compared to Prepregnancy Requirements

Mineral *Vitamin*	Recommended Increase During Lactation
iodine, chromium *vitamin A (beta-carotene)*	80–95%
copper, zinc *vitamin C, riboflavin, vitamin B$_6$, pantothenic acid*	40–60%
manganese, selenium *vitamin E, thiamin, folate, choline*	25–30%
niacin, vitamin B$_{12}$, biotin	about 20%
calcium, fluoride, magnesium, phosphorus *vitamins D and K*	0%

Fat. Though the amount of fat in breast milk stays fairly constant, providing about 54 percent of total calories, the composition and quality of that fat reflect the mother's diet. If mom eats lard, plenty of saturated fatty acids show up in the milk. Milk from vegetarian mothers contains less saturated fat and more of the polyunsaturated fatty acids found in natural plant oils. Of particular interest are two essential fatty acids, linolenic acid (LA) and alpha-linolenic acid (ALA), that were introduced in Chapter 6 (page 155).

LA, the "parent" in the omega-6 family, is abundant in seeds, nuts, soyfoods, and vegetable oils; it also is present in grains, legumes, and vegetables. Unless our diets are extremely low in fat, it is a simple task to get enough of this essential fat. In fact, most of us get far more omega-6s than we need, because on top of all the whole foods listed above, we get plenty from vegetable oils, including those added to processed foods. Sunflower, safflower, corn, sesame, and cottonseed oils are all high in LA. Vegetarians get plenty of LA, and this is reflected in our breast milk.

The other essential fatty acid, ALA, is the "parent" in the omega-3 family. Omega-3s are present in a limited number of foods. Vegetarian sources are flaxseeds, walnuts, butternuts, and unrefined canola, soybean, hemp, and flaxseed oil. We get very small amounts from soybeans, tofu, and leafy greens, too. As shown in Table 7.2, flaxseed oil is by far the most concentrated among these. For many people (both vegetarian and nonvegetarian), intake of omega-3 fatty acids tends to be low.

Getting Enough Omega-3 Fatty Acids. There are not yet firm recommendations for the amount of ALA we need daily. A reasonable estimate is at least 5 grams of alpha-linolenic acid during lactation. This is about double the amount needed by children, teens, and women who are not pregnant or lactating. We can meet these recommendations by regularly using flaxseed oil salad dressing, or by including ground flaxseeds in recipes such as Oatmeal Flax Porridge, page 252, Flaxen Hummus, page 276, and Crunchy Cornbread, page 268. We also could add ground flaxseeds to a smoothie, or sprinkle them on various dishes. *A simple and delicious solution is to keep Liquid Gold Dressing (page 290) on hand in the refrigerator and use 2 to 3 tablespoons daily on salads, baked potatoes, rice, pasta, and cooked veggies.*

DHA. One of the reasons we need ALA is to build the long-chain omega-3 fatty acid known as DHA (docosahexaenoic acid). DHA is found in all cells and is

TABLE 7.2

Foods to Provide 5 Grams of Alpha-Linolenic Acid

Food	Amount
flaxseed oil	2 tsp.
hempseed oil	2 tbsp.
walnut oil	3 tbsp.
canola oil	¼ cup
ground flaxseeds	2 tbsp.
walnuts	½ cup (2 oz.)
butternuts	½ cup (2 oz.)

especially abundant in the gray matter of the brain and retina of the eye. Research suggests that DHA plays an important role in the mental and visual development of infants.

Certain dietary habits affect the body's ability to convert ALA to DHA. We make DHA most efficiently when we limit our intake of other types of fats: high—omega-6 oils (sunflower, safflower, corn, sesame, and cottonseed oils), saturated fats, cholesterol, and trans-fatty acids. To assist conversion, we also should eliminate processed and deep-fried foods made with these, and avoid alcohol and smoking. When we cut back on these other fats and eat more of the ALA sources listed in Table 7.2, we increase the amount of DHA that is delivered to baby through breast milk. That's brain food for baby.

The amount of DHA in breast milk is related to the mother's intake of ALA and DHA. It also depends on the dietary fats and factors listed above that inhibit conversion of ALA to DHA. DHA has attracted interest because premature infants whose diets included DHA have scored better on developmental and intelligence tests later in childhood compared with those who received little dietary DHA.

DHA is present in cold-water fish, yet fish do not make DHA. Their source of DHA is marine microalgae that the fish have eaten. Besides adding ALA sources to our diets, another way to increase the amount of DHA in breast milk is to take DHA supplements that come directly from the source, microalgae. Two products that deliver this DHA—rich oil in vegetarian capsules are O-Mega-Zen3 and Genestra Neurogen, both listed in the Resources section.

Protein. We easily can meet protein needs while breastfeeding, as long as we get enough calories and make sure to include some of the higher-protein plant foods—legumes, tofu, meat analogs, and soyfoods. We won't meet recommended protein intakes with salads, bread, and pasta alone, or with a very low calorie diet. At the same time, this doesn't mean that we must eat tofu whether we like it or not, or use every one of the twenty types of beans, peas, and lentils that commonly are eaten. We have many options.

When we eat a whole-foods diet centered on whole grains, legumes, vegetables, nuts, and seeds, we need a little more protein than we do on a soy-based diet that includes plenty of tofu, other soyfoods, and meat analogs, or on an ovolacto diet with dairy products and eggs. Recommended protein intakes are about one gram of protein per kilogram body weight. The different protein recommendations for the two types of plant-based diets are based on slight differences in digestibility and amino acid patterns among the various high-protein foods. In practice, it's not difficult to meet and exceed recommended protein intakes by either type of diet. Table 7.3 shows the many protein sources in two 2,700-calorie menus—one centered on soyfoods and convenience foods, the other on whole foods.

We make it easy to meet protein recommendations when we eat a serving of Beans and Alternates at each meal. For breakfast we might have nut butter (spread on toast), fortified soymilk, or soy yogurt. Lunch and supper could include a bean burrito, falafel, hummus, tofu dish, tempeh, sprouted lentils, pea soup, or veggie "meats" (burgers, veggie dogs, slices, or veggie ground round, among others). Grains contribute about one-third of our daily protein. More comes from foods that many of us might never think of as protein sources. It's not difficult!

Iron. Generally, the high-protein foods listed above also are good sources of iron and zinc. Excellent examples are beans, split peas, lentils, tofu and soyfoods, and nuts and seeds. We get extra iron from whole and enriched grains and cereals, dried fruit (raisins, prunes, apricots), and some greens, such as kale and broccoli. Vitamin C–rich foods help us absorb iron, whereas cow's milk and the tannins in coffee and tea interfere with iron absorption. While breastfeeding, women need only 9 milligrams of iron daily, *less* than before pregnancy. This is because we are less likely to have the iron losses that occur with menstruation. Yet many women are low in iron right after giving birth and need to recover iron that has been transferred to the baby. Thus, the iron-rich foods listed above are very important at this time.

Zinc. Vegetarian or not, and lactating or not, the zinc intake of women tends to be below the recommended intake of 12 milligrams per day. Fortunately, our absorption of zinc seems to increase dramatically, as much as 75 percent, at this time of need. Zinc is needed for immune system support and has many other functions in the body; it's crucial for mom and baby. Our need for zinc is an excellent reason to include servings of Beans and Alternates at every meal. Good sources are cashew nuts, pumpkin seeds, sesame tahini, wheat germ, whole grains, and meat analogs that are zinc fortified. If you take a multivitamin-mineral supplement, make sure that it includes zinc, in an amount up to 15 milligrams. This is a better choice than a single-mineral zinc supplement because giving a single mineral can affect the absorption and use of other minerals.

Calcium. Though we are producing calcium-rich milk, our calcium requirements do not increase while breastfeeding. Why? As with zinc, we become more efficient at absorbing calcium during this time of need. At the same time, calcium is not a mineral to ignore, particularly since the majority of women have calcium intakes that are well below the recommended intake of 1,000 milligrams daily. Six studies in the United States, Canada, and Britain have reported intakes by vegan women averaging as low as 437 milligrams and as high as 900 milligrams. Some research has shown lower bone densities among vegan women. In contrast, lactovegetarian women tend to meet the recommended calcium intake. This does not mean that dairy products are essential as calcium sources. It means that vegan and near-vegan women need to take care to use the many calcium sources available.

The six studies were conducted between 1954 and 1995, and the availability of calcium-rich vegan foods has increased immensely over the past fifty years. Today, calcium-set tofu and calcium-fortified soymilk, rice milk, and orange juice are found in major supermarkets everywhere. Recent research has proven that calcium is extremely well absorbed from certain greens, including kale, collards, Chinese greens, broccoli, and okra. By relying on these and other calcium-rich foods, vegan women can fare as well as milk drinkers—or better! For added calcium, we can keep figs and almonds in our purses or glove compartments for quick snacks. We can bake with blackstrap molasses, and use the higher-calcium beans (such as soy, white, navy, great northern, and black turtle beans) in soups and casseroles. Also, some corn tortillas made with lime are high in calcium. Depending on overall calcium intake from these foods, a supplement may be a wise choice to reach the recommended intake.

Vitamin D. Vitamin D helps us absorb and use calcium and is essential to bone health. The amount of vitamin D in breast milk varies, depending on our two sources of this vitamin: our diets and exposure to sunlight. The daily intake should be 5 micrograms (also listed as 200 IU) of vitamin D from a supplement or fortified foods. This is the amount in 2 cups of fortified soymilk, rice milk, or cow's milk. Vitamin D also is added to some breakfast cereals (check labels for amounts).

To make sufficient vitamin D ourselves, we need an average of about ten to fifteen minutes of sun on the face and forearms daily if we are light skinned. If our skin is dark, we need about thirty minutes. The issue of getting vitamin D from sun exposure can be confusing. Aren't we supposed to avoid the sun? In truth, the time required to make vitamin D is very little. It can mean five minutes walking across the parking lot, plus another five minutes putting out the garbage bins. You might take a short walk at lunchtime. For longer exposure, it still is important to use sunscreen.

In the northern states and in Canada, where there is less ultraviolet light from November to February, it makes sense to use a supplement or fortified foods, especially in winter. To locate vegetarian (including vitamin D_2) supplements, see the Resources section.

Vitamin B_{12}. Breastfeeding women must include sources of vitamin B_{12} in their diets. Otherwise, levels in breast milk may be inadequate, and we need a regular supply ourselves. There's no sense in fooling around with this essential vitamin. Babies need vitamin B_{12} for the normal development of brain, nerve, and blood cells. During lactation, we require fortified foods or supplements that provide at least 2.8 micrograms of vitamin B_{12} per day, or 50 percent of the DV. (Check labels, and see Table 6.7 on page 154 for food sources.) Most supplements provide more than 2.8 micrograms, and it's fine to take a higher-dose supplement three times a week. Excess vitamin B_{12} does not cause problems.

Other Vitamins and Phytochemicals. Vegetables and other plant foods are rich in beta-carotene, vitamin C, folate, and a wealth of other protective substances. B vitamins are present in legumes and whole grains. The breast milk of vegetarian women reflects these healthful dietary choices.

Fluids. We should drink 8 to 12 cups of liquids each day. Water, fortified soy or grain beverages, juices, and soups are all good choices. A helpful motto from midwives is this: "When you sit down to nurse, bring your water."

Sample Menus

Table 7.3 presents two nutrition-packed sample menus. One is centered on whole foods; the other includes several soy foods and ready-to-eat items. Once you get the

TABLE 7.3

Two Menus for Lactating Moms (2,700 Calories)

Whole-Foods Menu	Protein, grams	Soy-Based Menu	Protein, grams
Breakfast			
2 slices whole-grain toast	5.5	1 whole-wheat bagel	12
2 tbsp. tahini	5	2 tbsp. almond butter	5
2 tsp. blackstrap molasses	0	2 tbsp. jam	0
1 cup Oatmeal Flax Porridge (page 252)	8	1 cup ready-to-eat cereal	4
		1 cup fortified soymilk	7–8
1 cup fortified rice milk	0.4	1 cup orange juice	1
2 tbsp. raisins	0.5		
Lunch			
1½ cups lentil soup	14	1 veggie burger	11
3 rye crackers	2	1 hamburger bun	4
1 cup Tricolor Quinoa-Corn Salad (page 301)	5	¼ cup lettuce, 1 slice tomato, 1 tbsp. eggless mayo, 2 tsp. mustard	1
1 banana or other fruit	1	4 small avocado slices	0.8
1 Muscle Muffin (page 265)	8	2 cups raw veggies (carrot, celery, red bell pepper, cucumber)	2
Supper			
2 cups African Stew (page 308)	12	½ cup tofu with 3 tbsp. barbecue sauce	11
1½ cups brown rice	7		
3 cups Five-Day Salad (page 298)	5	1 cup squash, broccoli, or other vegetable	2
3 tbsp. Beets-All Salad Dressing (page 292)	3	1 baked potato	5
		3 tbsp. Liquid Gold Dressing (page 290)	3
Snacks or Desserts (morning, afternoon, or evening)			
¼ cup walnuts	4	1 cup Crunchy Fruit Crisps (page 264)	5
1 cup Warm Cocoa with fortified rice milk (page 249)	4	1 serving Chocolate or Carob Shake with banana and fortified soymilk (page 242)	8
1 apple	0.4	1 tbsp. cashew nuts	1

Additional foods to meet energy needs: as desired.

(continued)

TABLE 7.3 (CONTINUED)

Nutritional Summary

Whole-Foods Menu		Soy-Based Menu	
calories	2,691	calories	2,718
protein (recommended is 68–72 g or more)	80 g	protein (recommended is 62–65 g or more)	84 g
calcium (recommended is 1,000 mg)	1,565 mg	calcium (recommended is 1,000 mg)	1,429 mg
iron (recommended for vegetarians is 16 mg)	32 mg	iron (recommended for vegetarians is 16 mg)	28 mg
zinc (recommended is 12 mg)	17 mg	zinc (recommended is 12 mg)	12 mg
omega-3 fatty acids (recommended is 5 mg)	5.6 g	omega-3 fatty acids (recommended is 5 mg)	7 g
vitamin B_{12} (recommended is 2.8 mcg)	6 mcg	vitamin B_{12} (recommended is 2.8 mcg)	5.5 mcg
vitamin D (recommended is 5 mcg)	5 mcg	vitamin D (recommended is 5 mcg)	5 mcg

Total Vegetarian Food Guide Servings

Whole-Foods Menu		Soy-Based Menu	
Grains	10	Grains	6
Vegetables	4	Vegetables	4
Fruit	2½	Fruit	3
Beans and Alternates	3	Beans and Alternates	4
Fortified Soymilk and Alternates*	6	Fortified Soymilk and Alternates	6½
Omega-3 Fatty Acids	2	Omega-3 Fatty Acids	2
Vitamin B_{12}	yes	Vitamin B_{12}	yes
Vitamin D	yes	Vitamin D	yes

* Fortified rice milk can be considered a serving of Fortified Soymilk and Alternates if protein needs are met. It contains much less protein (0.4 grams per cup) than soymilk (7 to 8 grams per cup).

basic idea, you can replace one type of grain or vegetable with another and use these as a general guide. These menus have been planned to give you all the nutrients you need without a supplement. See the summary of key nutrients at the end of each menu.

In a well-designed, nutritionally complete menu, there's not much room for "empty-calorie" foods that provide calories but little else. This holds true whether our diets are vegetarian or not. If we increase our activity level, we can afford a few more extras. These two menus do include sweets—a muffin, a fruit crisp, cocoa, a shake—yet even these include healthful ingredients. Though a diet that's this well balanced—or even close—meets our needs for vitamins and minerals, it can be a good idea to use a standard or prenatal multivitamin-mineral supplement several times a week. This can be done to provide vitamin B_{12} or D, to get a little extra calcium or zinc, or whenever our diets are less than ideal.

Breastfeeding Concerns and Questions

Does My Breastfed Baby Need Supplements?

For two vitamins (B_{12} and D) and two minerals (iron and fluoride), supplements given directly to the infant may be the simplest and most reliable way to provide them, although it's not the only way. (See Table 7.4 on the next page.)

Vitamin B_{12}. To make sure that our breastfed infants receive vitamin B_{12}, we can give them a supplement starting shortly after birth, or we can meet our requirements with a supplement or with foods containing B_{12} (see Table 6.7 on page 154). Some of this vitamin will pass to the baby though our breast milk. We also may supplement the infant *and* ourselves, which makes sense because we need this essential nutrient, too. Excess B_{12} is excreted and is not a problem.

Vitamin D. It is not certain whether sufficient vitamin D passes through breast milk to meet infants' needs. The most reliable way for infants to get vitamin D is from supplements, which can be started shortly after birth. For infants born in spring or summer to a mother who receives vitamin D from sunlight and fortified foods, breast milk provides an adequate supply of the vitamin, and the infant supplement may be delayed until three months of age. To find vitamin D_2 (instead of D_3, which is of animal origin), it may be necessary to call around to a few pharmacies or contact a supplier listed in the Resources section of this book.

TABLE 7·4

Recommended Vitamin and Mineral Supplements for Breastfed Infants

Nutrient	Age	Amount
vitamin B_{12}	If mother's diet does not include vitamin B_{12}, infant needs supplement beginning shortly after birth. (But note that mother needs B_{12} supplementation, too!)	0.4 mcg per day from birth to 6 months; 0.5 mcg per day after 6 months
vitamin D	Begin vitamin D at birth or 3 months for infants with insufficient sun exposure, or who live in northern climates.	5 mcg (200 IU) per day; take care not to overdose with this vitamin
iron	Begin at 4 to 6 months if iron-fortified cereal is not given.	1 mg per kg body weight per day

Infants can synthesize their own vitamin D if their skin is briefly exposed to sunlight on a regular basis. An estimate of the time required is a total of about two hours on face only, spread over the course of a week, or thirty minutes per week, wearing just a diaper. However, such care must be used in exposing babies to the sun, especially during the first six months of life, that a supplement seems a wiser choice. Using sunscreen that is specially formulated for a baby's skin is a possibility after six months of age; however, use of sunscreen will reduce vitamin D synthesis.

Iron. The iron in breast milk is very well absorbed; however, a baby's iron stores start to decline at about four months of age. For this reason, an iron supplement may be given, as shown in Table 7.4. Iron-fortified cereals, such as rice cereal, can provide dietary iron after about six months of age, although this iron is less well absorbed than that from supplements.

Fluoride. Many municipal water supplies are fluoridated. If yours is not, you may give a fluoride supplement starting at six months of age to help harden bones and tooth enamel and to increase resistance to decay.

Almost Ready to Give Up on Breastfeeding?

> Breastfeeding is the most healthy and natural way to feed a baby, but it doesn't always come automatically. For many babies and mothers, the learning process takes a little "hands-on" help.
>
> —*Dr. Jane Morton*

Breastfeeding is pleasurable—this is basic to the survival of our species. Yet it doesn't always start out that way. The first few days (or weeks) are a time for mother and baby to get the knack of this new process, and overcoming any obstacles is well worth it. If the baby doesn't latch on correctly, if nipples are sore, or if breasts become engorged, it's not the fault of either the mother or the baby. The necessary support system isn't in place. We may think breastfeeding should be instinctive, yet it is partly learned, and generally we have had few opportunities to observe this normal process.

It's okay to continue breastfeeding despite the mother having a minor illness such as a cold or influenza; breast milk continues to provide immune benefits to the infant. Generally, by the time she is aware of the illness, the most infectious stage has passed.

How Can We Find Local Breastfeeding Support?

We ensure our success by starting early. Attend a lactation support meeting before or during pregnancy, and arrange to have rooming-in at the hospital. La Leche League is an outstanding resource, though don't expect members to be up on the latest information on vegan diets for nursing mothers, as this is not their field of expertise. See the Resources section for contact information and for videos that give excellent, practical instruction. We also may find support through a local health clinic, a lactation consultant, or a knowledgeable friend or relative.

Several generations ago, new moms had experienced women within their communities to help them get started. However, many new mothers are geographically removed from this sort of help or lack this network for other reasons. If we don't have this support from friends or family, kind, caring consultants and lactation groups can help tremendously and have a great deal to offer.

How Long Shall I Breast-Feed?

Don't quit breastfeeding after a month or two. Continuing through the first year, or longer, clearly is beneficial for the baby's health and for the mother. Even if we must be apart from our babies because of work or other reasons, electric or manual breast pumps can simplify matters. While being hooked up to this apparatus may make you feel like a bionic woman, continuing with breastfeeding is a far better choice than substituting with formula, and it is well worth it.

Is Baby Getting Enough?

One of the best nursing tips is to let go of worrying about our milk supply. Immediately after birth there may be an initial drop of about up to 7 percent of birth weight. Following this, if our babies are producing about eight wet diapers daily and are gaining weight, we can be confident they are getting enough.

We can make sure they're latched on properly, do our best to get enough rest (though at times this may seem an impossible feat), and nurse them frequently through the day and night, along with many shared naps. Frequent feeders thrive, and rest helps our milk production. We can trust that our bodies know how to make enough milk, and a top-quality product at that!

The breast is not like a bottle that is full or empty. It produces instantly to meet the demand. Though our milk production tissues are fully capable, some of us need a little help with the delivery system. We also may wonder if the baby's appetite is "normal," especially during stretches when snack time seems to roll around every two hours. Be assured it is. Some infants get hungry every hour, whereas some will sleep for four or five hours; some are quickly satisfied, others are unhappy without a long, comforting period of closeness.

By twelve weeks of age, many babies can sleep at least six hours—and so can we! If we happen to have a night owl, we can adjust her to our preference for being awake during the daytime by waking her up every three hours during the day (instead of allowing five-hour sleeps). When baby wakes at night, we may keep the lights off and wait a little while before feeding, to see if he is ready to just go back to sleep.

What Are "Fuss Foods"?

Certain foods in the diets of breastfeeding mothers have been linked to colic, eczema, chronic congestion, or upset stomach in some, though not all, infants. Foods most commonly associated with these reactions are cow's milk (by far the most common, causing 75 to 80 percent of reactions), as well as onions, chocolate, eggs, wheat, soy, cabbage, cauliflower, and broccoli. Other foods that have been reported are garlic, spices, MSG, licorice, coffee, and artificial sweeteners. To determine whether a food is causing problems, we can eliminate it for seven days and see if the baby's symptoms vanish.

To Be Avoided. Don't use alcohol, tobacco, or drugs. If caffeine-containing coffee or tea is used, keep it to a minimum. When we are breastfeeding, our diets become our babies' diets, so we need to consider our own food and habits carefully.

Can I Regain My Prebaby Figure?

On the topic of "How to Get Your Body Back into Shape After Childbirth the Way All the Taut-Bodied Entertainment Personalities Such As Jane Fonda Do," here's a bit of advice from humorist Dave Barry:

> Don't kid yourself. Those women have never had babies. Their children were all borne by professional stuntwomen.
> —*Dave Barry*, Babies and Other Hazards of Sex

Actually, don't despair. Even without earlier assistance from a stuntwoman, we can get back into terrific shape, as good or better than before pregnancy. A total vegetarian diet is a tremendous help in supporting that gradual return. In addition, we can find ways to make exercise part of our routine. Weight loss is not recommended while nursing because drastic cuts in calories may affect the milk supply.

Diet for Role Models

Whether or not we are breastfeeding, our own diets matter and not just for our own health. Those little eyes take in every move made by caregivers, and we can be certain that our habits create a foundation for the lifelong patterns of the children in our lives. This often is a time when many of us make big improvements in the way we eat, knowing the impact our habits will have.

Taking Part

Those of us who are not breastfeeding—partners, the baby's brothers and sisters, grandparents—still can be a part of the process by cuddling close or sitting nearby and holding the baby's fingers. In this support, we become an integral part of the process, as we can when bottle feeding.

Weaning from the Breast

Weaning may be initiated by an independent child or by our choice as parents. Either way is fine. Difficulties can arise when we are undecided and waffle back and forth, so it's good to make a clear decision. Then, let the process be gradual, allowing the child to adjust to new options. We may start by eliminating the feeding that the little one cares about least. Perhaps we continue with one breastfeed a day for another year.

If we cut back to three feedings a day during the first year, we should supplement with iron-fortified formula. Formula also may be used as the main beverage for weaned children through the second and third years of life.

Infant Formula

There may be good reasons to use infant formula as your baby's primary source of nutrition or as an occasional option. The American Academy of Pediatrics advises that the *only* acceptable substitute for breast milk during the first year is iron-fortified infant formula.

Formulas: Vegan, Near-Vegan, and Vegetarian

Of the iron-fortified infant formulas available, one of the soy formulas is a good choice: Alsoy (Nestlé), Isomil (Ross), or Prosobee (Mead Johnson). Nursoy brand is not suitable for vegetarians as it contains beef fat. Lactovegetarians also may choose one of the formulas based on cow's milk. None of these soy formulas is entirely vegan at the time of writing this book, due to animal origin vitamin D_3, derived from the lanolin in sheepskin and wool. (With sufficient consumer demand, any of these companies could choose to use vitamin D_2 that is not of animal origin.)

The formulas listed above also contain soybeans that are genetically modified and are not organic. There is an organic powdered formula, Baby's Only Organic Soy, found at www.naturesone.com/soy.htm or phone (614) 898-9758. Vitamin D_2, which normally is derived from irradiated yeast, cannot be included in a product labeled "organic." This formula contains vitamin D_3 derived from wool, but no other animal source ingredients. Formula companies continually are making improvements in their products and consumer demand is likely to be the impetus to change this situation.

Though infant formula lacks some of the immune-protective compounds found in breast milk, it does supply adequate amounts of vitamins D and B_{12}. Regarding supplementary iron, see Table 7.4 (the same guidelines apply to formula-fed infants) or talk with your health care provider. Also see the comments about fluoride on page 173.

Is Fortified Commercial Soymilk Suitable as a Primary Beverage?

Fortified commercial soymilk should not be given before babies are one year of age; for the first year we should stay with breast milk or formula. After one year of age, soymilk that is fortified with calcium, vitamin D, and vitamin B_{12} may be used, although breast milk and formula are better choices until the age of two. Soymilk is lower in fat, so if you use it, be sure to include in the diet some of the higher-fat foods: tofu, nut butters, and a little flaxseed oil.

Is Cow's Milk Suitable as a Primary Beverage?

Before one year of age, cow's milk is not acceptable, according to the American Academy of Pediatrics; nor is goat's milk. Both have compositions that are quite different from human milk, including more than triple the protein content, much less of the essential fats, and less vitamin C and folic acid. After one year of age, whole, pasteurized cow's milk may be introduced, although breast milk and formula are better choices, as cow's milk lacks some nutrients found in breast milk and formula. Also note that for some children the protein in cow's milk may be linked to asthma, canker sores, ear infections, constipation, and Type 1 diabetes.

Are Other Milks Suitable as a Primary Beverage During the First Two Years?

No. Commercial or homemade milks from rice, oats, other grains, or nuts are low in protein, are no substitute for breast milk or infant formula, and should not be the primary beverage during the first two years, nor should unfortified soymilk.

Preparing and Giving Formula

Follow sterilization and mixing instructions as given by the formula company exactly, and take great care with washing and refrigerated storage of bottles. Use water that you know to be safe. Prepare only enough formula for one day at a time.

In determining amount, provide as much as your baby wants. During the first few weeks of life, babies are hungry often but will swallow just small amounts, so six to ten small feedings may be necessary. With time, the intervals between feedings become longer and the amount consumed at one time increases. From three months on, infants will drink about four or five bottles (32 to 40 ounces) over the course of a day and night, with the amount increasing as they grow bigger. Then, at about six months of age, with the right time varying from one infant to another, our babies will be ready to be introduced to a whole new world of flavor, aroma, and texture.

Chapter 8

Baby's Big Adventures: Introducing Solid Foods

Vegan and vegetarian diets are able to satisfy all infant nutritional needs and promote normal infant growth.
— *The American Dietetic Association and
the American Academy of Pediatrics*

Before about six months of age, most infants do not need foods other than breast milk or infant formula. It's time to start introducing solid foods when their nutritional needs are increasing and they are ready for new foods. Babies show their readiness when they can sit and hold their heads up, watch and open their mouths for the spoon, and do not push food out with their tongues. The recommended time to begin is about six months of age; earlier may encourage the development of food allergies. We shouldn't delay too long after six months, as this is a normal stage of learning for babies. When this normal stage of fascination with new tastes and textures is missed, a child may develop into a picky eater and reject new foods.

The sequence and timing in introducing solid foods are similar to those used for non-vegetarian infants. Table 8.1 on the next page is a general guide, not an absolute rule, as each infant is unique and many variations work well. Cooked and pureed kale is one good starter food as it is so rich in minerals. Iron-fortified commercial infant cereals have commonly been recommended as starter foods; however, recent research indicates that beginning with vegetables and then fruit is less likely to trigger food allergies. If you prefer to start with a well-cooked, pureed whole grain (brown rice or barley, mixed with breast milk or formula), also use an iron supplement (as shown in Table 7.4) or as advised by your doctor.

Initiate this great adventure at a time when baby is rested, awake, propped up comfortably, and ready to try a new experience: food from a spoon! Attempt it once a day for a while, with a half-teaspoon of food that has the consistency of cream soup. Your little one may take a few weeks to grasp the concept that food is supposed to end up inside the mouth and then be swallowed. Table 8.1 gives an approximate idea of how things *might* proceed.

TABLE 8.1

General Guide to the
Introduction of Solid Foods

Age (and amount of breast milk or formula)	Foods	Amounts
6–7 months (with 24–32 oz. breast milk or formula)	Vegetables and harder fruits (skin, seeds, and pits removed), cooked and mashed with potato masher or fork; straining is not necessary. Raw apple, peeled and grated. Soft fresh fruits, peeled, seeds and pits removed, and mashed. Iron-fortified, single-grain cereals (rice, barley), then mixed cereals, especially those that do not contain the protein gluten. Don't start with wheat, which can be a common allergen.	Feed solids once a day, gradually increasing to 3 to 4 times per day. Begin with 1 tsp. of vegetables and fruits; increase to 2 to 4 tbsp. With cereals, begin with 1 tsp.; increase gradually to ¼ cup and then ½ cup.

Age (and amount of breast milk or formula)	Foods	Amounts
6–7 months (with 24–32 oz. breast milk or formula)	Vegetables and harder fruits (skin, seeds, and pits removed), cooked and mashed with potato masher or fork; straining is not necessary. Raw apple, peeled and grated. Soft fresh fruits, peeled, seeds and pits removed, and mashed.	Feed solids 3 to 4 times per day. Begin with 1 tsp.; increase gradually to 2 to 4 tbsp.
7–8 months (with 24–32 oz. breast milk or formula)	Protein-rich foods: well-mashed tofu; well-cooked, mashed peas; beans and lentils; soy yogurt. Unsweetened fruit juice, offered in a cup (may be diluted with equal amount of water).	Feed solids 3 to 4 times per day. Begin with 1 tsp.; increase gradually to 2 to 3 tbsp. per meal. Begin with 1 oz.; increase to maximum of 4 oz. per day.
8–9 months (with 24–32 oz. breast milk or formula)	Finger foods and teething foods: cooked fruit and vegetable pieces; ripe, fresh fruit and vegetable chunks; dry toast; rusks. Well-cooked whole grains: rice, quinoa, millet, barley, or others; and pasta, mashed.	Feed solids 3 to 4 times per day. Give up to 2 to 4 tbsp. fruit and vegetable pieces, ½ slice toast, ¼ bagel. Begin with 1 tbsp.; increase gradually to 2 to 3 tbsp.
9–12 months (with 20–30 oz. breast milk or formula)	Family food, mixed dishes, stews, grated raw carrot and apple, veggie "meats," gluten, seed "creams" (blend tahini, sunflower, or pumpkin seed butter with soymilk, water, or juice). Offer water in a cup.	Feed solids 5 to 6 times per day (3 meals and 2 or 3 snacks). Begin with 1 tsp.; increase gradually to ¾ to 1 cup per meal.

Cautionary Notes for Infant Feeding

- *Avoid* small pieces of food that can cause choking, such as nuts, seeds, raw peas, corn kernels, popcorn, whole grapes (grapes can be cut in half or quartered), raisins, hard candies; a blob of peanut butter on a spoon; large chunks of hard, raw fruits and vegetables, such as carrots (grate carrots instead); veggie dogs (cut veggie dogs in half or quarters lengthwise).
- *Delay* solid food if baby frequently chokes or gags; its introduction may be too early.
- *Remove* pits from apricots, cherries, peaches, and plums.
- *Teach* children how to chew well. (Many adults could do this better, too!) Stay nearby while baby is eating.
- *Avoid* giving babies black or green tea, coffee, and foods with added salt, fat, sugar, honey, or corn syrup. Honey and corn syrup should not be given to babies under one year of age because they can support the growth of a type of food poisoning in the immature intestines of young infants.
- *Blend* smooth cashew or almond butters with fortified soymilk, water, or juice, for ease in swallowing.
- *Limit* juice to a maximum of ½ cup per day, as more can crowd out other important foods. It can be mixed with an equal amount of water.
- *Check* baby food jar labels to make sure they don't contain added sugar.
- *Choose organic* baby food (homemade or commercial).

After cereals, fruits, and vegetables, introduce well-cooked, mashed, and strained legumes: lentils, chickpeas, pink beans, and kidney beans, as well as tofu, which can be plain or mixed with pureed fruits or vegetables.

It is not essential that we puree all homemade baby foods, as was commonly done when we were babies. Foods with the consistency of mashed potato have value as they encourage the development of chewing skills. (Most commercial baby food is pureed, however.) Instructions for making your own wholesome baby foods can be found at www.vrg.org/recipes/babyfood.htm.

Prepared baby foods may be covered and kept refrigerated for up to three days. Don't feed directly from a baby food jar and then return an uneaten portion to the fridge, however, as bacteria from baby's saliva will spoil the remaining food. We could put one to two tablespoons of food in each section of a clean ice cube tray, cover,

> **For teething, a cool item baby will appreciate is a clean, cold, wet washcloth.**

and place the tray in the freezer. When frozen, the cubes can be transferred to a freezer bag or container, and a label attached showing the preparation date. Cubes can be thawed and used as needed, within four weeks.

How Do We Know How Much to Feed Our Babies?

Learning the baby's signals about food—such as turning the head away, spitting food out, or a message that means "more!"—will help us know when to begin or stop feeding. Healthy babies know how much to eat. Some eat a lot, some a little, and it is perfectly normal for their interest in food to vary from day to day. If they are sick or teeth are coming, they may not want much. Do not force solids; when your baby's intake is limited, focus on fluids instead.

As babies get older, we can serve small portions on a small plate or bowl. For example, a tablespoonful each of beans, potatoes, and carrots may be suitable for one-year-olds. When they finish, we can offer more. Breast milk or formula supply enough fluid; up to age six months or so, when these are the sole nourishment, water generally is not needed. After that, tiny sips may be offered from a cup, or water may be given daily in a bottle. It becomes more important as solid foods replace breast milk or formula. Water is especially important when the weather is hot or when your baby has a fever. Table 8.2 on the next page shows examples of meal plans that could be used as a general guideline, though you certainly may modify timing and quantities. Between twelve and eighteen months, amounts can be increased gradually. Have fun!

Finger Foods

At about eight months of age, or a little earlier, children discover their amazing ability to pick up things with their thumbs and forefingers. They often are so excited by this achievement that they'd rather explore this new skill than eat. When they eat, they want to feed themselves. What joy! What power!

TABLE 8.2

Sample Meal Plans for Babies from Six Months to Eighteen Months

	6–9 Months	9–12 Months	18 Months
			Offer water to drink throughout the day.
Early Morning	Breast milk or formula.	Breast milk or formula.	Sleep in!
Breakfast	4–8 tbsp. infant cereal mixed with breast milk, water, or formula. 1–4 tbsp. soft fruit in small pieces. Breast milk or formula.	4–8 tbsp. infant cereal mixed with breast milk, water, or formula. Soft fruit in small pieces. Breast milk, or formula in a cup.	1 small pancake, toast with spread, or ½ cup oatmeal. ½ banana or ½ cup applesauce. Breast milk, or ¾ cup formula or fortified soymilk.
Morning Snack	Breast milk or formula.	Breast milk or formula. Soft fruit in small pieces.	Small whole-wheat bun or 2–3 crackers spread with 2 tbsp. hummus. Breast milk, or 4 oz. formula or fortified soymilk.
Lunch	1–4 tbsp. mashed or soft vegetables. 1–6 tbsp. pureed cooked beans, peas, or lentils, steamed tofu or tempeh, or soy yogurt (starting at 7 months). Soft fruit in small pieces. Breast milk or formula.	2–4 tbsp. mashed or soft vegetables or fruit. 2–6 tbsp. soft cooked beans, peas, or lentils, steamed tofu or tempeh cubes, veggie burger cubes, or soy yogurt. Breast milk, or formula in a cup.	½ sandwich, or ½ cup Cheez-a-Roni (page 310), or 6 oz. soup. ½ tsp. flaxseed oil (mixed into one or more foods). ½ cup berries or fruit (such as ½ cooked, peeled pear). Breast milk, or 4 oz. formula or fortified soymilk.

	6–9 Months	9–12 Months	18 Months
Afternoon Snack	Breast milk or formula.	Breast milk or formula. Soft vegetable or fruit in small pieces.	4 oz. soy yogurt with fruit. Water in a cup.
Supper	1–4 tbsp. mashed or soft vegetables. 1–6 tbsp. pureed cooked beans, peas, or lentils, steamed tofu or tempeh, or soy yogurt (starting at 7 months). Soft fruit in small pieces. Breast milk or formula.	2–6 tbsp. cooked potato or pasta. 2–6 tbsp. pureed cooked beans, peas, or lentils, steamed tofu or tempeh, or soy yogurt. Soft vegetable or fruit in small pieces. Breast milk, or formula in a cup.	¼ cup tofu plus ½ cup rice, potato, or pasta, plus ⅓ cup stir-fried vegetables; or 1 to 1½ cups family entrée. Breast milk, or 4 oz. formula or fortified soymilk.
Evening Snack	Breast milk or formula. Infant cereal mixed with breast milk, water, or formula.	Breast milk or formula. Finger food such as oat cereal O's.	Breast milk, or ½ cup formula or fortified soymilk.

Finger foods should be given only when your baby is seated in a highchair, and those given at first should be soft enough to be gummed (rather than chewed). Finger foods can include toast, teething biscuits, different shapes of pasta, unsweetened ready-to-eat cereals, pieces of rolls or pancakes, unsalted crackers, steamed tofu cubes, well-cooked beans or lentils, soft-cooked vegetable or fruit cubes, and slices of raw, soft fruits such as avocado, banana, kiwi, mango, melon, or papaya. Our little ones will develop clear preferences, and these are likely to change over time.

TABLE 8.3

Foods of Low Allergenicity

Food Group	Low-Allergenicity Foods
vegetables	yams, sweet potatoes, squash, parsnips, carrots, green beans, beets, broccoli, potatoes
fruits	pears, cooked blueberries, cooked peaches, cooked apricots
grains	quinoa, tapioca, millet, rice, rice cakes, rice noodles

How Do We Prevent or Deal with Allergies?

When introducing solids to a baby with a family history of allergy, it helps to get expert advice from a dietitian, nurse, doctor, or clinic. One helpful reference is *Dietary Management of Food Allergies and Intolerances* by Dr. J. Joneja (J.A. Hall Publications, Vancouver, B.C., Canada, 1997). Signs of food allergy can appear on skin (red or itchy), in the respiratory tract (stuffy nose, wheezing, runny eyes), or in the gastrointestinal tract (colic that doesn't go away, frequent spitting up, diarrhea). Table 8.3 contains a list of "starter foods," foods that have proven less likely to trigger allergic reactions and can be introduced gradually.

When babies are nine to twelve months of age, we can add avocado, cauliflower, plums, prunes, cooked apple, oatmeal, and barley, as these are less likely to cause reactions. *For any infant, it is wise to introduce new foods one at a time and wait at least three or four days to see if there's any reaction.*

In situations in which allergies are more likely, it may help to wait longer to be certain the baby shows no reaction. For these infants, do not introduce soyfoods, beans, peas, lentils, wheat, corn, tomatoes, berries, melon, and citrus until after age one. Delay peanut butter, nut butter, or seed butter until three years of age. Milk, cheese, eggs, and dairy products also are common triggers for allergies.

In One End, Out the Other

Strained apricots and prunes may cause loose stools, in which case they can be left out of the diet until baby's digestive system has matured a little. These same foods, or a little prune juice, may be useful in preventing constipation. Beets or greens can have obvious, but harmless, color effects on the stool.

Ages One to Three

As toddlers make the transition from a reliance on breast milk or formula to family foods, we can have a wonderful time together exploring textures, tastes, and their newly discovered ability to feed themselves. Infants can be nutritionally vulnerable at this time of change. Our key to success is to have a good plan in mind, and at the same time be flexible. Table 8.4 on page 188 outlines a good plan.

Supplements

The guide in Table 8.4 has been planned around children's basic requirements for protein, minerals (such as iron, zinc, and calcium), and a host of vitamins. An additional multivitamin-mineral supplement is not necessary, although we may want to rely on a supplement when our children's food intake is insufficient. To boost a toddler's iron intake, you may use a supplement that includes iron. Kale and broccoli are iron-rich vegetables. Iron-fortified infant cereals or Cream of Wheat may be used to provide several of the Breads and Cereals servings, though the iron used to fortify these cereals is less well absorbed. A multivitamin-mineral supplement is an excellent way of providing vitamins B_{12} and D, especially if these are not supplied by fortified foods (or sunlight, in the case of vitamin D). If the amount of vitamin B_{12} is greater than 1 microgram, the supplement may be given less often; for example, three times a week. Take care not to give extra vitamin D, as excess can be toxic. Store all supplements safely away from children.

Flaxseed oil can be added to the diet after the age of one. Breast milk and formula provide omega-3 fatty acids. As these are replaced by solid foods, you can blend a half teaspoon of flaxseed oil into any smoothie, cereal, soup, or entrée. This oil should not be cooked, but mixed into the food when it is at serving temperature.

Meal and Snack Planning

Offer meals at regular times. Include foods from three to five food groups at every meal and at least two food groups at snack time. Though we always may have thought

Plant-Based Food Guide for Toddlers
(1–3 years)

Include a wide variety of foods.

Milk and Formula: Total 20–24 oz.
About three 6–8 oz. servings of breast milk, commercial formula, or full-fat fortified soymilk (or a combination of these).*

Breads and Cereals: 4–6 toddler-size servings.
1 toddler-size serving = ½ slice bread
 ¼ cup cooked grain or pasta
 ½ cup ready-to-eat cereal
 ¼ cup of cooked cereal**

Vegetables: 2–3 toddler-size servings.
1 toddler-size serving = ½ cup salad or other raw vegetable pieces
 ¼ cup cooked vegetables
 ⅓ cup vegetable juice

Fruits: 2–3 toddler-size servings.
1 toddler-size serving = ½ to 1 fresh fruit
 ¼ cup cooked fruit
 ¼ cup fruit juice (limit to about ½ cup per day)

Beans and Alternates: 2 toddler-size servings.
1 toddler-size serving = ¼ cup cooked beans, peas, or lentils
 2 oz. tofu
 ½ to 1 oz. veggie "meat"
 1½ tbsp. nut or seed butter
 2 oz. soy yogurt

Also Important:
Vitamin B$_{12}$: 1.0 mcg in fortified foods or supplement
Vitamin D: sunlight or at least 5.0 mcg in fortified foods or supplements
Omega-3 Fatty Acids: in ½ tsp. flaxseed oil or 2 tsp. organic canola oil

Source: Adapted from *Becoming Vegan,* The Book Publishing Company, Summertown, Tenn., 2000, by Vesanto Melina and Brenda Davis.

*Lactovegetarians can use 20–24 oz. full-fat cow's milk.

**Iron-fortified infant cereal and Cream of Wheat are excellent daily choices for good iron status.

of certain foods as "breakfast" or "supper" items, we can be much more flexible than that. In many parts of the world, it's common to have lentils at breakfast or cereal at supper. Look through the Recipes section for new ideas. Try Crunchy Fruit Crisps as a snack; start your day with Breakfast Burritos or Red Lentil Soup; and have Rice and Raisin Pudding or Warm Spiced Milk any time of day.

To prevent choking, make sure children sit down at the table while eating and that you or another adult are nearby. Eating while running or playing can cause choking.

How Can We Get Our Children to Eat More?

> Independence must win. Pushing a child to eat is the surest way to create a problem. Feeding has got to be pleasurable. If a mother thinks of feeding as a job instead of a fun time with her kid, she's going to make it a nightmare. She's also going to end up with a feeding problem, either undereating or overeating.
>
> —*T. Berry Brazelton, Pediatrician*

Feeding tends to be the arena (and note that arena can mean either playing field or battleground) in which children and parents work out issues of independence (feeding oneself) and dependence (being fed).

We're wise to make mealtime a quiet, relaxing, family occasion and a chance to talk about the day's activities—at least occasionally! (We may need to balance this with our children's natural urge to eat a bite, run off, and circle back for the next bite.) It's best to keep the television off or in another room. Children often take longer to finish their meals than we're accustomed to; however, this is natural. Our children also are our teachers. Leisurely mealtimes are thought to be one of the health benefits of "The Mediterranean Diet"—sitting, chatting, and taking time just to be with each other.

To keep active children with small stomachs well nourished, we need to serve meals or snacks every two to three hours. Keep muffins handy in the freezer, and have nutritious foods within reach for whenever hunger strikes: soy yogurt, a tray of cut-up veggies and an avocado or bean dip, or a fruit smoothie.

Who Decides?

As parents, we decide which foods will be served. Our children decide whether to eat and how much to eat. We can allow them choices within a food group, such as banana or kiwifruit; bread, tortillas, or noodles. Occasionally it is all right for them to completely refuse or miss a meal. We do not have to become short-order cooks, catering to their every wish. It's not wise to use dessert as a bribe for eating the rest of the meal, which can make sweets seem more special. Nor should we force children to eat or punish them for not eating, as when we do this we may override their natural hunger and fullness cues. It's best to remove uneaten food without comment. (Then, we might offer this food or perhaps Sneaky Dad's Pudding at snack time.)

Food Jags and Refusal: Is My Child's Diet Unbalanced?

By twelve months of age the natural order is that children feed themselves and become independent eaters, so it's best if we surrender our control. We can encourage autonomy by providing entire meals made of finger foods and allow children to accept or refuse what they wish. Though it helps to know what a "balanced diet" is for ages one through three years, we're wise to abandon the idea that our children's diets will always fit the guide. We can be grateful for the normal development of independence and model good eating habits ourselves, knowing that these patterns will take time to be adopted.

Messiness

Messy eating is normal and is a part of learning. Set up suitable protection for floors or walls, and relax. Though we may wonder if any food actually makes it into their stomachs, children often eat more when they are allowed to feed themselves.

Optimal Growth: The Middle Path

You needn't panic if your baby isn't quite as big as a neighbor's baby of the same age or is below the fiftieth percentile on growth charts. Many standard growth charts used in clinics and doctors' offices are based on weight-gain patterns of formula-fed infants from 1927 to the mid-1950s—a time when cereal was given as early as two to six weeks of age (with food allergy as one result). These growth charts, which are shown in Figures 9.1 to 9.4 in the next chapter, also can be obtained from health clinics or seen on the Internet (links are given in the Resources section, page 357, and a discussion of the use of these charts is given on page 195). We now suspect that the push toward maximum weight gain in infancy and childhood may even be linked to several types of adult cancers in later life. Also, note that small parents can expect to have a smaller infant.

All the same, we must ensure our children get enough calories, taking special care at the time of weaning. This is a particularly vulnerable period when children are switching from an easily digested fluid, which has over 50 percent calories from fat, to a variety of foods that can be more challenging to eat. Whereas low-fat meals are suitable for adults who are overweight or who want to reduce their risk of chronic disease, children's needs are somewhat different. Children certainly don't need hydrogenated fats in processed foods or the cholesterol and saturated fats in animal products. They thrive on the healthier plant foods that are higher in fat; for example, tofu, nut butters, mashed avocado, soy yogurt, puddings, and "good" oils (particularly flaxseed and olive oils), along with breast milk, formula, or fortified soymilk. We also may need to limit bulky foods such as wheat bran (in cereals or muffins) and big salads. These can fill up a child's small stomach without providing many calories. Though whole grains are excellent choices for youngsters, it can be valuable to include some refined breads, cereals, crackers, and pastas, which are lower in fiber and bulk.

Shall We Limit the Use of Bottles?

It's not a good idea to put children in bed with a bottle because of the damage to teeth that results from prolonged contact with sugars in formula, milks, and juice. At bedtime, you can offer a pacifier. We shouldn't allow a toddler to walk around all day with a bottle or use it as comfort. A bottle filled with water is not harmful, but it should be replaced with a cup when the child is ready and able to drink from one.

What's a Treat?

What springs to mind when we think of *treats?* Sugar? Fatty foods? Is a treat necessarily something that undermines our health or goes against our values? As we set life-long eating patterns in place, this is a good question to consider. If a child is upset, but not hungry, do we want to encourage the habit of using food as a remedy? If we comfort or reward our child with attention and affection instead of food, we'll be establishing more positive patterns.

Sometimes we need to say a gentle but firm "No!" (without wavering). Though children will ask, we don't need to buy unhealthful foods and beverages or keep them in the house. We can offer nutritious choices instead. It's important for us as parents to redefine for ourselves the meaning of *treats:* treating our family to organic foods, splurging on fresh berries, and sharing a bottle of juice are healthful pleasures about which we can feel good.

Will I *Ever* Have Enough Time?

Being a parent who has plenty to do around the house, and perhaps one who also works outside the home, can be quite overwhelming. However, tasks such as making lunch or clearing the table after dinner can be times for quality interaction. Because these jobs won't proceed as quickly as when we do them alone, we may need to lower some of our "house beautiful" standards. Nevertheless, we're likely to have much more fun when we make our children our top priority. Ensure that you get some rest, and let the tasks of lesser importance fall into place, even though some that were formerly "essential" now will remain undone.

Chapter 9

Children from Two to Twelve

Developing good food habits can be a wonderful adventure for our children *and* for us. Though adults and youngsters often are learning different things, the process of learning is something we can share.

When It Comes to Food

Differences Between Our Children and Ourselves

As children are growing rapidly, their nutritional needs are quite different from those of adults. At about two years of age, give or take a few months, a toddler may weigh about 27 pounds and be 34 inches tall. Three years later, that child may weigh 50 percent more and be 9 inches taller. To accomplish this, the child's diet must be rich in protein, minerals, and many other nutrients that build new cells. A child is involved in a remarkable bodybuilding project, which continues at varying rates through adolescence. In contrast, our adult diets simply provide materials for maintenance and repair; in fact, some of us would be happy if we lost a few pounds.

Outside forces impact our food choices in ways that vary from one time to another. Even more than adults, children are vulnerable to television advertising and store packaging. Because of what we have learned about farm practices, environmental concerns, or health matters, some family members may be highly motivated to be vegetarian or vegan, whereas others are responding to entirely different influences. Children and teens can be passionate about new belief systems or have a strong need to be distinct from family or friends and have their individuality respected. For other youngsters, a top priority can be the need to blend in at school and with peers.

The simple acts of making a shopping list, deciding how grocery dollars are spent, and what foods stock the refrigerator and pantry shelves involve complex decisions. We can help children meet all their nutritional needs in many different ways, whether their choices differ somewhat from ours; whether they have opted for vegan, ovolactovegetarian, or near-vegetarian diets; or whether their eating pattern involves foods prepared from basic grains, vegetables, and fruits, or includes plenty of quick, ready-to-eat items.

Similarities Between Our Children and Ourselves

As parents and caregivers, we are faced with the fact that unless we practice what we preach, it's difficult to insist on good habits of diet and exercise in children. Youngsters are sure to know where the cookies or chips are stored, and whether or not these are prized foods. When we try to numb our feelings with unhealthful foods or beverages, we pass the message that this is the best solution we could find.

Instead of being a daily burden, meal planning and preparation can become a fascinating and rewarding shared process. For this reason, the recipe section of this book is packed with highly nutritious foods that are simple to make and will appeal to children and adults alike. As parents and caregivers, we may find that as never before our senses open to the aroma, flavor, and texture of foods. The awe and excitement with which young children approach everyday experiences can help us look at fruits, vegetables, and grain products with a fresh and profound sense of wonder. Time spent with youngsters in shared food preparation will reap a great harvest in establishing good nutrition habits later.

Together: Creating Health

Though we may not have learned how to prepare wholesome and delicious food when *we* were children, there's no better time than now to develop this skill. Research linking food habits in the elderly with their diets as children shows that lifelong habits are set in place before the sixth grade. For our children's sakes, efforts to shape healthful patterns should be made before this stage.

The Weaning Period

At the time of weaning from breast milk or formula, a child can be nutritionally vulnerable. It's hard to beat the masterful mixture of human milk or infant formula, so well suited to the first months and years of life. Thus, our replacement pattern needs to be well balanced. A menu such as that in Table 8.2 on page 184 is equally nourishing and is actually better suited to the next stage of independence. With a little care, this transition will happen very smoothly. Of course, as in the rest of life, there could be a few challenges. (See Table 9.1 on page 196.)

Fast- and Slow-Growth Periods

At certain stages, children seem to shoot up a few inches overnight. Since we last looked, their bodies appear to have stretched out and changed from the roly-poly shape of a toddler to the lean torso of an older child. At other periods, increases in height or weight are tiny and development seems to occur primarily in other realms, such as language or motor skills.

There is no "ideal" rate of growth. Figures 9.1 to 9.4 on pages 198–201 show the typical weights and stature (height) of children as they grow from two to twenty years of age. These are the same charts that are used at health clinics. To read more about these charts, go to www.cdc.gov/growthcharts.

In using these charts, we may place the height of a girl at a certain age in years on the chart and see how her height compares with other girls of the same age. If her height is "average" for the general population of girls her age, her height will be at the fiftieth percentile. This means that 50 percent of the girls of that age will be taller and 50 percent will be shorter. The "average" is not the goal for a particular

TABLE 9.1

Food Challenges and Solutions

Normal Phases of Growing Up	As Your Child Sees It	As You May See It	What to Do About It
Refusal to eat	She or he may not be hungry, may be asserting independence, or may want attention.	You must somehow make her or him eat; growing children need food.	Respect the wisdom of the child's own body (and spirit). A skipped meal will not hurt a healthy child, so remove the food without fuss after a reasonable length of time. If you're concerned about weight gain, see your doctor or health clinic.
Food jag; getting hooked on one food	What a wonderful new food this is!	Children need balanced diets.	Food jags aren't unusual in children; they occur in adults, too. If no issue is made of them, eating patterns tend to balance out after a few days.
Dislike of new foods	Your child may not like the taste or may not feel up to trying something new today.	Children should learn to like everything and adjust to family eating patterns.	Children have a right to a few dislikes. You don't need to become a short-order cook, but if you have time, you might provide a substitute from the same food group. If the dislike is treated casually, the same food may be accepted at a later date. Also, your youngster may eat that food without question when it is offered at school or at the home of a friend.

Normal Phases of Growing Up	As Your Child Sees It	As You May See It	What to Do About It
Dislike of cooked vegetables	Those aren't appealing.	Vegetables are packed with good nutrition. Furthermore, we're told to give variety.	Vitamins, minerals, and all those protective nutrients come in all sorts of foods. If your child rejects everything except raw peas from a pod, or carrot sticks, or papaya cubes, or bananas, you can feel grateful that each of these is highly nutritious. It's not essential to eat cooked vegetables every day. Perhaps that will come later on.
Dawdling, or playing with foods	The color, taste, texture, and squishiness of foods is fascinating! Also, he or she may not be hungry.	Food is not a toy. Besides, we can't wait around all day.	If you're a fast eater, you might use this as an opportunity to slow down a little yourself. When the child is clearly finished eating, simply remove the food.

child at a certain age. To put these charts in perspective, note that "the general population" includes the one child in seven who is overweight. We are coming to understand that bigger is not always better and that more gradual development may well be healthier overall. For example, physicians are concerned that the fastest rates of growth and increasingly early puberty in girls may be linked to a higher risk of breast cancer later on. There may be similar concerns for males and eventual prostate cancer. If one or both parents are small or very tall, we may expect their genetic influence to be reflected in the next generation.

FIGURE 9.1

Weight Chart for Boys

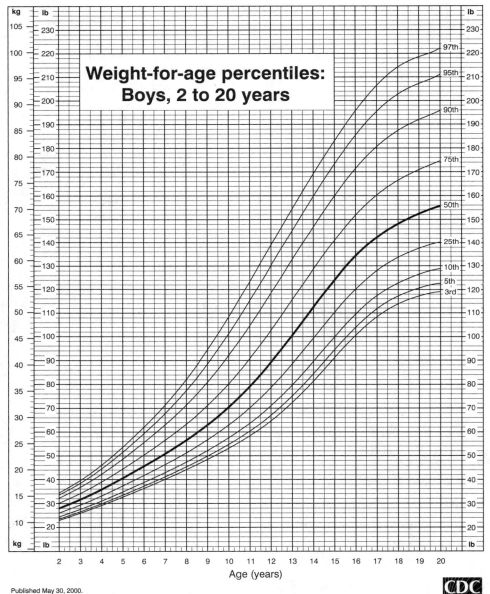

Weight-for-age percentiles: Boys, 2 to 20 years

Published May 30, 2000.
SOURCE: Developed by the National Center for Health Statistics in collaboration with
the National Center for Chronic Disease Prevention and Health Promotion (2000).

FIGURE 9.2

Weight Chart for Girls

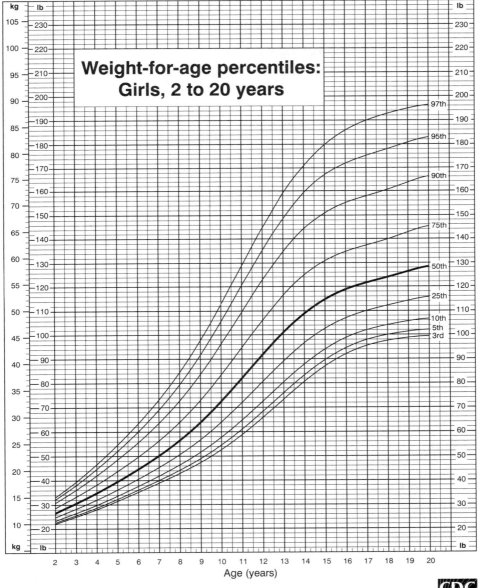

Weight-for-age percentiles: Girls, 2 to 20 years

Published May 30, 2000.
SOURCE: Developed by the National Center for Health Statistics in collaboration with
the National Center for Chronic Disease Prevention and Health Promotion (2000).

FIGURE 9.3

Stature Chart for Boys

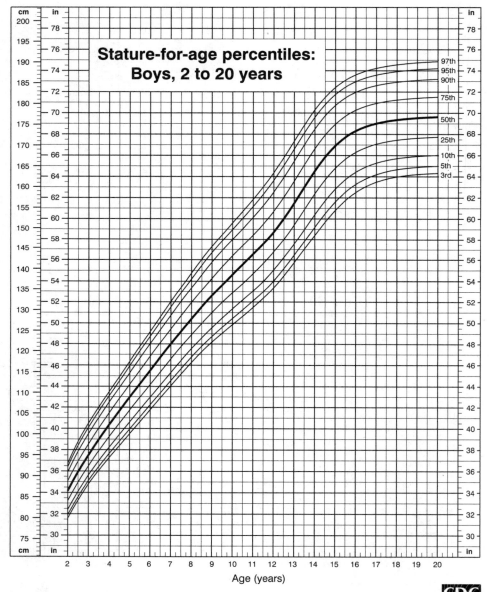

Stature-for-age percentiles: Boys, 2 to 20 years

Published May 30, 2000.
SOURCE: Developed by the National Center for Health Statistics in collaboration with
the National Center for Chronic Disease Prevention and Health Promotion (2000).

CDC
SAFER · HEALTHIER · PEOPLE™

FIGURE 9.4

Stature Chart for Girls

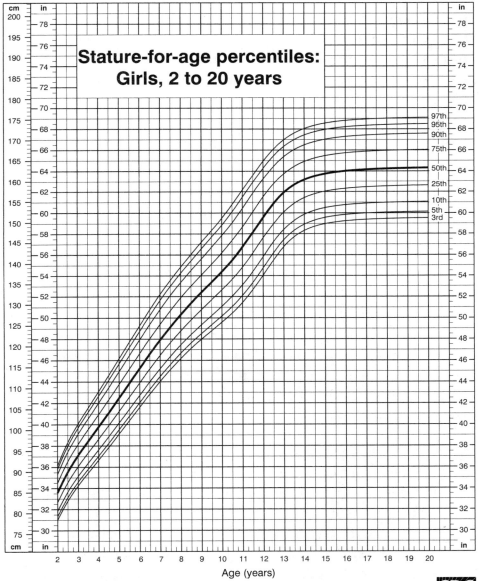

Stature-for-age percentiles:
Girls, 2 to 20 years

Age (years)

Published May 30, 2000.
SOURCE: Developed by the National Center for Health Statistics in collaboration with
the National Center for Chronic Disease Prevention and Health Promotion (2000).

SAFER · HEALTHIER · PEOPLE™

At each office visit, physicians, public health nurses, and other health professionals write a child's current height and weight on these charts. When we have a record of a child's height at several ages, we can link the dots and trace the child's growth; the same can be done for weight. If a child's measurements place him at the twenty-fifth percentile at three years of age, it will not be surprising if his measurements at later ages continue along the same percentile line. If we see a sudden, significant change in pattern, we may consider the possible causes. For example, if a child is usually at the fiftieth percentile, showing "average" height and weight, and then drops to the twentieth percentile (in which 80 percent of children of the same age group are larger) a year later, we wonder what changes have occurred in health or food intake. If our child is in the lowest fifth percentile (the smallest 5 percent for that age group), this can be cause for concern. A remedy may be to pack more calories into meals and snacks.

Providing Enough Calories

Some active children simply don't get enough calories, especially right after weaning. This can happen if the diet is high in salads, raw fruits and vegetables, sprouts, and whole grains. Such foods are ideal for weight-conscious adults who want bulky, high-fiber foods to fill them up without making them fat. Make no mistake, these are highly nutritious for children, too, and are important as a significant part of the day's menus. But note that in breast milk or formula, 54 percent of the calories are derived from fat (very high-quality fat, tailored to our needs). So we need to include foods and beverages that are concentrated sources of calories, along with the minerals and vitamins. Here are some examples:

- Provide about 3 cups of fortified full-fat soymilk each day. We may give a serving at each meal. In case of soy allergy, we may use fortified rice milk; however, we will need to boost the protein and calories in other ways.
- Rely on avocados, nut and seed butters, soy yogurt, and tofu.
- Include some refined grain products (such as pasta) in addition to whole grains, as these less fibrous foods may help children to eat more.
- Pack in the calories with cooked foods, such as thick soups or stews. A cup of pea soup provides 136 calories and 9 grams of protein, whereas a cup of snow pea pods provides 26 calories and 2 grams of protein.

- Start thinking of cookies, muffins, puddings, and shakes as highly nutritious foods. If you make them with healthful ingredients, they *will* be highly nutritious! All of these are excellent between-meal snacks.

Picky Eaters

Though children may *appear* to be picky eaters, diligent detective work often will prove that they are managing very well; in fact, they may be thriving. It is important to watch both food intake *and* growth. It may seem that a child's favorite five foods can't possibly sustain life. For example, if, over the course of a day, a 29-pound toddler gets 3 cups of fortified soymilk, two peanut butter sandwiches, two sliced bananas, and a half cup of peas, he or she receives enough calories and twice the necessary calcium and protein. These five foods give more than enough B vitamins, vitamin C, and iron, plus 80 percent of the zinc requirement. Even though every other food in the house is firmly rejected, these simple choices are packed with vitamins and minerals.

One Louisville lawyer overcame concerns about his daughter's lack of interest in food by inventing Sneaky Dad's Pudding (page 338). It may seem an unusual combination, but it's surprisingly tasty. If our children avoids vegetables, we can put grated carrot or cooked squash or pumpkin into muffins (page 266). We may watch television with a platter of veggies nearby. (This is a great choice for adults, too.) Children often will add avocado, tomato, or sprouts to a burger or taco, whereas they might shun a salad.

We can make sure that mealtimes are pleasant. Children's food choices shouldn't become a topic for dispute. As parents, we always will lose. One of our best tools is perseverance. For example, we may remove an untouched meal without comment, place it in the refrigerator, and then serve it later when hunger strikes. We can offer at least one favorite food at each meal. We can encourage our child's successes in trying new foods and ignore the unwanted behaviors.

Keeping It Simple

We certainly don't need to create exotic meals that are complicated to prepare. In fact, most youngsters will reject a fancy casserole and instead go for finger foods that they easily can identify: raw veggies, chunks of tofu, fruit, and toast or crackers with a spread.

Breakfasts

Breakfast helps children pay attention and do better at school. Problem-solving ability is improved in those who start the day fueled with a good meal. Teachers report that the breakfast-eaters in the class have better attitudes. Though sugar-laden, fluorescent cereals may be the rage in television commercials, it's not difficult to come up with highly nutritious breakfasts that appeal to children. It helps to be a bit adventurous in allowing new choices. Also, let's consider how we prefer our days to begin.

Is our priority to get a peaceful start, even though family members must be out of the house early? If so, we may set out dishes and ready-to-eat foods the night before and avoid the rush hour. Good choices are Granny's Grand Granola (page 253), Swiss-Style Muesli (page 254), or one of the truly nutritious whole-grain flaked cereals from the supermarket. Creamy Multigrain Porridge (page 250) can be simmering in a crock-pot overnight. Fruit can be on the table or Freestyle Fruit Salad (page 262) can be ready in the refrigerator.

If your youngsters thrive on a high-protein start, rely on Vegetable Tofu Scramble (page 261). A Purple Protein Power Shake (page 243) is good in warm weather. You can invent variations for both recipes, too. If you prefer a traditional breakfast with lots of staying power, Oatmeal Flax Porridge (page 252) or Creamy Multigrain Porridge, plus fortified soymilk, are ideal. For big appetites, add toast, nut butters, and fruit.

For children who are too sleepy to eat before heading to school or day care, choose a grab-and-go breakfast. Muscle Muffins (page 265) or a nut butter sandwich can be eaten during a long drive in the car or during morning break. A chocolate or carob shake in a thermos or jar provides fruit (banana) and fortified soymilk; added protein powder is an option. Sneaky Dad's Power Punch Smoothie (page 244) was developed as a quick breakfast, though it's also helpful at other times of day.

If you have time for a leisurely and companionable start to your day, it's fun to sit with toddlers and breakfast on finger foods. Try Apples and Tahini (page 264), Crunchy Fruit Crisps (page 264), or Breakfast Burritos (page 263).

On weekends, you can try every one of the recipes for pancakes, French toast, and toppings on pages 259 to 260. These are such fun to make that they can motivate children of both sexes to become good cooks later in life.

Bag Lunches

Packing those brown bags or lunch boxes can be a very pleasant evening (or morning) task. Some children want the security of the same nut butter and jam sandwich every single school day. Alternatively, we may find that lunch retains its appeal only if we come up with new ideas every few weeks. Nutritionally, one of the most important things about a lunch is that it gets eaten.

Another important factor is that lunch should include some protein-rich foods and whole grains, which supply continued energy over a long afternoon. At first it may seem that if we've given up meat slices and aren't keen on cheese, there's not much left with which to make a sandwich. Fortunately, that is not the case; dozens of sandwich possibilities are listed on pages 269 to 282.

Soy yogurt is a welcome choice in lunches. We also can provide wonderful grain salads—especially handy for those with wheat allergies. Potato salads and pasta salads are good choices, too. (For tips on packing "food safe" lunches, see page 110.)

If our children aren't fond of homemade soups or cooked vegetables, they may become more "vegetable friendly" when they help with the preparation. We can encourage them to help wash the carrots. When they are a little older and able to handle knives safely, they may assist with chopping. We'll likely find that half the carrot coins are eaten long before the soup starts cooking. Alphabet Minestrone (page 283) is a good choice for beginning readers.

Top Ten Meals for Children

It is well known that most people live on six to ten favorite meals, repeated over and over. The following are time-tested meals that children love. As it happens, each provides at least 15 to 20 grams of protein, plus one-third or more of the day's requirements for iron, zinc, and calcium for a child six to ten years of age. Each is superbly balanced nutritionally.

- African Stew (page 308), brown rice, fruit soy yogurt
- French Bread Pizza (page 319), raw veggies
- Cheez-A-Roni (page 310), fortified nondairy milk
- spaghetti, Chunky Tomato Pasta Sauce (page 322), fortified soymilk
- baked potato, Liquid Gold Dressing (page 290), Crispy Tofu Fingers (page 315), and broccoli florets (steamed or raw)

- Chili with Veggie Wieners (page 311) or baked beans, Crunchy Cornbread (page 268), calcium-fortified juice
- veggie burger, Oven Fries (page 329), Rice and Raisin Pudding (page 340)
- Protein-Rich Stir Fry (page 314), fortified rice milk
- Grandma's Noodles (page 309), carrot sticks, tofu cubes (marinated, as for Colorful Kabobs, page 318)
- Taco or Burrito (page 326 or other recipe), fortified nondairy milk

For ethnic or international meals, it can be fun to have a theme day. We might play music, show a movie, or even invite a dinner guest from that part of the world.

The few desserts listed in this "Top Ten" make significant contributions nutritionally. It's not necessary to serve desserts, and certainly not as an everyday occurrence. In some families, dessert is a semiannual event. However, in the dessert section (pages 338 to 347) you'll find a selection of cookies, puddings, squares, and "ice creams" made with such healthful ingredients that you'll feel good about serving them. They taste terrific, too.

Snacking

Keep small portions of leftover grains, pasta, and tasty entrées from yesterday's lunch and supper. In fact, prepare amounts so that you will always have a little left over. These make ideal "instant" snacks when hunger strikes midafternoon, or any other time. Although many children don't mind them cold, they also may be warmed and a sauce added, such as Nutti Sauce (page 293). This gives an alternative to peanut butter and jelly sandwiches or expensive junk food snacks. To satisfy the sweet tooth, keep ripe bananas in a bowl on the countertop and jars of dried dates, apricots, figs, or other fruit handy (and make sure that teeth get brushed after these sweet treats are eaten).

The "Perfect" Day

Table 9.2 on page 207 presents menus that meet the nutrient needs of children at three different stages of growth. At the end of Table 9.2, we show amounts of calories, protein, and certain minerals and vitamins provided by each menu and how each meets the Total Vegetarian Food Guide on page 126. Robin's menu doesn't contain any soyfoods, yet it provides plenty of protein and minerals. Pat's menu would be a

TABLE 9.2

Three Menus for Children

Robin, 44 pounds	Protein grams	Pat, 62 pounds	Protein grams	Jamie, 80 pounds	Protein grams
Breakfast					
1 English muffin	4	1 cup oatmeal with 1 tbsp. ground flaxseed stirred in	6	1 cup fortified ready-to-eat cereal	4
1½ tbsp. almond butter	3	1 cup fortified soymilk	7–8	½ cup berries	0.5
¾ cup (6 oz.) calcium-fortified orange juice	0.5	½ banana	0.6	1 cup fortified soymilk	7–8
Lunch					
¾ cup Red Lentil Soup (page 285)	6	1½ cups Alphabet Minestrone (page 283)	6	2 slices whole-grain bread	5
½ sandwich (1 slice bread, veggie seitan "meat" slice, tomato slices)	8	4 crackers	1–2	2 tbsp. peanut butter	8
½ cup raw veggies	0.5	1 orange or kiwifruit	1	1½ tbsp. jam	0.1
½ cup fortified rice milk	0.5	1 cup fortified soymilk	7–8	1 carrot	1
				6 oz. grape juice	0
Supper					
1 cup pasta with ¾ cup Chunky Tomato Pasta Sauce (page 322)	9	1 tortilla	1–3	1 veggie burger	8–18

(continued)

TABLE 9.2 (CONTINUED)

Robin, 44 pounds	Protein grams	Pat, 62 pounds	Protein grams	Jamie, 80 pounds	Protein grams
		Supper (cont.)			
1 tsp. flaxseed oil (stirred into pasta just before serving)	0	¾ cup refried beans	9	1 hamburger bun	4
½ cup fortified rice milk	0.5	¼ cup chopped tomato	0.4	¼ cup chopped lettuce	0.2
½ cup fresh fruit salad	1	¼ cup chopped lettuce	0.2	2 slices tomato	0.3
		¼ avocado	1	2 tbsp. ketchup	0.5
		1 tbsp. salsa	0.2	½ cup Oven Fries (page 329)	3
		1 cup fortified chocolate soymilk	7–8	1 cup fortified soymilk	7–8
		Snacks			
1 cup fortified chocolate rice milk	1	1 Strawberry Popsoycle, (page 347)	2	1 cup Warm Cocoa (page 249)	8
1 tbsp. almond butter with 1 tbsp. applesauce on toast	5	¼ cup raisins	1	¼ cup walnuts	4
water	0	water	0	water	0

Additional foods to meet energy needs: as desired.

Nutritional Summary

Robin, 44 pounds		Pat, 62 pounds		Jamie, 80 pounds	
calories	1,382	calories	1,443	calories	1,815
protein (recommended minimum is 26–28 g)	42 g	protein (recommended minimum is 31–34 g)	54 g	protein (recommended minimum is 40–44 g)	60–70 g
calcium (recommended is 500 mg)	955 mg	calcium (recommended is 800 mg)	1,256 mg	calcium (recommended is 1,300 mg)	1,479 mg

Nutritional Summary (*continued*)

Robin, 44 pounds		Pat, 62 pounds		Jamie, 80 pounds	
iron (recommended for vegetarians at age 3 is 12 mg)	13 mg	iron (recommended for vegetarians at ages 4–8 is 18 mg)	18 mg	iron (recommended for vegetarians at ages 9–12 is 14 mg)	15–40 mg
zinc (recommended is 5 mg)	5 mg	zinc (recommended is 5 mg)	5 mg	zinc (recommended is 8 mg)	8–33 mg
omega-3 fatty acids (recommended is at least 1.2–1.6 g)	2.9 g	omega-3 fatty acids (recommended is at least 1.2–1.6 g)	1.6 g	omega-3 fatty acids (recommended is at least 2.2 g)	2.4 g
vitamin B_{12} (recommended is 1.2 mcg)	2.4 mcg	vitamin B_{12} (recommended is 1.2 mcg)	9 mcg	vitamin B_{12} (recommended is 1.8 mcg)	9–20 mcg
vitamin D (recommended is 5 mcg— or less with sunlight)	4 mcg	vitamin D (recommended is 5 mcg)	7.5 mcg	vitamin D (recommended is 5 mcg)	8 mcg

Total Vegetarian Food Guide Servings

Robin, 44 pounds		Pat, 62 pounds		Jamie, 80 pounds	
Grains	6	Grains	6	Grains	6
Vegetables	3	Vegetables	3	Vegetables	3
Fruit	2	Fruit	2+	Fruit	2
Beans and Alternates	2	Beans and Alternates	2+	Beans and Alternates	3
Fortified Soymilk and Alternates	6	Fortified Soymilk and Alternates	6+	Fortified Soymilk and Alternates	6
Omega-3 Fatty Acids	yes	Omega-3 Fatty Acids	yes	Omega-3 Fatty Acids	yes
Vitamin B_{12}	yes	Vitamin B_{12}	yes	Vitamin B_{12}	yes
Vitamin D	yes	Vitamin D	yes	Vitamin D	yes

little light on the calories for some children, yet it meets nutrient needs. In all menus, the fortified milks supply vitamins B_{12} and D; this also would be the case if cow's milk were used. Although the meals in all three menus are simple, Jamie's meals are particularly fast and easy. The range of protein, minerals, and vitamins will depend on which cereals and veggie burgers are chosen; fortified cereals and burgers are used sometimes, but are not essential. Very active children will burn more calories than the amounts supplied by these menus and can add other foods as desired. Children who are more sedentary do not have many calories to spare for "empty-calorie" foods if nutrient needs are to be met. For some children, one item a day may be appropriate; for others, one a week.

Vitamins—Essential to Life

The first four letters of the word *vitamin* are the Latin word for life. All vitamins are essential, and most are supplied in great abundance by vegetarian diets. Two need special attention: vitamins B_{12} and D.

> All vegetarian children should have a reliable source of vitamin B_{12} and, if sun exposure is limited, vitamin D supplements or fortified foods should be used.
>
> —*Position of the American Dietetic Association: Vegetarian Diets*

Vitamin B_{12}. Vitamin B_{12} is added to meat analogs, fortified (enriched) soymilks and rice milks, some breakfast cereals, and nutritional yeast that has been grown on a B_{12}–enriched medium (Red Star Vegetarian Support Formula). Ovolactovegetarian children also get vitamin B_{12} from eggs and dairy products. With total-vegetarian and vegan children, we must ensure that sources of vitamin B_{12} from fortified food or supplements are regularly received.

Vitamin D. Regular exposure to sunlight, totaling one or two hours per week of sunlight on the face and hands, is an excellent way to get vitamin D. For those in northern states and in Canada, the amount of sunlight is insufficient for several months of the year. Here, the "vitamin D winter" (when there is minimal vitamin D production from sunlight) lasts about two to five months, from October or

November through February or March. Thus in northern climates, vitamin D supplements or fortified foods are important. Fortified soymilk, rice milk, and cow's milk contain vitamin D. Many types of soymilk and rice milk use vitamin D_2, the vegan-friendly form of vitamin D. Many margarines and most brands of cow's milk are fortified with vitamin D_3, derived from fish or from the oily wool of sheep.

Supplements

When vegetarian children's diets are loosely built around the Total Vegetarian Food Guide on page 126, including B_{12}-fortified foods and vitamin-D fortified foods or sunlight, a multivitamin-mineral supplement is not essential and children should meet recommendations. If a multivitamin-mineral supplement is used to provide vitamins B_{12} and D, make sure it also contains iron, zinc, and calcium, as these minerals often are in short supply in children's diets, whether the children are vegetarian or not. (Good sources of zinc are legumes, whole grains, cashew nuts, and seeds; these same foods, as well as other nuts and fortified foods, also provide iron.) Because of lower iron absorption from plant foods, it is recommended that vegetarian children get somewhat higher intakes of iron compared to children on meat-based diets. For children whose diets generally are good, a daily supplement is not necessary. However, it can work well to take a supplement every few days or during periods when intake is less than adequate; for example, while on a trip.

Eating Away from Home

We may anticipate that a vegetarian diet will make life difficult for our little ones by setting them apart. Many parents find this isn't such a big hurdle after all. For example, one parent thought that her daughter might be singled out as unusual at their co-op preschool because of her vegan diet. Yet they soon found that several other children had food allergies and a number of parents wished to avoid sugar and hydrogenated oils for snacks and holiday treats. The group decided to avoid bringing birthday cupcakes, opting instead for a special nonfood birthday ritual the teacher devised and the kids enjoy. The vegetarian parent let the teacher know that she would be glad to check food labels and help modify recipes that were used at the preschool, where appropriate. The outcome was that the family's dietary choice was easily accepted and other parents were very supportive.

To ensure success, we may need to be resourceful so that our vegetarian children are well nourished in assorted environments. Invest in containers of various sizes, with tight-fitting, spill-proof lids. These are available from outdoor equipment stores and make it easy to send along a serving of fortified soymilk, a protein-rich soup or stew, hummus, a veggie wiener, or marinated tofu. Hot foods—such as soup, stews, chili, beans, and tofu dogs—can be packed safely in a thermos and will keep for several hours. Preheating the thermos with boiling water prior to packing the food will help the thermos better retain heat. Perishable cold foods should be put in an insulated cooler (or insulated lunch box or bag designed for this purpose) along with frozen gel packs. When children are dining away from home, if we supply the high-protein items, often the rest of the meal will come together fairly easily. Breakfast can be as simple as oatmeal, cereals, fruit, toast, jam, peanut butter, and juices, all of which are widely available. For lunch and dinner, there's generally rice, baked potatoes, or pasta, along with salad or vegetables, at school or at public functions. By providing just one or two items from home, we allow our children to take part in school or day care meals without compromising our dietary choices.

For more on the process of bridge-building with staff and parents at preschools and schools, see Chapter 3, pages 52 to 54.

School Meals

If you hope to make positive changes in local school meals, your first step may be to gather a few allies. These may be a vegetarian-friendly teacher, school food service personnel, or other parents. Before talking to the administration, find out whether or not the school receives United States Department of Agriculture reimbursement. Such food services may face tighter restrictions and be less flexible. Whatever the situation, you are part of a movement across the country to improve the healthfulness of school meals and to include entirely vegetarian options for those who want them. Once you have located an interested ear among the school food service administration, provide the excellent brochure *Tips for Introducing Vegetarian Options into Institutions*, available from the Vegetarian Resource Group. For ideas and support material, see the Resources section (page 360) under School Meals. If food ordering for school meals has been done a year in advance, change can be slow. On the other hand, you may be pleasantly surprised to find that significant changes occur within several months. Naturally, school food service staff appreciates supportive ideas and input, encouragement, and appreciation for their efforts.

Restaurant Eating with Children

Dining out can be a pleasure or a nightmare when children are involved. If we want good nutrition to be a part of meals away from home, preplanning is almost essential. A meal at a vegetarian restaurant is likely to be a success because there will be a variety of healthful options and relatively few junk foods. If you're heading out of town, look at the Resources section for Web sites, books, and periodicals that can direct you to vegetarian restaurants at your destination and en route. Sometimes the best choice will be an ethnic restaurant: Mexican, Chinese, Thai, Middle Eastern, or East Indian. Any restaurant that has a salad bar is a possible source of chickpeas, tomatoes, corn, and perhaps other well-accepted veggies, along with rolls, bagels, or rice. Even though these items are not listed on the menu, many restaurants will be able to provide you with dry cereal at any time of day and can serve plain pasta, steamed vegetables, peanut butter and jelly sandwiches, or baked potatoes.

Travel Tips

Some children are natural explorers; others want familiar foods when they venture out into the world. For them, it can make a big difference to bring along their favorite brand of crackers, individual packs of chocolate soymilk, miniportions of peanut butter, a well-liked sandwich, and a favorite trail mix combination. For car travel, carry a big bottle of water to wash berries, cherry tomatoes, or peas in the pod that you purchase from a farmer's market or grocery store en route, plus a knife to cut fresh fruit or veggies.

When you have requested the vegetarian option prior to your airplane flight, you generally can count on fresh fruit and a roll or crackers, as well as plenty of juice. By adding a little peanut butter to the tray given to your little ones, they will survive the trip pretty well, even if they decide the entrée looks "yucky."

How "Normal" Do We Want to Be?

Trips to the grocery store can be challenging when our children push for brands or products that we don't want to buy. When we feel torn, it helps to review the Standard American Diet and some of its effects.

During the past decade, the number of American children who are overweight has doubled. One child in seven is overweight or obese. Compared to children of normal weight, those who are overweight are more likely to become obese adults, with greater likelihood of coronary heart disease, hypertension, diabetes, gallbladder disease, osteoarthritis, and some cancers. Children who carry excess weight often experience psychological stress, poor body image, and low self-esteem.

Studies of diet show that the increased weight is accompanied by high intakes of dietary fat from poultry, cheese, and snacks, and plenty of carbonated beverages. Overweight children also eat less fiber from vegetables, fruits, and grains.

Six-year-olds put themselves on diets (though the diets are not well balanced or effective). Girls begin menstruation at the age of nine. Preadolescent boys want to bulk up.

Of children aged six to ten years, two out of three participate in school lunch programs daily. Of American children aged six to eleven years, 91 percent do not get the minimum "five-a-day" servings of vegetables and fruits; the average intake is half this amount (two-and-a-half servings per day). One-third of calories children get are from foods eaten away from home. One-fifth of the day's calories come from snacks.

Sometimes it can take a little more work or be a challenge to our creativity to make meals and snacks truly nutritious and life supportive. But the extra effort we expend will reap valuable rewards in taste, appeal, and healthfulness—and aren't our precious children worth it?

Chapter 10

The Unique Needs of Teens

The teen years often are regarded as a period of great challenge for parents—a close reenactment of the "terrible two's," but this time with someone who's just become several inches taller than you. Parents who felt confident about their parenting skills with preteens may find that a formerly compliant and well-behaved child suddenly has become a stranger. As with other aspects of life, nutrition-related issues can become an arena for conflict—or for growth—for all concerned.

Teens are striving to achieve a sense of identity and individuality. If parents and caregivers simultaneously are struggling to maintain the same measure of control they had in earlier years, clearly they are headed for confrontation. Yet if we relax and increasingly allow adolescents greater input, hand in hand with more responsibility, this typically challenging stage of life can become a time of enhanced freedom and joy.

One goal we can share with our teens is a common desire to help them make decisions on their own, without direct adult intervention. As we might recall, some of our most important life lessons were learned when we landed nose-down in the mud.

We need to let teens make similar mistakes and watch and love them through the process without interfering, while we learn our own lessons about boundaries and letting go.

The following food- and nutrition-related concerns commonly arise during adolescence:

- the need for increased nutrients during a major growth spurt
- rebellion about family food rules (along with other rules)
- reluctance to take responsibility for food preparation and nutrition needs
- other matters receiving much more attention than good nutrition
- distress about acne, premenstrual syndrome, and weight (whether under- or overweight)
- emergence of eating disorders
- a consuming focus on sports

These issues are the focus of this chapter.

Nutrition and the Teenage Growth Spurt

Growth Spurts for Boys

Between the ages of eleven and fourteen, a boy may weigh 100 pounds and be 5 foot 2 inches tall. Four years later, he may have gained 50 pounds and be 7 inches taller. His body will have created many new cells and used plenty of protein, vitamins, minerals, carbohydrates, and essential fats in the process. Not surprisingly, this growth is reflected in his appetite. Boys have been known to consume a dish intended for the whole family, mistaking it for a single portion. They may eat a big dinner at a friend's place, then return home and repeat the process that same evening. You may notice that our recipes describe the yield in volume measures (such as "cups") rather than "servings." This is done because of the vast difference between a "serving" for a two-year-old and a serving for a seventeen-year-old boy!

The weight and stature charts shown on pages 198 to 201 show typical growth curves during childhood through adolescence. You can plot the growth of teens on these charts. (Use of the charts is described on page 195.)

Table 10.1 on the next page presents menus that meet daily nutritional needs for three teens at different stages of growth and leading quite different lives. The choices for

TABLE 10.1

Three Menus for Teens

Instant Eric (or Erin), 100 pounds	Protein, grams	Slim Sarah, 115 pounds	Protein, grams	Fit Freddie, 155 pounds	Protein, grams
Breakfast					
1 cup dry cereal (e.g., ready-to-eat bran flakes)	4	1 cup Cream of Wheat cereal, with 1 tbsp. ground flaxseeds stirred in	4	1½ cups Granny's Grand Granola (page 253)	22
1 cup fortified rice milk or soymilk	0.5–8	1 cup fortified soymilk (part used to make cereal)	7–8	1 cup fortified soymilk	7–8
		½ cup blueberries		1 sliced banana	1
Lunch					
2 veggie wieners	16–22	1 cup Flaxen Hummus (page 276)	19	1 Hero Sub sandwich (page 280)	24
1 hot dog bun	7	1 whole-wheat pita bread	6	1 cup potato salad	4
2 tbsp. chopped onion, 2 tbsp. ketchup, and 2 tsp. mustard	1	1 cup raw vegetable sticks	2		
1 oz. potato chips	2				
12 oz. calcium-fortified orange juice	1				

(continued)

Instant Eric (or Erin), 100 pounds	Protein, grams	Slim Sarah, 115 pounds	Protein, grams	Fit Freddie, 155 pounds	Protein, grams
Supper					
2 cups pea soup (canned or homemade), with 1 tbsp. ground flaxseeds stirred in	19	12 Simple Nori Roll pieces with tofu, carrot, red pepper (page 316)	16	2 servings French Bread Pizza (page 319) or commercial vegetarian pizza	14
1 oz. pretzels	3	2 tbsp. pickled ginger	0	2 cups green salad, plus 1 cup chickpeas, and ¼ cup Liquid Gold Dressing (page 290)	22
1 cup fortified rice milk or soymilk	0.5–8	1 cup fortified soymilk, vanilla or chocolate	7–8	1 cup fortified soymilk	7–8
1 Very Best Chocolate Chip Cookie (page 344)	2	2 slices watermelon (each ⅟₁₆ melon)	4		
Snacks					
½ bagel with 1 tbsp. peanut butter	8	shake made with 1 banana, 1 cup fortified chocolate soymilk	8–9	2 Muscle Muffins (page 265)	16
2 Carrot Cake Muffins (page 266)	8	water	0	1 cup fortified soymilk	7–8
water	0			trail mix: ¼ cup nuts and seeds, ¼ cup dried fruit	7
				water	0

Additional foods to meet caloric needs: as desired.

Nutritional Summary

Instant Eric (or Erin), 100 pounds		Slim Sarah, 115 pounds		Fit Freddie, 155 pounds	
calories	2,234	calories	1,864	calories	3,288
protein (recommended minimum is 50–55 g)	72–87 g	protein (recommended minimum is 52 g)	73 g	protein (recommended minimum is 70–77 g; for athlete increase to 105 g)	131–134
calcium (recommended is 1,300 mg)	1,398 mg	calcium (recommended is 1,300 mg)	1,623 mg	calcium (recommended is 1,300 mg)	2,158
iron (recommended for vegetarian boys or girls at age 9–13 is 14 mg)	28 mg	iron (recommended for vegetarian girls at age 14–18 is 27 mg)	34 mg	iron (recommended for vegetarian boys at age 14–18 is 20 mg)	41 mg
zinc (recommended is 8 mg)	10 mg	zinc (recommended is 9 mg)	9 mg	zinc (recommended is 11 mg)	20 mg
omega-3 fatty acids (recommended is at least 2.2 g)	2.7 g	omega-3 fatty acids (recommended is at least 2.2 g)	2.2 g	omega-3 fatty acids (recommended is at least 2.2 g)	9 g
vitamin B_{12} (recommended is 1.2 mcg)	7 mcg	vitamin B_{12} (recommended is 1.2 mcg)	9 mcg	vitamin B_{12} (recommended is 1.8 mcg)	17 mcg
vitamin D (recommended is 5 mcg)	6.9 mcg	vitamin D (recommended is 5 mcg)	7 mcg	vitamin D (recommended is 5 mcg)	9 mcg

Total Vegetarian Food Guide Servings

Instant Eric (or Erin), 100 pounds		Slim Sarah, 115 pounds		Fit Freddie, 155 pounds	
Grains	6+	Grains	6	Grains	11+
Vegetables	3	Vegetables	3	Vegetables	8
Fruit	2	Fruit	4	Fruit	2
Beans and Alternates	3+	Beans and Alternates	2	Beans and Alternates	4
Fortified Soymilk and Alternates	7	Fortified Soymilk and Alternates	6	Fortified Soymilk and Alternates	7
Omega-3 Fatty Acids	yes	Omega-3 Fatty Acids	yes	Omega-3 Fatty Acids	yes
Vitamin B_{12}	yes	Vitamin B_{12}	yes	Vitamin B_{12}	yes
Vitamin D	yes	Vitamin D	yes	Vitamin D	yes

Instant Eric (or Erin) reflect the joint influences of a youngster determined to survive, at least in part, on chips, pretzels, and fast foods, plus an adult who is resolved that the intake for the day meet nutritional requirements. Though servings of vegetables aren't obvious, they consist of onion and ketchup on the hot dogs, veggies in the pea soup, and carrot in the Carrot Cake Muffins (page 266). These muffins are kept in individual plastic bags at the front of the freezer so they are easy to grab on the way out the door. Because of the veggie wieners and pea (or bean or lentil) soups, the protein intake isn't dependent on soymilk; thus, either fortified rice milk or soymilk may be used.

Fit Freddie is on a school sports team and works out at the gym. He's interested in being vegetarian, but not at the expense of his growing muscles. He wants his protein intake to be at least 1.5 grams per kilogram body weight. Not a problem! On this particular day it is 1.9 grams per kilo, derived from foods throughout the day. He doesn't have a lot of time for meals, but he eats big portions of baked potatoes, rice, pasta, cereal, breads, and whatever else is handy to provide a constant stream of energy. His teammates like to add soy protein to their diets, and they all enjoy Muscle Muffins (page 265) and variations of the Purple Protein Power Shake on page 243. Freddie has learned a few quick ways to prepare tofu; the Crispy Tofu Fingers on page 315 are a real favorite. Marinated tofu from the deli, cut-up raw veggies and a protein-rich dip, or a bean salad are almost always in the fridge.

More isn't necessarily better, and this is true when it comes to protein. Athletes need a little more protein than the 0.9 grams per kilogram body weight that generally is recommended. However, once basic requirements are met, excess protein must be broken down and eliminated, leading to calcium losses in the urine and putting stress on the kidneys. It's not the ideal fuel, whereas the carbohydrates in Freddie's diet are.

Growth Spurts for Girls

Girls aged eleven to fourteen begin their growth spurt at about the same average weight (100 pounds) and height (5 foot 2 inches) as the boys in their class, or they might be an inch or so taller. However, during the four-year period of the growth spurt, their average gains are likely to be less than those of the boys—about 20 pounds and 2 inches. This 20 percent increase in weight still requires plenty of nutritious food. In addition, their iron requirements will be greater with the onset of menstruation.

Girls confront a different set of social pressures than boys. Whereas boys are likely to welcome changes that will give them a bigger, more manly body, girls are well aware of the cultural emphasis on females staying slim. In addition to issues of image, they may want to limit their weight due to participation in gymnastics, dance, swimming, or skating. It may come as little surprise that the proportion of North American girls who fail to meet recommended intakes for iron, zinc, and calcium increases dramatically after age eleven.

It's important that we work *with* our daughters, helping them achieve their goals while packing all the nutrition we can into their meals and snacks. Fortunately, a diet of whole-plant foods, along with a few fortified foods, is ideal for building bodies that are both lean and strong, as shown in Slim Sarah's menu in Table 10.1. Sarah knows the caloric content and hidden fats in everything. At the same time, she wants to eat healthfully. She appreciates that fruits and vegetables are a foundation for clear, glowing skin. To get enough iron, she relies on Cream of Wheat (as well as whole-grain cereals and ready-to-eat cereals that are fortified with iron and zinc) in addition to hummus, tofu, and soymilk. Her calcium comes mainly from fortified soymilk, calcium-set tofu, beans, and tahini. On the day shown here, she not only meets but significantly exceeds her nutrient requirements.

In these three menus, the omega-3 fatty acids primarily come from flaxseed (or its oil) and walnuts. Vitamins B_{12} and D come from nondairy milks that are fortified with these nutrients plus calcium. Water is important.

Good Nutrition: Authority and Responsibility

What's a good solution if our teens want to follow an eating pattern that is different from the rest of the family? What if their chosen diets are more (or less) vegetarian than those of other family members? What if their food choices are downright unhealthful? Adolescents are likely to experiment—to explore what feels right for them and to "try on" different behaviors for size. (For more information on this topic, please refer to Chapter 2.)

Part of our responsibilities as caregivers is to provide basic nutritious food. When teens assume more authority over their food choices, their growing autonomy should be accompanied by increased responsibility. For example, if they want veggie burgers instead of the usual family dinner, and we feel overwhelmed by their demands, it's time for a few informal cooking classes (if they haven't learned already) so they can prepare the items they want independently. If they prefer to stray from family eating patterns when away from home, we can learn to relax and let them follow their wishes. Nevertheless, this doesn't mean we must buy or prepare foods for them at home about which we don't feel good.

Our most effective course is to keep the lines of communication open, to briefly let teens know our views, and especially to exercise our listening skills. (See Chapter 2, and Chapter 4.) We want to encourage teens to be comfortable with who they are, rather than attempt to mold them into who we think they should be. Adults can support the adolescents in their lives by providing plenty of love, examples of healthful eating, and the opportunity to experiment with various foods and eating styles. All these factors play a powerful role in developing lifelong habits of good nutrition.

Social Life, Independence, and Mealtimes

Circumstances of life may mean that our teens spend a great deal of time away from us. Perhaps they ride the bus to school, or maybe they fill afternoons and evenings with sports, drama, and other demanding activities. Their desire to socialize and be with friends may interfere with family mealtimes. Teens are on the brink of adulthood, so although it may be tough for us to pull back, we need to find a midpoint between being *autocratic* (you'll eat what, when, and where I say) and *permissive* (I'll be your short-order cook and give you plenty of money for fast food). As parents and caregivers, our lives may be extremely busy as well. A smart strategy is to ensure that our family comes together often for meals, even if this is not possible every day. Solo microwaved dinners can lead to feelings of isolation at all ages. Mealtime offers a special and safe occasion for adolescents to share their days with us.

Some teens spend much of their time in their bedrooms alone—listening to music, watching television, using the computer, or talking on the phone—emerging only at the point of near-starvation. They may want to take meals back to their rooms to eat in privacy. It's important that we give teens responsibilities that involve them with the rest of the family; for instance, setting the table for dinner, washing dishes, making muffins, or preparing bag lunches. We can recognize and respect their need for time alone or on the phone while tempering this separation with a required half hour together at dinner.

Nourishing Healthy Skin

Along with other issues of appearance, skin health becomes a major interest during adolescence. A surge in the level of sex hormones (androgens) can enlarge and stimulate oil glands in the skin, particularly around the nose and on the neck, chest, and back. Despite similar levels of hormones, some people produce more oil than others, and some people's skin is less efficient at exfoliation (clearing away discarded cells). The result can be acne and pimples. It is important to clean the skin gently and regularly with water and mild soap, to avoid oil-based cosmetics, and to keep skin dry. Some teens find that certain foods (sweets, processed foods, artificially flavored beverages, fried foods, whey, or cow's milk, for example) can result in skin reactions. (Nonvegetarian teens may find that fish causes skin problems, too.)

Water is an important cleanser for the inside as well as the outside of our bodies; it carries away toxins that are flushed out through the kidneys. The effectiveness of drinking water in promoting skin health should not be underestimated. The recommended amount is 8 cups of water per day. Fruits and vegetables help keep skin clear and healthy, too, in part because they consist of at least 80 percent water by weight, and partly because they contribute vitamins that directly nourish the skin.

Premenstrual Syndrome (PMS)

Some girls and women experience excruciating cramps at the onset of menstruation. A low-fat vegetarian diet has been shown to reduce symptoms of premenstrual syndrome: pain (both intensity and duration), behavior changes, water retention, and weight gain. A study conducted at Georgetown University found that when those who experienced mild to moderate PMS pain switched from meals that included animal products and fats to a pattern of whole grains, beans, vegetables, and fruit, they had more energy and their premenstrual problems diminished. A vegetarian diet may help in two ways, both related to the hormone estrogen, which is linked to PMS symptoms. Whereas fatty foods drive estrogen levels up, a low-fat, plant-based diet helps reduce the production of this hormone. Also, the fiber in plant foods assists the body in eliminating excess estrogen.

Improving calcium intake also may reduce menstrual pain and PMS. This mineral is abundant in calcium-fortified beverages (orange juice, soymilk, rice milk); high-calcium greens (kale, collards, Chinese greens, broccoli, okra); beans (soy, white, navy, Great Northern, black turtle); blackstrap molasses; and figs. Some corn tortillas and textured soy protein are high in calcium, too; check labels. The menus in Table 10.1 meet or exceed calcium recommendations. The vitamin D present in fortified soymilks and rice milks is beneficial, too. It promotes calcium absorption and helps retain and use the calcium that already has been absorbed. Outdoor activities are advantageous in two ways: they encourage the body's own production of vitamin D (under the influence of sunlight), and they provide the bone-building rewards of weight-bearing exercise.

A well-planned diet may lessen PMS in other ways. Some research has shown vitamin B_6 to be effective in reducing pain and improving mood. Yet taking large amounts of vitamin B_6 in pills can lead to problems. Fortunately, this vitamin is found abundantly in beans, peas, lentils, and whole grains.

Though the overall PMS prevention diet for teens should be moderately low in fat, essential fatty acids have demonstrated their effectiveness in the treatment of PMS symptoms. Include a tablespoon or two of ground flaxseeds or 2 teaspoons of flaxseed oil for essential omega-3 fatty acids. Borage oil and primrose oil also have proven their worth for many young women; both contain an omega-6 fatty acid known as GLA. Take a supplement that provides 500 to 1,000 milligrams of GLA per day. Soyfoods and moderate amounts of nuts and seeds have a lot to offer nutritionally and are valuable parts of the diet.

Weight Management: Controlling Gains

In the general population of children and teens between the ages of six and seventeen, one in three is overweight. This is less likely to be the case with vegetarians, and it is rarer still for vegans to carry excess body fat. These findings are not surprising, because plant foods tend to be low in total fat and in saturated fat. In addition, the fiber in plants contributes to a feeling of satiety, yet it passes through the body without being absorbed.

Nonetheless, it is possible for vegetarians to be overweight. Two-thirds of the calories in eggs come from fat; three-quarters of the calories in cheese come from fat, and most of it is saturated. The majority of chips, fries, cakes, pies, doughnuts, soft drinks, candy, cookies, and granola bars are vegetarian. To make matters even tougher, these come in "super sizes," with 40-ounce drinks at the corner store and bottomless tubs of popcorn at the movies.

Over the past two decades, the percentage of teens who are overweight has doubled. Certainly this is linked to inactive pastimes. For many, a sedentary lifestyle is accepted as normal: school curricula place less emphasis on physical education, teens ride to school instead of walk, and parents prefer to keep teens safe at home rather than allow them to roughhouse outdoors.

For teens who are struggling with excess weight, here are some useful tips:

1. *Focus on the plant foods in the Total Vegetarian Food Guide (page 126).* Use these to replace foods that are high in fats, refined carbohydrates, and sugar.

2. *Cut down on sugar and fats.* Our bodies convert sugar directly to fat. Satisfy that craving for sweets with fruit. Note that a vegetarian who eats plenty of fried foods, eggs, and high-fat dairy products is courting obesity in the same way as someone on the Standard American Diet.

3. *Drink noncaloric beverages.* Aim for six to eight glasses of water throughout the day. This can include herbal teas (but avoid drinks with artificial sweeteners).

4. *Eat when hungry, not otherwise.* Eating can be a solace for feelings of depression or loneliness. Unfortunately, "comfort foods" are no solution, and they usually cause the situation to get worse.

5. *Make physical activity a priority.* Restricting food intake can adversely affect growth and generally is not recommended for teens. Instead, start habits of fun fitness with family and friends. It may be necessary to limit time spent sitting with television, video games, or the Internet, in addition to the necessary school, homework, and meals.

Body Image and Eating Disorders

With our culture's heightened emphasis on physical appearance and slimness, dissatisfaction with body image now is described as a "normative discontent." One out of every two women dislikes her body and is afraid of being overweight, including a significant number who actually are at healthy weights. It shouldn't startle us that this attitude is reflected in two-thirds of our teenage and preteen daughters—and even in some of our sons. Eating disorders can be present in teens who are underweight, of normal weight, or are overweight. The conditions can range from very mild to life threatening.

Some teens with eating disorders may call themselves *vegetarian*, yet the underlying motive is not a sincere interest in vegetarianism. Instead, it is an obsession with food, with avoiding eating, and with becoming excessively thin. The vegetarian label is chosen as a pretense that allows these teens to avoid fatty animal products and limit their food intake as much as possible. In these cases, the diet chosen is unlikely to be a nourishing and balanced vegetarian way of eating.

Recovery from the more serious eating disorders includes some or all of the following:

- a visit to a family doctor
- referral to a treatment center and perhaps hospitalization
- therapy (including family therapy)
- nutrition counseling

Since the teen's natural signals of hunger and satiety may be suppressed, a period of "mechanical eating" often is necessary during recovery. This entails eating a balanced diet that gradually increases to "normal" amounts, while the teen involved is relearning how to follow hunger cues.

Those who were vegetarian prior to their eating disorder or have chosen to be vegetarian for ethical or other personal reasons should not be forced to consume unwanted animal products during recovery and treatment. Recovery from an eating disorder is no more problematic for vegetarians or vegans than meat-eaters, and their diets may prove more healthful in the long run. As they return to normal eating, their eventual goal should be to eat according to the Total Vegetarian Food Guide.

> Adopting a vegetarian diet does not lead to eating disorders.
> —Journal of the American Dietetic Association, *November 1997, page 1318.*

To prevent these difficulties, we can allow children to respond to their natural feelings of fullness, hunger, high energy, and fatigue; to pay attention to physical needs; and to experience and express feelings. As usual, this is a place where we can learn with them. For more on weight management and eating disorders in vegetarians, read Chapters 13 and 14 in *Becoming Vegan,* by Brenda Davis and Vesanto Melina.

Weight Management: Bulking Up

Some teens, often boys, are engaged in an ongoing struggle to gain weight. They want to fill out their frames and wonder if it's possible to get all the calories and protein they need from plant foods. Fortunately, vegetarian diets can be custom-made for their needs—and it won't take a lot of time. It may help to acquire a few kitchen skills and learn how to whip up a shake, prepare hummus, bake a batch of cookies, heat up a veggie burger or dog, bake potatoes, cook pasta, and assemble a burrito.

Whether vegetarian or not, some people have trouble putting on as many pounds as they'd like. Frequently, even for some who think they are "eating all the time," it turns out they simply are not eating enough. If an exact food record is kept and the calories for the day are tallied, they may discover that what they have consumed is insufficient to meet the needs of an active, growing teen. With the hectic schedules so prevalent among young people, meals easily could be missed. Perhaps there's no time for breakfast; snacks or lunches are forgotten; and when they look in the fridge, there's nothing really substantial that's ready to grab. In some cases, everyone else in the house is calorie conscious, and any food that's readily available is low in fat. Maybe plenty is eaten at family dinners, but when dining alone, meals aren't so appealing.

Naturally, an underweight teen with a slim family can expect that genetics have some part to play. Yet consistent effort will result in added pounds and increased muscle mass. Here are tips for adding weight to a slight build.

1. *To gain 1 to 2 pounds a week, consume an increase of 500 to 1,000 calories per day above usual food intake.* (One pound of body weight is the energy equivalent of 3,500 calories.) Look at the calories listed below each recipe in this book. Check Granny's Grand Granola (page 253), Sneaky Dad's Power Punch Smoothie (page 244), Warm Sesame Noodles (page 303), Monster Mash Roll-Up (page 279), Time-Saving Tacos and Bean Burritos (pages 326 and 282), and some of the bars or cookies (pages 341 to 345). Keep leftover baked potatoes in the fridge; they're good topped with Sesame Tahini Salad

Dressing (page 289) or Liquid Gold Dressing (page 290). For meals and snacks, make your servings a little bigger than usual.

2. *Aim for intakes at the high end of the ranges suggested in the Total Vegetarian Food Guide (page 126).* This means eating significantly more of the Grains category (bread, cereal, whole grains, and pasta). These provide energy, B vitamins, and protein (about 10 to 15 percent of the calories in grains come from protein). To get in eleven servings a day, you might have 1½ cups of granola or cooked cereal (three servings), two sandwiches (four servings, provided by the slices of bread), and 2 cups of pasta (four servings). It's not so difficult.

3. *Include nuts, seeds, tofu, and beans at most meals and for snacks.* As you can see from Eric's snack in Table 10.1, a half bagel spread with peanut butter provides 8 grams of protein; it also supplies 200 calories. For variety, try other nut and seed butters and add jam or banana slices. Keep hummus, seasoned tofu (marinated or from the deli), and the ingredients for a shake (pages 241 to 245) available for instant use. Trail mix travels well and is great to keep in a backpack.

4. *Don't be fat-phobic.* Whereas health agencies recommend a maximum of 30 percent of calories from fat for adults, this is arbitrary and is based on the fact that most people include plenty of saturated fats from animal products and trans fats in their diets, not the healthful oils found in nuts, seeds, avocados, olives, soyfoods, flaxseeds, and other plant foods. For a vegetarian teen whose goal is to gain weight, the ideal intake may consist of 35 percent of calories from fat.

5. *Plan to eat more often.* This means three meals and two to three snacks *every day.* To guarantee that your plan succeeds, make sure important foods get onto the shopping list. To remind you of all the possibilities, see the food lists on pages 61 to 67.

6. *Include moderate resistance training in your exercise program.* It's a basic fact that muscles grow with regular use of weights and by doing push-ups and pull-ups.

Nutrition for Athletes

> With guidance in meal planning, vegetarian diets are appropriate and healthful choices for adolescents. Vegetarian diets can also meet the needs of competitive athletes.
>
> —*Position of the American Dietetic Association:*
> *Vegetarian Diets*

When we look among marathon runners, sprinters, bodybuilders, football players, swimmers, and skaters, we find many examples of athletes whose physical excellence is supported by a plant-based diet. In fact, it turns out that vegetarian diets are ideal for building and fueling strong bodies.

Carbohydrates are widely recognized as the ideal, clean-burning fuel. This doesn't mean sugar or highly refined foods, however. The best carbohydrates for athletes are whole-grain breads, cereals and pasta, peas, lentils, beans, potatoes, other root vegetables, corn, and fruit. These provide a steady source of energy that is balanced with protein and doesn't contain excess fat. They help us to stock up on glycogen. A diet based on the food groups in the Total Vegetarian Food Guide (page 126) can provide plenty of protein per kilogram of body weight, as shown in Fit Freddie's menu in Table 10.1. This same menu supplies 41 milligrams of iron, 20 milligrams of zinc, and over 2,000 milligrams of calcium. The Nutritional Summary below the three menus in Table 10.1 shows their contributions of calories, protein, certain minerals, vitamins, and omega-3 fatty acids. (Also see Chapter 6 for food sources of these nutrients.)

Can you train and compete while maintaining a vegetarian diet? You certainly can! Whether your goal is endurance, strength, or keeping your weight within a certain range, it's not difficult to tailor a vegetarian diet to meet your needs. It usually turns out that the challenges are practical. The solution involves having nutritious foods handy when needed, and this is managed easily with a little advance planning. Many top athletes are particular about the foods that go into their bodies and consider this preparation to be a basic part of their peak performance.

Whether you're involved in an after-school team sport or have plans to travel out of town, arrange to take along some healthful foods. Get an assortment of containers with leak-proof, screw-top lids; these are available at outdoor equipment stores.

Such containers make it simple to carry a takeout meal from a restaurant or from home. Keep muffins (such as Muscle Muffins, page 265, or Carrot Cake Muffins, page 266) in the freezer in individual bags to make it easy to carry them with you for snack breaks. Foods that don't require refrigeration include fruit, bread, rye crackers, and nut and seed butters. Be creative with trail mix by visiting the bulk food section at the supermarket and making your own glorious combination of dried fruits, nuts, seeds, soynuts, candied ginger, chocolate bits, and granola. Review the tips listed under Weight Management: Bulking-Up (page 227); most apply here as well.

For details on the nutrient requirements of athletes, pre- and postevent meals, supplements, and sports energy bars, one helpful reference is *The Vegetarian Sports Nutrition Guide* by dietitian and athlete Lisa Dorfman. Another good resource is *Becoming Vegan* by Brenda Davis and Vesanto Melina (Chapters 9, 15, and 16), where you'll find high-calorie menus; tips on carbohydrate loading, keeping hydrated, and meeting mineral needs; plus practical pointers for competition athletes. The Veggie Sports Association, online at www.veggie.org, is another useful resource.

Part Three

Recipes for Every Occasion

Chapter 11

Kitchen Magic: Harmonizing Good Health and Great Food

Four Keys to Enjoying Cooking

For many parents with bustling households and infinite to-do lists, preparing food is deemed a necessary ordeal rather than one of the great sensory delights. If you are among this group, know that cooking offers a grand opportunity to add joy to your life at regular intervals. Step away from your old mind-set, and allow yourself to appreciate, savor, and indeed relish your time in the kitchen. Here are a few suggestions to make meal preparation a pleasure instead of a chore. You needn't adopt all of these ideas at once. Talk with family and friends who enjoy vegetarian cooking, and unlock the secret of their exuberance. Watch the fun your little ones have when they explore new foods, and rejoice in their amusement. Begin to view cooking as a celebration and a tangible expression of the love you have for your family. We don't need to be gourmet chefs to prepare dishes that are well received. Simple foods often are the most requested and appreciated, and almost any effort we put forth will be met with praise and gratitude. Here are four keys that will help ensure satisfaction and success in the kitchen.

Invest in a Few Good Pieces of Kitchen Equipment

Using good-quality equipment greatly increases the enjoyment of meal preparation and allows the cook(s) to work with ease and speed. Here are the essentials:

- an 8-inch knife that holds its edge, stays sharp, and feels good in your hand
- one or more plastic or wooden cutting boards
- a large and a small stainless steel saucepan
- a frying pan (a cast-iron skillet will help add extra iron to your family's diet)
- a blender or food processor, or both
- a set of four glass, stainless steel, or lead-free ceramic mixing bowls in graduated sizes
- at least two saucepans (sizes will depend on the number of people in your household)
- a colander
- a mesh strainer (for rinsing grains)
- hand tools: can opener, paring knife, vegetable peeler, measuring cups and spoons, wooden spoon(s), grater, metal spatula, and rubber spatula(s)

Begin Cooking by Reading Your Recipe Through and Gathering Ingredients

It is immensely frustrating to discover partway through a recipe that an essential ingredient is missing from your cupboard. Therefore, it's a smart strategy to assemble all the items needed beforehand and prevent this problem from occurring. To avoid mistakes, read through the recipe directions to become familiar with the steps and determine if any advance preparation is required. Something as simple as preheating the oven can make or break your success with a recipe. For instance, muffins won't rise well if the batter is mixed and losing its leavening power while we wait for the oven to heat. Investing a few extra minutes to get everything in order will actually save time in the long run by averting potential disasters and enhancing the odds of a satisfactory outcome.

Learn to Make a Few Things Well

If cooking is new for you, choose just a few appealing recipes and master them. With time and experience, you will gain the confidence to be more daring. Don't fret if you have a few failures. Although cooking is an art, it's one that people of all ages and abilities can learn. We each can progress at our own pace and achieve excellence—not by attaining anything spectacular but merely by satisfying our own family's tastes (which is a spectacular accomplishment in itself!).

Create Cooking Experiences You Enjoy

Make some of the time spent in food preparation high-quality family time. When children, teens, or adults wander by the kitchen to tell you about their school or work days, invite their help. Put on music everyone enjoys or that suits the mood you want to create. By making meal preparation (and cleanup) a family affair, we'll have a chance to enjoy each other's company and our children will associate cooking with positive experiences while gaining valuable kitchen sense.

Even when we work in the kitchen alone we can have a pleasant time. As much as possible, try to prepare food when you can enjoy the process, instead of when you rush in the door, starving. This may mean:

- cooking fewer times a week (perhaps on an evening or weekend), but making larger quantities of food (such as rice, stews, chili, or casseroles) that can be eaten throughout the week
- freezing batches of beans, muffins, and soups
- preparing salads that last four or five days (see page 287)

Have fun, be creative, and discover the joy in preparing food that can nourish body, mind, and spirit.

Making Healthful Changes

When we start to change the way we cook, we often find we can adapt old favorite recipes by making a few simple substitutions. Table 11.1 on the next page shows some of the basic ways we can do this.

TABLE 11.1

Basic Substitutions for Dairy, Eggs, Meat, and Sugar

Instead of Dairy Products

1 cup cow's milk	1 cup fortified soymilk or grain milk
1 cup buttermilk	1 cup soymilk + 2 teaspoons lemon juice or apple cider vinegar
1 cup yogurt	1 cup soy yogurt
1 ounce cheese	1 ounce casein-free soy cheese, nut "cheese," or home-made "uncheese" (See *The Uncheese Cookbook* by Joanne Stepaniak.)
1 cup cottage cheese	1 cup mashed regular tofu, mixed with a little lemon juice and salt
1 cup ricotta cheese	1 cup mashed regular tofu, mixed with a little lemon juice and salt; for creamy ricotta, mix with a little vegan mayonnaise and a pinch of salt
1 cup ice cream	1 cup frozen soy or rice dessert, dairy-free fruit sherbet, or sorbet
1 cup whipped cream topping	12 ounces firm silken tofu + ¼ cup maple syrup + 1 tablespoon lemon juice + 1 teaspoon vanilla, blended well
1 tablespoon butter	1 tablespoon olive oil, vegan margarine, or soy spread

Instead of Eggs

Note: Sometimes just leaving out the 1 or 2 eggs in a recipe makes very little difference.

1 egg	1 tablespoon ground flaxseeds mixed with 3 tablespoons water
	2 to 4 tablespoons soft tofu
	¼ cup mashed, very ripe banana
	1 teaspoon starch-based egg substitutes (or see package directions)
	⅛ teaspoon baking powder added to dry ingredients to replace leavening action of each egg or egg white in baking

Instead of Meat Products

1 tablespoon gelatin	½ teaspoon agar-agar powder (thickens 1 cup liquid)
	1 tablespoon agar-agar flakes (thickens 1 cup liquid)
1 cup meat or chicken stock	1 cup liquid vegetable stock
	1 cup water + vegetable stock cubes or powder (see package directions)
	1 cup water + Bragg Liquid Aminos or tamari (to taste)
	1 cup water + miso (to taste)
1 serving meat, chicken, fish	equal weight or volume of meat analog, beans, tofu, marinated tofu, tempeh, gluten (seitan), portabello mushrooms
1 cup ground beef	1 cup vegetarian "ground round"
	½ cup dry TVP + (½ cup less 1 tablespoon) boiling water, soaked for 10 minutes
1 serving sausage or smoked meat	equal weight or volume of meat analogs or crumbled, seasoned tofu (season with sage, savory, thyme, parsley, garlic, ground fennel seeds, and liquid smoke)

Instead of Sugar

1 cup white sugar, 1 cup brown sugar, or ¾ cup honey	*Note: The following will replace the sweetening power of sugar and honey. To substitute the white sugar called for in recipes with a natural liquid sweetener, reduce the total amount of other liquid ingredients in the recipe by about ¼ cup for each cup of liquid sweetener used. Some experimentation will be necessary, as results will vary depending on the recipe.*
	⅔ to ¾ cup maple syrup or fruit juice concentrate
	¾ cup agave nectar
	2 cups fruit juice
	1 cup dried, granulated cane juice or unbleached sugar
	¼ cup blackstrap molasses + ½ cup sweet molasses
	1 to 1½ cups barley malt syrup or rice malt syrup (these are less sweet)
	½ to ¾ cup granulated fructose

(continued)

TABLE 11.1 (CONTINUED)

Instead of White Flour	
1 cup all-purpose white (refined) wheat flour (bleached or unbleached)	Note: Generally, if flour in recipe is all whole grain, fat can be reduced in breads. ⅞ cups whole-wheat flour 1 cup whole-wheat flour; increase liquid in recipe by 2–4 tablespoons

Working with Herbs

If a recipe calls for dried herbs, you may replace these with fresh herbs and triple the quantity. For example, 1 teaspoon of dried basil would be replaced by 1 tablespoon of fresh basil. The opposite is true as well: 1 tablespoon of fresh herbs may be replaced with 1 teaspoon dried.

Use of Oils in Food Preparation

Here are a few simple guidelines regarding the use of oils in preparing food. All whole-plant foods contain healthful oils, and it's best to rely on these for the bulk of the fat in our diets. When we wish to give a rich, creamy texture to foods, our best option is to use the higher-fat plant foods—nuts, seeds, avocados, and tofu—as ingredients, wherever possible. We can keep our use of oils to a few straightforward choices. For any frying or sautéing, and for use in savory dishes, olive oil is our best bet as it is monounsaturated and is not damaged by heat. Safflower oil, which has very little flavor, is a good choice for use in desserts, as are sunflower and sesame oils. Organic canola oil is a possibility; generally nonorganic canola is genetically modified.

For use in salad dressing, your best choice is flaxseed oil. This will give you your daily quota of essential omega-3 fatty acids. Flaxseed oil should never be heated, as the omega-3s are easily damaged by heat and oxygen. Flaxseed oil must always be stored in the refrigerator or freezer and used by the expiration date stamped on the package. If the taste of flaxseed oil is too strong for you or your children, mix it with a small amount of milder oil, such as olive or sesame. For all the oils you use, select organic oils that are processed without heat extraction, rather than highly refined commercial oils. The latter may have been subjected to hexane solvent extraction and to temperatures from 130°F to over 500°F while the oils are degummed, bleached, and deodorized. The resulting oil contains molecules that are rearranged and has lost antioxidant vitamins and other protective substances that were originally present in the food source from which it is derived.

Nutritional Analysis of Recipes

The recipes that follow have been carefully designed to combine great taste, simple preparation, and excellent nutrition. Below each, you will find a nutritional analysis. For example, below the recipe for African Stew (page 308) you will see:

Per Cup: calories 309; protein 9 g; carbohydrate 49 g; fat 10g;
dietary fiber 6 g; sodium 75 mg
Percent calories from: protein 12 percent; fat 27 percent; carbohydrate 61 percent

The analysis does not include optional ingredients. Where there is a range in amounts for an ingredient, the lower amount is used for analysis. Below the grams of protein, carbohydrate, fat, fiber, and salt, we show the percentage of calories that come from protein, fat, and carbohydrate. You may read more about the recommended guidelines for these nutrients on page 157.

Chapter 12

Recipes

BEVERAGES

Fruit Smoothie

Makes about 2 cups

Frozen bananas make Fruit Smoothies extra thick and creamy. If your children prefer beverages that aren't ice cold, just use a fresh banana instead. Made with grape juice and blueberries, it's an excellent source of vitamin C, magnesium, and potassium, and a wealth of protective antioxidants; with orange juice and strawberries it's rich in folate, too. Experiment with peaches, kiwifruit, melons, and apple or pineapple juice to find new favorites.

> 1 frozen or fresh banana (see Tip, below)
> 1½ cups fruit juice of your choice
> ½ cup sliced fresh or frozen fruit, or berries

Break the banana into chunks and place in a blender along with the remaining ingredients. Process until very smooth and creamy. Serve at once.

Tip

With a few bananas in your freezer, you can create a creamy shake, or frozen banana ice cream, at a moment's notice. Simply peel ripe bananas, place them in plastic bags, and store in your freezer. Bananas will last for several weeks, depending on your freezer temperature.

Per Cup: calories 170; protein 2 g; carbohydrate 43 g; fat 0.5 g; dietary fiber 3 g; sodium 3 mg
Percent calories from: protein 5 percent; fat 3 percent; carbohydrate 92 percent

Orange Banana Whirl

Makes about 2 cups

This simple, nutritious treat makes orange juice special any time of the day. Use calcium-fortified juice, if you prefer, for an added calcium boost. (From *The Vegan Sourcebook,* by Joanne Stepaniak.)

> 1 frozen or fresh banana (see Tip, page 241)
> 1⅔ cups orange juice (or ½ cup frozen orange juice concentrate plus
>   1⅓ cups water)
> ¼ to ½ teaspoon vanilla extract, to taste

Break the banana into chunks and place in a blender along with the remaining ingredients. Process until very smooth and creamy. Serve at once.

Per Cup: calories 150; protein 2 g; carbohydrate 36 g; fat 0.4 g; dietary fiber 2 g; sodium 3 mg
Percent calories from: protein 5 percent; fat 2 percent; carbohydrate 93 percent

Chocolate or Carob Shake

Makes 1½ cups

This creamy shake is so simple that a toddler can place the ingredients in a blender, put on the lid, and push the button—as long as she's prepared for the big noise! Using your favorite fortified nondairy milk, this shake is a good source of calcium, vitamins B_{12} and D, and riboflavin. The banana adds potassium and vitamin B_6. With rice milk, you'll get a little less protein (4 grams) than with soymilk. This also is a fine, low-fat treat for weight-conscious adults.

1 fresh or frozen ripe banana (see Tip, page 235)

2 teaspoons cocoa or carob powder

¾ cup fortified nondairy milk

Break the banana into chunks and place in a blender along with the cocoa and about ½ cup of the milk. Process for a minute or until smooth. Add remaining milk and blend briefly.

Per Cup*: calories 224; protein 6 g; carbohydrate 50 g; fat 3 g; dietary fiber 4 g; sodium 69 mg
Percent calories from: protein 11 percent; fat 12 percent; carbohydrate 77 percent

*Nutritional analysis done using fortified soymilk.

Variation

To get your omega-3s for the day, add 2 tablespoons ground flaxseeds.

Purple Protein Power Shake

Makes about 2½ cups

Need a simple protein boost? Try this shake with or without the protein powder; it's good both ways. Blueberries provide a wealth of antioxidants that protect cells from disease.

1 cup grape juice

1 cup blueberries

6 to 8 ounces cherry or blueberry soy yogurt

¼ cup (1 scoop/30 grams) soy protein powder

Place all ingredients in a blender and process until smooth and creamy.

Per Half Recipe: calories 209; protein 16 g; carbohydrate 36 g; fat 3 g; dietary fiber 2 g; sodium 154 mg
Percent calories from: protein 30 percent; fat 13 percent; carbohydrate 57 percent

Sneaky Dad's Power Punch Smoothie

Makes 2 servings (about 3½ cups)

This recipe was developed by Louisville lawyer John Borders as a nutrient-dense breakfast for his three children, in particular for one who is a persistent picky eater. He guarantees this recipe will reduce stress for concerned parents who worry that their children have eaten little else all day. If you like, any needed supplements may be added to it.

1 cup calcium-fortified orange juice
1 cup fortified vanilla soymilk
1½ bananas, peeled and frozen (see Tip, page 241)
1 cup frozen strawberries
1 to 2 tablespoons ground flaxseeds (or 1 to 2 teaspoons flaxseed oil)
1 tablespoon nut butter (such as cashew or almond butter)
¼ avocado, peeled (optional)

Pour juice and soymilk into a blender; then add all remaining ingredients. Blend until thoroughly smooth and creamy, with no lumps. Serve with a straw.

Per Half Recipe: calories 300; protein 8 g; carbohydrate 54 g; fat 8 g; dietary fiber 6 g; sodium 80 mg
Percent calories from: protein 10 percent; fat 22 percent; carbohydrate 68 percent

Per Half Recipe with Avocado: calories 341; protein 8 g; carbohydrate 56 g; fat 12 g; dietary fiber 7 g; sodium 82 mg
Percent calories from: protein 9 percent; fat 29 percent; carbohydrate 62 percent

Note

Raw nut butters are preferable as they don't really affect the flavor of the smoothie much. Roasted nut butters (such as cashew, almond, peanut, etc.) are fine, too, but they tend to overpower the flavor of the fruit. Experiment with different nut butters to see which one your children like best.

For a child weighing about 30 pounds, a serving of this smoothie provides 20 percent of the day's requirement for protein; 25 percent of the calories, zinc, vitamins A and D, and omega-3 fatty acids; 40 percent of the iron, zinc, manganese, thiamin, riboflavin, niacin, folate, and fiber; 50 percent of the calcium, phosphorus, and vitamin E; 100 percent of the copper, magnesium, and vitamins B_6, B_{12}, and C.

Variations

Many variations are possible as long as you maintain the 1:1 ratio of total liquids and total frozen fruit. Here are just a few possibilities:

- Double the amount of avocado or nut butter.
- Replace strawberries with frozen pitted cherries or frozen raspberries.
- Add ¼ cup cooked carrots.

Sweet Almond Milk

Makes about 3 cups

Almond milk is sweet and delicate, and a favorite among children. Nut milks cannot take the place of fortified rice milk or soymilk as good sources of calcium, vitamin D, and riboflavin for your youngster. However, they are delicious for occasional use as a beverage and in recipes such as the Coconut Squash Icing on page 335. To prepare other nut milks, see *Vegan Vittles,* by Joanne Stepaniak.

> ⅓ cup blanched almonds
> 3 cups almost-boiling water
> 2 tablespoons sweetener of your choice
> ½ teaspoon vanilla extract (optional)

Grind the nuts to a fine powder or paste in an electric coffee grinder or in a dry blender, stopping to stir frequently until the nuts are finely ground. Blend the nut meal with ½ cup of the hot water, sweetener, and vanilla, if using. Process on medium speed to make a smooth, thick cream. Add the remaining hot water, one cup at a time, and blend on high until creamy.

Strain the milk through cheesecloth or a very fine mesh strainer, pressing firmly to remove as much liquid as possible. Discard the nut residue. Transfer the milk to a beverage container and store in the refrigerator for five to seven days. Shake well before using.

Per Cup: calories 132; protein 3 g; carbohydrate 12 g; fat 8 g; dietary fiber 2 g; sodium 8 mg
Percent calories from: protein 10 percent; fat 54 percent; carbohydrate 36 percent

Pretty Party Punch

Makes 8 cups

This colorful punch adds the natural sweetness of fruit to special occasions. With an inexpensive ice cube tray, you can make the event extra special with ice stars or trees, or freeze a berry or grape in each cube.

8 to 16 ice cubes made from purple grape juice
2 cups pineapple juice
2 cups orange juice
2 cups sparkling apple juice or sparkling cider
1 cup seedless green grapes

Using grape juice, make ice cubes. Combine other juices in a punch bowl or pitcher. If using punch bowl, add ice cubes and grapes. If serving in glasses, distribute ice cubes and grapes among glasses, add punch, and serve.

Per Cup: calories 128; protein 1 g; carbohydrate 31 g; fat 0.2 g; dietary fiber 0.4 g; sodium 4 mg
Percent calories from: protein 2 percent; fat 2 percent; carbohydrate 96 percent

Warm Red Cider

Makes 3¾ cups

This warming, aromatic drink is a welcome addition to a frosty afternoon of hiking or skating. By using whole cloves and cinnamon sticks, you can show children that spices are parts of plants. Cinnamon comes from the bark of an evergreen tree that grows in Indonesia and South Vietnam. The bark is harvested during the rainy season, when it comes off the tree easily. It is then rolled into slender tubes called cinnamon sticks. Cloves are unopened buds that grow in clusters on trees in mountainous regions of East Africa and India. If you prefer, you may replace the cinnamon sticks and whole cloves with ¼ teaspoon of ground cinnamon and a pinch of ground cloves. As cranberry cocktail is usually sweetened with sugar, you may prefer to replace both juices with a sugar-free apple-cranberry-grape juice blend.

> 2 cups apple juice
> 2 cups cranberry cocktail
> 2 cinnamon sticks
> 5 whole cloves

In a saucepan, combine juices, cinnamon, and cloves. Bring just to a boil, reduce heat, and simmer for 5 minutes. Serve warm.

Per Cup: calories 139; protein 0 g; carbohydrate 35 g; fat 0.3 g; dietary fiber 0.4 g; sodium 6 mg
Percent calories from: protein 0 percent; fat 2 percent; carbohydrate 98 percent

Warm Spiced Milk

Makes 1 cup

This hot drink contains soothing Indian spices for a relaxing before-bed treat or warm morning beverage. It is easy to double, triple, or quadruple the quantities. Black pepper is traditional, but it may be omitted for children and others who prefer milder flavors. (Adapted from *The Vegan Sourcebook*, by Joanne Stepaniak.)

1 cup fortified nondairy milk
¼ teaspoon ground cinnamon
⅛ teaspoon ground cardamom
Pinch of ground black pepper (optional)
Pinch of saffron threads (optional)
Sugar, as desired

In a small saucepan, whisk together the milk and spices. Heat on medium, stirring occasionally until steaming and hot. Do not boil. Pour the milk through a fine mesh strainer to filter out the spices (you can put the strainer over your cup or mug and pour the hot milk directly into it). Stir in as much sugar as necessary to achieve the desired sweetness. Serve hot.

Per Cup*: calories 154; protein 8 g; carbohydrate 21 g; fat 5 g; dietary fiber 0.4 g; sodium 154 mg
Percent calories from: protein 19 percent; fat 28 percent; carbohydrate 52 percent

*Nutritional analysis done using fortified soymilk.

Warm Cocoa

Makes 2 cups

Hot cocoa is always a favorite with children of any age. If you prefer that your youngsters avoid caffeine, the cocoa may be replaced with carob.

    3 tablespoons unsweetened cocoa or carob powder
    3 tablespoons sugar
    ½ cup water
    2 cups fortified vanilla nondairy milk

Combine the cocoa or carob, sugar, and water in a small saucepan, and whisk until smooth. Heat on medium, stirring constantly, until the mixture comes to a boil. Simmer, stirring constantly, for 1 minute. Whisk in the milk and cook, stirring often, until steaming and hot. Do not boil. Pour into mugs and serve at once.

Per Cup*: calories 245; protein 9 g; carbohydrate 43 g; fat 6 g; dietary fiber 3 g; sodium 157 mg
Percent calories from: protein 14 percent; fat 21 percent; carbohydrate 65 percent

*Nutritional analysis done using fortified soymilk.

BREAKFAST

Creamy Multigrain Porridge

Makes 3½ cups

Health experts advise us to eat whole grains—but how can we prepare them quickly and easily, in a way the whole family will enjoy? Here's a solution to that challenge, and one that works well for people with sensitivities to wheat and soy. Using a double boiler, you can let this cereal simmer during the evening, chill it according to the directions on page 107, then warm it for breakfast the next morning. Or, with a crock-pot, cook it overnight and it will be ready when you wake up. With a pressure cooker, you can have the porridge ready to serve in under an hour. Leftovers make a fine dessert, plain or with fruit topping. Experiment with combinations of amaranth, buckwheat, quinoa, spelt, or wheat berries, or you may use a single grain instead of three. Chopped dates, dried cranberries or apricots (cut into pieces), sunflower seeds, or chopped almonds may also be added before cooking or when served. One cup of this cereal provides 107 milligrams calcium—plus the calcium in the fortified beverage you pour over it. It also contains iron (1.6 milligrams), zinc (1.4 milligrams), and plenty of other minerals and B vitamins.

> ¼ cup brown rice
> ¼ cup millet
> ¼ cup barley, kamut, or other grain
> ¼ to ½ cup raisins or currants
> ¼ teaspoon salt (optional)
> ½ teaspoon cinnamon
> 3 cups boiling water
> 1 cup fortified nondairy milk

Double Boiler Method

Place grains, raisins, salt (if using), cinnamon, and water in the top section of a double boiler, and bring to a boil over direct heat. Place pan over lower section of double boiler, which should contain several cups of boiling water, cover, and cook for 2 hours.

Crock-Pot Method

Place grains, raisins, salt (if using), cinnamon, and water in a crock-pot and cook on low heat overnight, or on high for about 4 hours.

Pressure Cooker Method

Place grains, raisins, salt (if using), cinnamon, and water in a 4-quart or larger pressure cooker and bring up to high pressure over high heat. Reduce heat just enough to maintain high pressure and cook for 35 to 45 minutes (use the longer cooking time for mixtures that contain hulled barley, whole kamut, whole spelt berries, or whole wheat berries). Remove from heat and let the pressure come down naturally for 10 minutes. Use a quick-release method (see your cooker's instruction booklet) to release any remaining pressure. (Note: If you are using a first-generation "jiggle top" pressure cooker, add an additional ½ cup of water.)

For All Three Methods

Fifteen to 30 minutes before serving, stir in nondairy milk and warm through. Serve warm or cold.

Per Cup*: calories 223; protein 5 g; carbohydrate 48 g; fat 2 g; dietary fiber 5 g; sodium 36 mg
Percent calories from: protein 8 percent; fat 8 percent; carbohydrate 84 percent

*Nutritional analysis done using fortified soymilk.

Oatmeal Flax Porridge

Makes 1 cup, 2 cups, or 4 cups

Oatmeal provides a soothing and nourishing beginning to your day. With ground flaxseeds, it's also an excellent way to get your supply of omega-3s. Testers proclaimed this to be the best oatmeal they'd ever tasted.

1 serving	2 servings	4 servings
1 cup water	2 cups	4 cups
⅓ cup quick-cooking oats	⅔ cups	4⅓ cup
1 tablespoon currants or other dried fruit	2 tablespoons	¼ cup
⅛ teaspoon ground cinnamon	¼ teaspoon	½ teaspoon
2 tablespoons ground flaxseeds	¼ cup	½ cup

In a saucepan with lid, bring water to boil over high heat. Stir or whisk in rolled oats, currants, and cinnamon. Reduce heat, cover, and simmer for 2 to 4 minutes, stirring occasionally. Transfer to serving bowl and stir in ground flaxseeds. Serve with a teaspoon of maple syrup or other sweetener, if desired, and your choice of fortified soymilk or other milk.

Per Cup: calories 199; protein 9 g; carbohydrate 24 g; fat 7 g; dietary fiber 10 g; sodium 9 mg; omega-3 fatty acids (linolenic acid) 2.6 g

Percent calories from: protein 18 percent; fat 33 percent; carbohydrate 49 percent

Variations
Microwave Method for One Serving

Place water, oats, dried fruit, and cinnamon in microwave-safe bowl, stir to mix, and cook on high for 3 minutes. (You may need to adjust time for your microwave.)

Slow-Cooking Oats Method

Proceed as in basic method, but simmer for 15 minutes.

Granny's Grand Granola

Makes about 11 cups

Grand in winter, great on a camping trip, and most agreeable as an after-school or evening snack, this energy- and protein-packed cereal really sticks to your ribs.

   7 cups rolled oats
   1 cup oat bran or wheat germ (or another cup oats)
   1 cup sunflower seeds
   ½ cup tahini
   ¼ to ½ cup maple syrup, rice syrup, or barley malt syrup
   1 cup chopped dates, raisins, or other dried fruit

Preheat oven to 300°F. In a roasting pan or large (14-inch diameter) metal bowl, combine oats, wheat germ, and seeds. In a cup, combine tahini and syrup, then pour over oat mixture and mix well. In the roasting pan or large bowl, roast oat mixture for 45 minutes, removing from the oven every 15 minutes to stir, moving granola that has browned to the center.

Add dried fruit and store in a covered container. Serve with fortified nondairy milk or apple juice.

Per ½ Cup: calories 211; protein 7.5 g; carbohydrate 31 g; fat 8 g; dietary fiber 5 g; sodium 4 mg
Percent calories from: protein 13 percent; fat 32 percent; carbohydrate 55 percent

Swiss-Style Muesli

Makes 2½ cups

This breakfast has an ideal balance of protein, fat, and carbohydrate, and provides 11 grams of protein per half recipe. A hungry teen who eats the whole recipe will start his day with 22 grams of protein.

¾ cup rolled oats
2 tablespoons raisins
2 tablespoons chopped nuts or sunflower seeds
¼ teaspoon cinnamon
1 cup fortified nondairy milk
2 tablespoons frozen fruit juice concentrate
1 small apple or pear (peel if not organic), grated or finely chopped

In a medium bowl, combine all ingredients, cover, and refrigerate overnight. Alternatively, the fresh fruit may be stirred in just before serving.

Per Half Recipe (1¼ Cups)*: calories 335; protein 11 g; carbohydrate 55 g; fat 10 g; dietary fiber 6 g; sodium 80 mg

Percent calories from: protein 12 percent; fat 25 percent; carbohydrate 63 percent

*Nutritional analysis done using orange juice concentrate and fortified soymilk.

Fabulous French Toast

From toddlers to teens and beyond, French toast is always a welcome treat. This scrumptious, egg-free version is quick, easy, and healthful. Serve plain or with your favorite syrup or topping. (From *Vegan Vittles*, by Joanne Stepaniak.)

> 1⅓ cups fortified nondairy milk
> 3 tablespoons flour
> 1 tablespoon nutritional yeast flakes
> Pinch of salt (optional)
> 8 slices whole-grain bread

In a medium bowl, beat together milk, flour, yeast flakes, and salt (if using) to make a smooth, thin batter. Pour into a wide shallow bowl or pan. Dip bread slices, one at a time, into batter, making sure both sides are well saturated.

Oil a large, heavy griddle or skillet and heat on medium-high. When hot, add one or two soaked bread slices in a single layer. When bottoms are well browned, carefully turn over and cook the other side until golden. To prevent sticking, oil griddle well between batches. Serve hot.

Tip

While the remainder cook, keep the finished French toast slices hot by placing on a lightly oiled baking sheet in a preheated 300°F oven. For easier cleanup, line baking sheet with parchment paper instead of using oil.

Per Slice*: calories 109; protein 5 g; carbohydrate 19 g; fat 2 g; dietary fiber 2 g; sodium 175 mg
Percent calories from: protein 17 percent; fat 17 percent; carbohydrate 66 percent

*Nutritional analysis done using fortified soymilk.

Peanut Butter and Banana Hotcakes

Makes about 18 pancakes

A satisfying and tasty choice for children. A small dab of fruit-sweetened jam is the perfect topping! (Adapted from *Table for Two*, by Joanne Stepaniak.)

> 1½ cups whole-wheat flour
> 2 teaspoons baking powder
> 2 small, ripe bananas, mashed (about ⅔ cup)
> 1½ tablespoons smooth peanut butter
> 1 cup fortified vanilla nondairy milk

In a medium bowl, combine flour and baking powder. In a separate bowl, cream together banana and peanut butter; stir in milk. Pour banana mixture into flour mixture and stir until well combined.

Oil a large, heavy skillet or griddle and place over medium-high heat. When hot, spoon in batter using 2 tablespoons for each pancake. Spread out using the back of a spoon. Cook until bottoms are brown, adjusting heat as necessary. Turn over and cook other side briefly, just until golden. To prevent sticking, oil skillet well between batches.

Per Hotcake*: calories 61; protein 2 g; carbohydrate 11 g; fat 1 g; dietary fiber 2 g; sodium 41 mg
Percent calories from: protein 14 percent; fat 16 percent; carbohydrate 70 percent

*Nutritional analysis done using fortified soymilk.

Flaxjacks

Makes about 12 3-inch pancakes

These light, fluffy pancakes are a great way for children to enjoy a whole-grain breakfast. Five flaxjacks provides the day's supply of 2 grams of omega-3 fatty acids, along with 12 grams of protein, 150 milligrams of calcium, 3 milligrams of iron, and 2 milligrams of zinc.

> 1 cup whole-wheat flour
> 2 tablespoons finely ground flaxseeds
> 2 teaspoons baking powder
> ⅛ teaspoon salt
> 1 cup fortified vanilla nondairy milk
> 1 tablespoon vegetable oil (plus extra as needed for cooking)

In a large mixing bowl, combine flour, ground flaxseeds, baking powder, and salt. Pour in milk and oil and mix just until everything is evenly moistened. Let rest for 5 minutes, then stir again.

Oil a large, heavy griddle or skillet and place over medium-high heat. When hot, spoon in batter using 2 tablespoons for each pancake. Cook until bubbles pop through top of the pancakes and bottoms are brown, about 2 to 3 minutes. Adjust heat as necessary. Turn over and cook other side briefly, just until cooked through and golden, about 1 minute longer. To prevent sticking, oil griddle well between batches.

Per Flaxjack*: calories 65; protein 2 g; carbohydrate 10 g; fat 2 g; dietary fiber 2 g; sodium 77 mg
Percent calories from: protein 14 percent; fat 30 percent; carbohydrate 56 percent

*Nutritional analysis done using fortified soymilk.

Wheat-Free Minipancakes

Makes about 18 small pancakes

Did you think you could have scrumptious pancakes without a trace of wheat or gluten? Here they are! A trick to good pancakes is to preheat the skillet so that a drop of water dances across the surface. Oil the skillet well so the pancakes don't stick. Chickpea (garbanzo) flour is the main ingredient in the large, thin crackers from India known as papadoms; it can be found in East Indian and Asian stores.

> ½ cup brown rice flour
> ½ cup chickpea flour
> 1½ teaspoons baking powder
> ½ cup blueberries (optional)
> ¾ cup fortified nondairy milk
> 1 tablespoon vegetable oil (plus extra as needed for cooking)

In a medium bowl, combine flours, baking powder, and blueberries (if using). In a small bowl or measuring cup, mix milk and oil, then pour into flour mixture and stir to combine.

Oil a large, heavy skillet or griddle and place over medium-high heat. When hot, spoon in batter using about 1 tablespoon to make each 2-inch pancake. Cook pancakes until lightly browned and bubbles pop through top of the pancakes, about 2 minutes per side, turning carefully. To prevent sticking, oil griddle well between batches. Serve warm with Hot Cinnamon Apple Topping (page 260) or one of the maple toppings that follow.

Per Mini-Pancake*: calories 38; protein 1 g; carbohydrate 6 g; fat 1 g; dietary fiber 0.5 g; sodium 23 mg
Percent calories from: protein 10 percent; fat 25 percent; carbohydrate 65 percent

*Nutritional analysis done using fortified rice milk.

Maple Syrup–Based Toppings

Pure maple syrup is delectable, but it also is expensive, and too much of it can give little ones a "sugar rush." There are a few ways we can "stretch" pure maple syrup so it can go a little farther and have less of an impact on our bodies and moods. Below are some simple ways to do that. Fruit and Maple Blend is a painless way to add more fruit to your children's diets, and Flaxen Maple Syrup is a great way to incorporate omega-3 fatty acids.

Fruit and Maple Blend

Combine equal parts of pure maple syrup and berries or peeled and finely chopped fresh fruit. Serve as is or blend for a smoother texture.

Per 2 Tablespoons*: calories 57; protein 0 g; carbohydrate 15 g; fat 0.1 g; dietary fiber 0.2 g; sodium 2 mg
Percent calories from: protein 0 percent; fat 1 percent; carbohydrate 99 percent

*Nutritional analysis done using blueberries.

Flaxen Maple Syrup

Makes about ⅔ cup

Each tablespoon provides 1.5 grams of essential omega-3 fatty acids.

For each ½ cup pure maple syrup, stir in 2 teaspoons flaxseed oil. Mix until well blended.

Per 2 Tablespoons: calories 67; protein 0 g; carbohydrate 11 g; fat 3 g; dietary fiber 0 g; sodium 1 mg
Percent calories from: protein 0 percent; fat 37 percent; carbohydrate 63 percent

Extended Maple Syrup

Makes about 1¼ cups

⅔ cup water
1 tablespoon cornstarch
⅔ cup pure maple syrup

Combine water and cornstarch in a medium saucepan and stir until cornstarch is dissolved. Stir in maple syrup and bring to a boil, stirring constantly. Reduce heat to low and cook, stirring constantly, until mixture is clear and slightly thickened.

Per 2 Tablespoons: calories 59; protein 0 g; carbohydrate 15 g; fat 0 g; dietary fiber 0 g; sodium 2 mg
Percent calories from: protein 0 percent; fat 1 percent; carbohydrate 99 percent

Hot Cinnamon Apple Topping

Makes about 2 cups

This chunky sauce made with fresh apples is a tempting topping for pancakes, French toast, or hot porridge. It's also delicious on nondairy frozen dessert and has a gentle, mellow sweetness that is not overpowering.

2 Granny Smith apples, peeled, cored, and cut into 12 equal slices
per apple
1⅓ cups frozen apple juice concentrate
¼ cup raisins or chopped dates
1 tablespoon fresh or frozen lemon juice
½ teaspoon cinnamon

Place all ingredients in a medium saucepan and bring to a boil. Reduce heat to medium-low and simmer, stirring occasionally, until apple is soft but not mushy. Serve hot or warm.

Per ½ Cup: calories 218; protein 1 g; carbohydrate 56 g; fat 0.4 g; dietary fiber 2 g; sodium 25 mg
Percent calories from: protein 2 percent; fat 1 percent; carbohydrate 97 percent

Vegetable Tofu Scramble

Makes 1⅓ cups

This is a great way for athletes, teens, and younger children to enjoy a protein-powered breakfast, with 19 grams of protein in a half recipe, and 38 grams for someone who eats the whole thing. When calcium-set tofu is used, this dish is also an excellent source of calcium. Vegetable Tofu Scramble makes a hearty brunch, lunch, or supper item, and can be accompanied by sliced tomatoes, veggie bacon, and whole-grain toast or bagels.

> 1 teaspoon vegetable oil (or as needed)
> ½ cup sliced mushrooms (optional)
> ¼ cup grated carrot
> ¼ cup finely chopped scallions
> ⅛ teaspoon turmeric
> ½ pound firm tofu, rinsed, patted dry, and crumbled
> 1 or 2 teaspoons nutritional yeast flakes
> Salt, or your favorite seasoned salt
> Pepper
> 1 tablespoon minced fresh parsley (optional)

Oil a large, heavy skillet and place over medium-high heat. When hot, add mushrooms (if using), and sauté until lightly browned, about 2 minutes. Add carrot, scallions, and turmeric, and sauté for 2 minutes longer.

Add tofu, yeast flakes, and seasoning to taste. Mix well and continue to cook, stirring constantly, for 5 minutes or until heated through. Stir in parsley (if using) just before serving.

Per Half Recipe (⅔ Cup): calories 200; protein 19 g; carbohydrate 8 g; fat 12 g; dietary fiber 4 g; sodium 24 mg
Percent calories from: protein 35 percent; fat 51 percent; carbohydrate 14 percent

Freestyle Fruit Salad

Fruit salad is a real favorite with children, especially when they help to cut it up. Various fruits contain the same protective vitamins and phytochemicals that are found in vegetables. For example, carotenoids are not only in carrots, squash, sweet potatoes, and green vegetables; they're in apricots, cantaloupe, guavas, mangoes, papaya, peaches, strawberries, and watermelon, too. So if your child is going through a stage of rejecting vegetables, don't despair. Just create a colorful fruit salad!

Apple, chunked
Grapefruit, peeled, sectioned, seeded and pith removed
Orange, peeled and sectioned, seeded, and chopped
Banana, peeled and sliced
Melon chunks or balls
Blueberries
Papaya, mango, or other fruits, peeled and cut into chunks
Orange juice

Combine fruits of choice in a large, nonmetallic bowl. Add orange juice to cover. Serve at once, or cover and chill.

Per Half Cup*: calories 56; protein 1 g; carbohydrate 14 g; fat 0.2 g; dietary fiber 2 g; sodium 3 mg
Percent calories from: protein 5 percent: fat 3 percent; carbohydrate 92 percent

*Nutritional analysis done using equal amounts of fruits listed.

Breakfast Burritos

Makes 4 burritos

These simple, nutritious roll-ups make a substantial morning meal. For a wheat-free version, use corn tortillas.

> 4 whole-wheat or corn tortillas
> ¼ cup smooth or crunchy peanut butter
> ¼ cup fruit-sweetened jam or jelly
> 4 very small, thin bananas, or 2 medium bananas cut in half lengthwise

Warm tortillas, one at a time, in a dry skillet over medium-high heat for about 1 minute or until just heated. Spread one side of each tortilla evenly with peanut butter. Then carefully spread jam over the peanut butter. Place one banana (or banana half) on the edge of each tortilla on top of the jelly, and roll tortilla around banana to enclose it. Serve at once.

Per Burrito: calories 317; protein 8 g; carbohydrate 61 g; fat 9 g; dietary fiber 6 g; sodium 181 mg
Percent calories from: protein 9 percent; fat 23 percent; carbohydrate 68 percent

Crunchy Fruit Crisps

This is a fun finger food that both children and adults love making and eating. Beyond breakfast, these Fruit Crisps make a quick, healthful snack or not-too-sweet dessert. Whereas parents are wise to be cautious about introducing nuts to toddlers who might choke on them, nut butters are a wonderful way to serve youngsters these energy- and protein-rich foods, so packed with protective phytochemicals.

> 1 crisp eating apple, cored and sliced into rings or wedges
> 1 pear, cut into four wedges
> 1 banana, sliced lengthwise and cut in half widthwise to make 4 pieces
> ¼ cup peanut butter or almond butter
> ½ cup crisp rice cereal, as needed

Spread a thick layer of nut butter on one side of each piece of fruit. Place cereal in a small bowl and press nut-buttered side of fruit firmly into it.

Per ¼ Recipe: calories 181; protein 5 g; carbohydrate 25 g; fat 9 g; dietary fiber 4 g; sodium 29 mg
Percent calories from: protein 10 percent; fat 40 percent; carbohydrate 50 percent

Apples and Tahini

This is a light, quick breakfast or snack, especially for young children who love simple finger food that involves dipping.

> 4 crisp eating apples, cored and sliced into 8 wedges each
> ¼ to ½ cup tahini

Put apple slices on serving plates and spoon a portion of tahini onto one side of the plate.

Per ¼ Recipe: calories 170; protein 3 g; carbohydrate 24 g; fat 8 g; dietary fiber 4 g; sodium 5 mg
Percent calories from: protein 6 percent; fat 41 percent; carbohydrate 53 percent

QUICK BREADS

Muscle Muffins

Makes 12 muffins

These muffins are quite different from cake-type muffins—they're more hearty, satisfying, and nutritious, making them perfect for sports-minded teens. Every muffin provides 8 grams of protein, 3 milligrams of iron, and 150 milligrams of calcium. Store them in individual plastic bags in your freezer to grab for a midmorning snack, hiking treat, or boost after the gym.

   1 cup whole-wheat flour
   1 cup unbleached flour
   2 teaspoons baking powder
   1 teaspoon baking soda
   1 teaspoon cinnamon
   2 frozen or fresh, ripe bananas
   ¾ cup fortified soymilk
   ½ cup soy protein powder (2 scoops)
   ¼ cup safflower oil
   ¼ cup blackstrap molasses
   ¼ cup pure maple syrup
   2 teaspoons apple cider vinegar
   1 cup raisins or chopped dates

Preheat oven to 350°F and oil muffin tins or mist them with nonstick cooking spray for easier cleanup. In a large bowl, combine flours, baking powder, baking soda, and cinnamon, and mix well. In a smaller bowl, mash bananas; then stir in soymilk, protein powder, oil, molasses, syrup, and vinegar. (Alternatively, you may puree these together in a blender.) Add banana mixture to dry ingredients, stir until just blended, then stir in raisins. Fill muffin tins and bake for 30 to 35 minutes or until done. You can tell muffins are done when they pull away from the sides of the tin and when the dent made by a finger pressed in the center of a muffin pops up again to its original shape.

Per Muffin: calories 223; protein 8 g; carbohydrate 40 g; fat 5 g; dietary fiber 3 g; sodium 194 mg
Percent calories from: protein 14 percent; fat 19 percent; carbohydrate 67 percent

Carrot Cake Muffins

Makes 12 muffins

Are you looking for ways to get your youngsters to eat their veggies? In each one of these muffins they'll get 3 tablespoons of carrot.

> 2 cups whole-wheat pastry flour
> 1 tablespoon baking powder
> 1 teaspoon baking soda
> 1 teaspoon cinnamon
> ½ teaspoon salt
> ¼ teaspoon allspice
> 2¼ cups shredded carrots
> 8 ounces unsweetened crushed pineapple in juice (do not drain)
> ½ cup sugar
> 2 tablespoons safflower oil
> ½ cup raisins
> ½ cup chopped walnuts

Preheat oven to 350°F. Lightly oil 12 muffin cups or mist with nonstick spray for easier cleanup. In a medium bowl, combine flour, baking powder, baking soda, cinnamon, salt, and allspice. Place remaining ingredients in a separate large bowl and stir until well combined. Gradually stir dry ingredients into wet ingredients, sprinkling in about ⅛ at a time. Mix until well combined. Batter will be thick. Immediately spoon equally into muffin cups. The cups will be quite full. Bake for about 20 to 25 minutes or until a cake tester or toothpick tests clean, or until tops are beginning to brown, muffins pull away from the sides of the cup, and top springs back when dented with a fingertip. Gently loosen muffins and turn them on their sides in the muffin tin. Cover with a clean kitchen towel and let rest for 5 minutes. (This will keep them from developing a hard crust.) Transfer to a cooling rack.

Per Muffin: calories 167; protein 4 g; carbohydrate 28 g; fat 6 g; dietary fiber 4 g; sodium 368 mg
Percent calories from: protein 8 percent; fat 28 percent; carbohydrate 64 percent

Variation

Carrot Cake

This same recipe can be made into a carrot cake by pouring the batter into an 8 × 8-inch baking pan that has been lightly oiled or misted with nonstick spray. Bake for 35 to 40 minutes or until a cake tester or toothpick tests clean or top is beginning to brown, cake pulls away from the sides of the pan, and top springs back when dented with a fingertip.

Crunchy Cornbread

Makes one 9-inch loaf

Here's a delectable treat that's eggless, wheat free, and dairy free. Although spelt contains gluten, some people who are wheat intolerant find spelt easier to digest. If you prefer, you may replace the spelt with whole-wheat pastry flour. This quick bread has a delicate sweetness and a lovely texture when you bite into it. Flaxseeds, as an egg replacer, give lightness.

> 1½ cups fortified rice milk
> 3 tablespoons ground flaxseeds
> 3 tablespoons vegetable oil
> 2 tablespoons pure maple syrup or other sweetener
> 1 cup spelt flour
> 1 cup cornmeal
> ½ teaspoon salt
> 2½ teaspoons baking powder

Preheat oven to 400°F. In a small bowl, combine rice milk, flaxseeds, oil, and maple syrup. In a medium bowl, mix flour, cornmeal, salt, and baking powder. Add liquid mixture to flour mixture and combine thoroughly with minimal mixing. Pour into oiled 9 × 5-inch loaf pan (or 8-inch square pan). Bake for 30 minutes or until cornbread pulls away from the sides and a dent made by a finger pressed in the center of the loaf recovers its shape.

Per ¾-Inch Slice or ¹⁄₁₂ Recipe: calories 140; protein 4 g; carbohydrate 21 g; fat 5 g; dietary fiber 3 g; sodium: 163 mg

Percent calories from: protein 10 percent; fat 32 percent; carbohydrate 58 percent

SPREADS AND SANDWICHES

What Shall I Spread on My Bread?

Finding a suitable spread for bread or toast can seem a challenge, especially if you don't want cholesterol-laden butter or the trans-fatty acids found in many margarines. Here are some flavorful alternatives that provide plenty of nutritional pluses. Almond butter is a tasty source of calcium. Cashew butter provides zinc. Peanut butter is economical and high in protein. Gee Whiz Spread is high in nutritional value, yet low in calories. A thin layer each of sesame tahini and blackstrap molasses is great on morning toast. Here are some super spreads that provide plenty of nutrition and wonderfully satisfying flavor:

- nut and seed butters made from almonds, cashews, sunflower seeds, sesame seeds, or other nuts and seeds
- peanut or soynut butter
- Nutti Whip (page 274)
- mashed avocado
- miso (bean paste made from soybeans or chickpeas), thinly spread
- mustard, plain or seasoned, thinly spread
- fruit jams, spreads, butters, and conserves
- rice syrup or barley malt syrup, thinly spread

Sandwiches

When you're faced with a decade or so of bag lunches to make, it certainly helps to have a few new ideas!

The Breads

- whole-grain or multigrain breads
- soft or crusty rolls
- whole-wheat pita bread
- bagels
- Indian roti or chapatis
- tortillas (flour or corn)
- rice cakes
- lavash
- whole-grain crackers or matzoh

The Condiments

- mustard, plain or seasoned
- barbecue sauce
- ketchup
- vegan mayonnaise
- yeast spreads (such as Marmite or Vegemite)
- miso (bean paste made from soybeans or chickpeas)
- mashed avocado
- Sesame Tahini Salad Dressing (page 289)
- Ranch-Style Dressing and Dip (page 295)

Protein-Rich Fillings

- hummus
- Red Bean hummus (page 275)
- Flaxen Hummus (page 276)
- Tofu-Vegetable Spread (page 277)
- nut and seed butters
- peanut or soynut butter
- Gee Whiz Spread (page 273)

- Gooda Uncheese slices (page 278)
- Nutti Whip (page 274)
- seasoned or marinated tofu
- bean salad
- marinated and baked or sautéed tempeh
- sliced seitan (wheat "meat")
- veggie deli slices
- hot or cold cooked veggie burgers
- hot or cold cooked veggie dogs

Even More to Chew On
- grilled vegetables
- grated or thinly sliced raw vegetables
- lightly steamed vegetables
- salad greens
- raw spinach
- cooked greens, such as kale or collards (well drained)
- seasoned potatoes
- leftover casseroles
- leftover thick stew or chili

Winning Combos
- marinated tofu (page 314), tomato slices, lettuce or alfalfa sprouts, vegan mayo
- mashed avocado, slices of red bell pepper or pimento, sprouts
- hummus (pages 275 or 276), tomato or cucumber slice, avocado slices
- hummus (pages 275 or 276), sprouts, chopped olives, Sesame Tahini Salad Dressing (page 289)
- Tofu-Vegetable Spread (page 277), lettuce
- Gee Whiz Spread (page 273), cucumber slices
- Gooda Uncheese (page 278), alfalfa sprouts, vegan mayo
- veggie burger (warmed or not), red onion slice, tomato, ketchup, relish, mustard, sprouts
- vegetarian pepperoni or deli slices, dill pickle slices, tomato slices, mustard, vegan mayo

- nut or seed butter, jam, or rice syrup
- nut or seed butter, sliced banana
- nut or seed butter, thinly sliced strawberries or orange sections
- nut or seed butter, grated carrot, sliced cucumber, red onion slice
- nut or seed butter, raisins or other chopped, dried fruit
- nut or seed butter, steamed broccoli florets, tamari
- steamed vegetables, thick salad dressing or vegan mayo
- mashed beans, lettuce, red onion slice, barbecue sauce
- mashed beans, lettuce, tomato, scallions, vegan mayo
- tahini, sauerkraut, mustard
- tahini, steamed kale, mustard
- tahini, blackstrap molasses
- steamed greens (such as kale or collards), grilled onions, mustard
- raw spinach, thinly sliced mushrooms (raw or sautéed), red onion slice, dressing
- grilled or broiled portobello mushrooms, barbecue sauce
- salad greens, chopped raw veggies, dressing

Sandwiches with an International Flair
- Bean Burritos (page 282)
- Simple Nori Rolls (page 316) or from a deli or Japanese restaurant
- Veggie Rice Roll (page 298)
- French Bread Pizza wedge (page 319)
- Monster Mash Roll-Ups (page 279)
- Fabulous Fajitas (page 323)
- falafels
- Time-Saving Tacos (page 326)

Gee Whiz Spread

Makes about 2 cups

A phenomenal cheeseless "cheese" spread that will have the whole family begging for more. Stir a little into pasta, soups, or sauces for added protein and a burst of rich, cheesy flavor. (Adapted from *The Uncheese Cookbook*, by Joanne Stepaniak.)

2 cups cooked white beans, drained (15-ounce can)

⅓ cup nutritional yeast flakes

¼ cup fresh or frozen lemon juice

3 tablespoons tahini or cashew butter

¾ teaspoon paprika

½ teaspoon prepared yellow mustard

½ teaspoon salt

¼ to ½ teaspoon onion or garlic powder (optional)

Place all ingredients in a food processor and process until completely smooth. Chill thoroughly before serving. Keeps five to seven days in the refrigerator.

Per 2 Tablespoons: calories 58; protein 4 g; carbohydrate 8 g; fat 2 g; dietary fiber 3 g; sodium 77 mg
Percent calories from: protein 23 percent; fat 26 percent; carbohydrate 51 percent

Creative Grain Spread

Makes 1 to 1½ cups

This is an exciting way to use up small amounts of leftovers, although you might enjoy this spread so much you'll want to cook grain specifically for it. Use your imagination to turn whatever you have in the fridge or pantry into a special and original sandwich filling. This recipe can be easily doubled or tripled, if desired.

> 1 to 1½ cups cooked grain (rice, barley, bulgur, polenta, quinoa, etc.)
> 1 to 2 tablespoons nut or seed butter or vegan mayo
> 1 small carrot, shredded
> Water, as needed
> Salt, tamari, and pepper

Place all ingredients except the salt, tamari, and pepper in a food processor fitted with a metal blade. Process until grain is coarsely chopped but not pureed. Add about a tablespoon of water, if needed, to facilitate processing. Mixture should be thick, not runny. Season with salt, tamari, and pepper to taste.

Per ¼ Recipe*: calories 84; protein 2 g; carbohydrate 14 g; fat 2 g; dietary fiber 1 g; sodium 8 mg+ (sodium content will be higher depending on amount of salt or tamari used)
Percent calories from: protein 11 percent; fat 26 percent; carbohydrate 63 percent

*Nutritional analysis done using brown rice and peanut butter.

Nutti Whip

Makes about ¾ cup

A deceptively simple spread that cuts the fat of nut butter while adding the natural sweetness of apples. It's a protein-packed spread that is great on sandwiches, bagels, toast, crackers, and rice cakes, or even stuffed into celery sticks for a wholesome snack. Other unsweetened fruit butters may be used instead of apple, if preferred. (From *Delicious Food for a Healthy Heart*, by Joanne Stepaniak.)

4 tablespoons unsweetened applesauce or apple butter

2 tablespoons nut or seed butter

Combine applesauce or fruit butter and nut or seed butter in a bowl, stirring until thoroughly blended. Cover leftovers and store in refrigerator.

Per 2 Tablespoons: calories 86; protein 3 g; carbohydrate 5 g; fat 7 g; dietary fiber 1 g; sodium 3 mg
Percent calories from: protein 14 percent; fat 22 percent; carbohydrate 64 percent

Red Bean Hummus

Makes about 1½ cups

This hummus of a different color can be as spicy or mild as you and your family like. It is simple but tantalizing. Best of all, it takes mere minutes to prepare. (Adapted from *Vegan Deli*, by Joanne Stepaniak.)

2 cups cooked pinto beans, drained (15-ounce can)

2 tablespoons tahini

2 tablespoons balsamic vinegar

¼ to ½ teaspoon bottled hot sauce

¼ teaspoon ground cumin

Salt

2 to 4 tablespoons sliced scallions

Combine beans, tahini, vinegar, hot sauce, cumin, and salt to taste in a food processor. Blend into a smooth paste. Pulse in scallions until finely chopped and evenly distributed.

Per 2 Tablespoons: calories 56; protein 3 g; carbohydrate 8 g; fat 1 g; dietary fiber 3 g; sodium 5 mg+
   (sodium content will be higher depending on amount of salt used)
Percent calories from: protein 19 percent; fat 23 percent; carbohydrate 58 percent

Flaxen Hummus

The oils in this hummus are from healthful seeds: sesame and flax.

2 tablespoons ground flaxseeds
¼ cup warm water
2 cups cooked garbanzo beans, drained (15-ounce can)
2 tablespoons tahini
¼ cup fresh or frozen lemon juice
2 cloves garlic, chopped
1 to 2 tablespoons tamari or Bragg Liquid Aminos
½ teaspoon ground cumin
1 or 2 pinches cayenne pepper
Pinch black pepper

Place flaxseeds and water in a small bowl and let soak for about 10 minutes. Meanwhile, put beans, tahini, lemon juice, garlic, tamari, cumin, cayenne, and pepper into food processor. Add soaked seeds and process until smooth. Adjust seasoning.

Per 2 Tablespoons: calories 46; protein 2 g; carbohydrate 6 g; fat 2 g; dietary fiber 2 g; sodium 58 mg
Percent calories from: protein 19 percent; fat 32 percent; carbohydrate 49 percent

Tofu-Vegetable Spread

Makes 3 cups

This quick and easy protein-rich spread is a winner with both children and adults. It makes a substantial filling for a sandwich, yet it is sufficiently elegant for a party pâté. Use the Chinese-style (regular) water-packed tofu, rather than the Japanese-style (silken) tofu. Also, to increase your family's calcium intake, look for calcium on the ingredient panel of the tofu package. (From *The Vegan Sourcebook*, by Joanne Stepaniak.)

> 1 pound firm regular tofu, drained and rinsed
> ¼ cup tahini
> 2 tablespoons light miso
> 1½ tablespoons tamari, or to taste
> 1 cup shredded carrots
> ½ cup sliced scallions

Simmer tofu in fresh water to cover for 10 minutes. Slice, arrange in single layer in a metal pan or on plates, and cool in refrigerator until completely cold to the touch. When cool, crumble and place in a food processor fitted with metal blade. Add tahini, miso, and tamari and process into a thick paste. Add carrots and scallions and pulse until evenly distributed. Chill several hours before serving to blend flavors.

Per 2 Tablespoons: calories 48; protein 4 g; carbohydrate 2 g; fat 3 g; dietary fiber 1 g; sodium 121 mg
Percent calories from: protein 29 percent; fat 53 percent; carbohydrate 18 percent

Gooda Uncheese

Makes one 3-cup dome

A creamy, golden-colored, dairy-free "cheese" that is sliceable and delicious. Using a round-bottomed mold, such as a small mixing bowl, will give this unique uncheese a lovely domed shape.

1¾ cups water

½ cup chopped carrots

5 tablespoons agar flakes (or 2 tablespoons agar powder)

½ cup raw cashew pieces

¼ cup nutritional yeast flakes

3 tablespoons tahini

3 tablespoons fresh or frozen lemon juice

1 tablespoon prepared mustard

2 teaspoons onion powder

1 teaspoon salt

½ teaspoon each of garlic powder and dry mustard

¼ teaspoon each of turmeric, paprika, ground cumin

Place water and carrots in a saucepan and bring to a boil. Reduce heat, cover, and cook for 15 minutes. Remove lid and stir in agar flakes or powder. Bring to a boil again, then reduce heat and simmer 15 minutes longer.

Transfer water, cooked carrots, and agar to a blender and add remaining ingredients. Process until very smooth.

Pour immediately into a lightly oiled, 3-cup bowl or mold with a rounded bottom. Smooth the top. Cool, cover, and chill several hours or overnight. To serve, turn out of mold onto plate or serving platter and slice into thin wedges. Store leftovers covered in the refrigerator. Will keep for about seven days.

Per 2 Tablespoons: calories 35; protein 1 g; carbohydrate 3 g; fat 2 g; dietary fiber 1 g; sodium 116 mg
Percent calories from: protein 15 percent; fat 58 percent; carbohydrate 27 percent

Monster Mash Roll-Up

Here is a creative bean spread that offers endless ideas for fillings for rice paper roll-ups, taco shells, tortillas, and lavash. Kids in particular enjoy inventing their own Monster Mash recipes, and it's fun for parents and youngsters of any age to make these together.

2 cups cooked or canned beans of your choice, drained (15-ounce can)

Optional Ingredients
barbecue sauce
capers
carrots (minced or shredded)
citrus juice (lemon, lime, or orange)
garlic
herbs (fresh or dried)
horseradish
ketchup
mayonnaise (vegan)
mustard (prepared or dry)
nut or seed butter
nutritional yeast flakes
oil (olive or flaxseed)
onion
pickles (chopped or relish)
salad dressing (nondairy)
salt and pepper
spices
tamari
tomato paste
vegetables (cooked)
vegetables (raw, minced or grated)
vinegar (apple cider, balsamic, rice, or wine)

Place beans in a food processor fitted with a metal blade and process until ground. Add optional ingredients of your choice, adding a small amount of water, if needed, to facilitate processing. Taste, adjust seasonings, and add more optional ingredients as necessary to achieve the flavor and texture you desire.

Hero Sub

Makes 1 big sandwich

For growing teens, athletes, and people who want to get about half the day's protein in a single sandwich, here's a recipe that's a snap to make. It provides a teenage girl (or woman) with half of her protein for the day and supplies 40 percent of a boy's or man's requirement. Use one type of slice or a variety, choosing from veggie "chicken," "turkey," "salami," "pepperoni," "ham," or deli slices. Some brands are fortified with iron and zinc.

1 Kaiser roll or sub bun (2 ½ ounces)
1 to 2 tablespoons each of two of the following spreads: mustard, barbecue sauce, ketchup, or vegan mayonnaise
4 slices veggie "meat" (2 ounces)
3 slices tomato
3 slices red onion
3 slices avocado (¼ avocado)
½ cup alfalfa sprouts or chopped lettuce

On the top half of a bun, spread one of the sauces chosen. Spread the other sauce on the bottom half. Arrange veggie "meat" slices on bottom half of bun, followed by tomato, onion, avocado, and sprouts. Cover with other half of bun. Slice sub in half for easy handling.

Per Sub Sandwich: calories 431; protein 24 g; carbohydrate 64 g; fat 10 g; dietary fiber 6 g; sodium 1,488 mg
Percent calories from: protein 22 percent; fat 19 percent; carbohydrate 59 percent

Grilled Cheeze Sandwiches

Makes 4 sandwiches

These yummy, grilled sandwiches have all the goo and glory that made them so out-rageously popular, but now they're low in fat, high in protein, and dairy free! Leftover filling can be stored in the refrigerator for several days, so last-minute sandwiches can be pulled together in a snap. (From *Vegan Vittles*, by Joanne Stepaniak.)

⅔ cup water

3 tablespoons nutritional yeast flakes

2 tablespoons oat flour (see Tip, below)

2 tablespoons fresh or frozen lemon juice

2 tablespoons tahini

1½ tablespoons tomato paste or ketchup

2 teaspoons cornstarch

1 teaspoon onion powder or granules

¼ teaspoon each of garlic powder, turmeric, dry mustard, salt

8 slices whole-grain bread

Combine all ingredients except bread in a medium saucepan and whisk until smooth. Bring to a boil, stirring constantly with the wire whisk. Reduce heat to low and cook, stirring constantly, until thick and smooth. Remove from heat. Spread a few table-spoons between two slices of bread and grill in small amount of oil until both sides are well browned. Slice in half diagonally. Serve hot.

Tip

If you don't have oat flour, you can make it yourself from rolled oats. Just put ¾ cup rolled oats in a dry blender and process until powdery. This will yield about ½ cup of oat flour. Store unused oat flour in an airtight container in the refrigerator or freezer.

Per Sandwich: calories 231; protein 10 g; carbohydrate 36 g; fat 7 g; dietary fiber 6 g; sodium 452 mg
Percent calories from: protein 16 percent; fat 25 percent; carbohydrate 59 percent

Bean Burritos

Makes 4 burritos

These quick, nutritious roll-ups have a mild but flavorful filling. They are certain to become a lunch box staple. Omit the hot sauce for those with sensitive palates.

The Wraps
4 whole-wheat flour tortillas, chapatis, lavash, or corn tortillas

The Bean Filling
2 cups cooked pinto beans, drained (15-ounce can)
⅔ cup tomato sauce
⅓ cup finely chopped red or green bell pepper
1 teaspoon chili powder
¼ teaspoon each of garlic powder, dried oregano, ground cumin
Several drops bottled hot sauce

The Topping Options
avocado
cilantro
lettuce
olives
onion
scallions
tomato

Warm the wraps in a dry skillet, if desired. Keep warm by stacking and wrapping in a clean kitchen towel. Place all filling ingredients in a medium saucepan and bring to a boil. Reduce heat and simmer uncovered for 5 minutes, stirring occasionally. Remove from heat and mash beans coarsely with fork or potato masher. Place one-quarter of the filling onto each wrap, placing it in a strip along one side, slightly off center. Add your favorite toppings and roll the wrap around the filling.

Per Burrito, Without Optional Toppings: calories 370; protein 14 g; carbohydrate 66 g; fat 6 g; dietary fiber 11 g; sodium 600 mg
Percent calories from: protein 15 percent; fat 14 percent; carbohydrate 71 percent

SOUPS

Alphabet Minestrone

Makes 9 cups

There are at least as many versions of minestrone as towns in Italy, so feel free to use your creativity by trying different beans, herbs, vegetables, and other shapes of pasta. It is best to cook vegetables and pasta until just tender-crisp and add fresh basil near the end of the cooking time. Canned tomatoes and stock may contain salt, so check flavor before adding salt. Stock may be homemade, purchased, or prepared using cubes or powder. This nourishing soup keeps in the refrigerator for four or five days. Soups that contain pasta don't freeze well.

1 onion, diced
1 tablespoon olive oil
1 cup carrot coins (sliced carrots)
1 cup chopped celery
2 cloves garlic, minced
4 cups vegetable stock or broth
2 cups chopped fresh or canned tomatoes
Pinch or 10 grinds pepper
1 cup sliced zucchini
1 cup green beans, cut diagonally
1 cup cooked or canned beans (white, kidney, pinto, or garbanzo)
1⅓ cup cooked alphabet macaroni (¾ cup dry)
¼ cup fresh basil
Salt
¼ cup chopped parsley

In a large saucepan, sauté onions in oil over medium heat for 5 minutes or until beginning to brown. Add carrots, celery, and garlic, and sauté for another 5 minutes. Stir in stock, tomatoes, and pepper and bring to a boil. Cover, reduce heat, and simmer for 15 minutes. Add zucchini and beans. Cook another 5 to 7 minutes or until vegetables are tender-crisp. Add macaroni, basil, and salt and warm through. Garnish with parsley.

Per Cup: calories 104; protein 4 g; carbohydrate 18 g; fat 2 g; dietary fiber 5 g; sodium 144 mg
Percent calories from: protein 15 percent; fat 19 percent; carbohydrate 66 percent

Variations

- Substitute or add chopped cabbage, okra, or red or white potatoes, added at the same time as the tomatoes.
- Add chopped bell peppers, added along with the beans.
- Cut vegetables in ¼-inch dice instead of larger pieces.
- Replace fresh basil with 1 teaspoon each of dried basil, oregano, and celery seed, added at the same time as the tomatoes.
- Instead of wheat pasta, use corn or rice pasta.

Split Pea Soup with Veggie Dogs

Makes about 10 cups

Here's an appetizing soup to be enjoyed by children and adults alike at any time of the year, but it is especially inviting on cold or rainy days. It provides the minerals iron, zinc, and magnesium and is an excellent source of vitamin A, thiamin, and folate.

3 tablespoons olive oil
1 large onion, chopped
2 carrots, diced
2 cups yellow or green split peas, soaked overnight
8 cups water
Salt and pepper
8 veggie dogs, sliced
2 to 4 tablespoons fresh or frozen lemon juice

Heat the oil in a large soup pot. When hot, add the onion and carrots and sauté until soft. Drain the peas, rinse well, and add to the pot along with the water. Bring to a boil, reduce heat to low, cover and simmer, stirring occasionally, until peas have practically disintegrated, about 1½ to 2 hours. Season with salt and pepper, and simmer 30 minutes longer. Add sliced "hot dogs" and lemon juice and cook a few more minutes. Serve hot.

Per Cup: calories 229; protein 19 g; carbohydrate 29 g; fat 5 g; dietary fiber 12 g; sodium 289 mg
Percent calories from: protein 33 percent; fat 18 percent; carbohydrate 48 percent

Red Lentil Soup

Makes about 8 cups

This soup is very simple—but scrumptious! Red lentils take far less time to cook than green, gray, or brown lentils and provide an extremely low-fat source of protein.

7 cups water
2½ cups dried red lentils, rinsed
1 large onion, finely chopped
2 to 4 tablespoons fresh or frozen lemon juice
1 teaspoon ground cumin
Salt and pepper

Combine the water, lentils, and onion in a large soup pot and bring to a boil. Reduce heat, partially cover, and simmer until the lentils have disintegrated, about 30 to 60 minutes. Stir in the lemon juice, cumin, salt, and pepper.

Per Cup: calories 199; protein 14 g; carbohydrate 36 g; fat 0.1 g; dietary fiber 9 g; sodium 26 mg
Percent calories from: protein 28 percent; fat 0 percent; carbohydrate 72 percent

Variation
Add 2 chopped tomatoes just before serving.

Cheeze Please Soup

Makes 5 cups

This healthful dairy-free soup satisfies even the deepest cheese urges and will fool the most discriminating palate. It is low in fat, but its luscious texture and incredibly rich flavor make this hard to believe. Made with Red Star Vegetarian Support Formula nutritional yeast, a cup of this soup provides your day's supply of vitamin B_{12}, plus plenty of other B vitamins and zinc. (From *The Uncheese Cookbook*, by Joanne Stepaniak.)

1 medium potato, peeled and coarsely chopped
1 medium carrot, peeled and coarsely chopped
1 medium onion, coarsely chopped
1 cup water
1½ cups silken tofu, crumbled (12 ounces)
½ cup nutritional yeast flakes
2 tablespoons fresh or frozen lemon juice
1¼ teaspoons salt
1 teaspoon onion powder or granules
¼ teaspoon garlic powder or granules
1 cup fortified nondairy milk

Combine the potato, carrot, onion, and water in a large soup pot and bring to a boil. Reduce heat, cover, and simmer, stirring once or twice, until vegetables are tender.

Combine the remaining ingredients, except the milk, in a large bowl. Mix well, and stir into the cooked vegetables. Puree this mixture in batches in a blender. Process until completely smooth. Pour the blended mixture into a clean, large bowl or soup pot and add each blended batch to it as it is finished. Stir the milk into the blended soup and warm over low heat until hot.

Per Cup[*]: calories 139; protein 12 g; carbohydrate 17 g; fat 3 g; dietary fiber 4 g; sodium 619 mg
Percent calories from: protein 33 percent; fat 21 percent; carbohydrate 46 percent

*Nutritional analysis done using fortified soymilk.

Creamy Butternut Squash Soup

Makes about 14 cups

This satisfying, golden soup has a delicate, natural sweetness and is packed with protective antioxidants. Use soymilk for an effortless protein boost.

      3½ pounds butternut squash (about 4 cups cubed)
      4 medium potatoes, peeled and cubed (about 4½ cups)
      10 cups fortified vanilla nondairy milk
      Salt and pepper

Peel squash, scrape away the seeds and fibers, and cut into cubes. Place in a large soup pot with the potatoes, milk, salt, and pepper. Bring to a boil, reduce heat to low, cover, and simmer until squash and potatoes are very soft, about 30 minutes. Mash the vegetables in the pot with a potato masher. Adjust the seasonings, if necessary, and simmer a few minutes longer. Serve hot.

Per Cup*: calories 47; protein 2g; carbohydrate 12g; fat 0g; dietary fiber 2g; sodium 2 mg
Percent calories from: protein 11 percent; fat 1 percent; carbohydrate 88 percent

*Nutritional analysis done using fortified vanilla soymilk.

Green Potato Soup

Makes about 8 cups

This nutritious, easy-to-make soup adds visual appeal whether as a first course for a St. Patrick's Day "Green Dinner" or any day just for the fun of it. (From *Vegan Deli*, by Joanne Stepaniak.)

> 2 tablespoons olive oil
> 1 large onion, coarsely chopped
> 1 teaspoon crushed garlic
> 6 cups water
> 4 large potatoes, peeled and chopped
> Salt and pepper
> 1 large bunch fresh parsley, washed, stems removed (about 2 ounces or
>   1½ cups, chopped)
> 1 to 1½ cups fortified nondairy milk, as needed

Heat oil in a large soup pot. Add onion and sauté until tender. Add garlic and sauté for 1 minute. Stir in water, potatoes, salt, and pepper, and bring to a boil. Reduce heat, cover, and simmer until the potatoes are tender and starting to fall apart, about 45 minutes. Remove from heat and puree in batches in a blender along with the parsley. Return to the pot and add enough milk to thin to your liking. Heat through, stirring often, but do not boil. Serve hot.

Per Cup*: calories 129; protein 3 g; carbohydrate 21 g; fat 4 g; dietary fiber 2 g; sodium 18 mg
Percent calories from: protein 10 percent; fat 28 percent; carbohydrate 62 percent

*Nutritional analysis done using fortified soymilk.

DRESSINGS, DIPS, AND SAUCES

Sesame Tahini Salad Dressing

Makes 1⅓ cups

This dressing is traditionally used with falafels. However, it will soon become a favorite on baked potatoes, salads, Veggie Rice Rolls (page 298), steamed broccoli, and other vegetables. You may prefer to replace half of the tahini with flaxseed oil. With a little less water, it makes a terrific dip.

½ cup sesame tahini
¼ cup fresh or frozen lemon juice
1 teaspoon Dijon mustard or other mustard
1 clove garlic, chopped
2 tablespoons tamari or Bragg Liquid Aminos
¼ teaspoon pepper (or to taste)
½ cup water

Place all ingredients except water in a blender and blend until smooth. Add water and blend. This dressing may be kept in a jar, refrigerated, for several weeks.

Per 2 Tablespoons: calories 69; protein 2 g; carbohydrate 3 g; fat 6 g; dietary fiber 0.6 g; sodium 198 mg
Percent calories from: protein 12 percent; fat 71 percent; carbohydrate 17 percent

Liquid Gold Dressing

Makes 2 cups (4 cups doubled)

This dressing is named "Liquid Gold" for reasons beyond its color. Because of the flaxseed oil, 2 tablespoons of the dressing provide 3.8 grams of omega-3 fatty acids, about double the amount (2 grams) needed by growing children and enough to meet the daily needs of teens and adults. Using the higher amount of Red Star Vegetarian Support Formula nutritional yeast ($\frac{1}{2}$ cup per single batch), you'll also meet the child's daily requirement for vitamin B_{12} and 80 percent of the B_{12} needed by an adult or teen. It's packed with riboflavin and other B vitamins, too. Luckily, it's so tasty that it's a pleasure to use it on a daily basis, on salads, baked potatoes, rice, steamed broccoli, and other veggies. Finely ground psyllium or flaxseed is not essential; however, it imparts an even creamier consistency.

Single Batch		Double Batch
½ cup	flaxseed oil	1 cup
½ cup	water	1 cup
⅓ cup	fresh or frozen lemon juice	⅔ cup
2 tablespoons	balsamic or raspberry vinegar	¼ cup
¼ cup	Bragg Liquid Aminos or tamari	½ cup
¼ to ½ cup	nutritional yeast powder or flakes	½ to 1 cup
2 teaspoons	Dijon mustard	4 teaspoons
1 teaspoon	ground cumin	2 teaspoons
½ tablespoon	ground psyllium or flaxseed (optional)	1 tablespoon

Place all ingredients in a blender and blend until smooth. Dressing can be kept in a jar with lid, refrigerated, for two weeks.

Per 2 Tablespoons: calories 72; protein 1 g; carbohydrate 2 g; fat 7 g; dietary fiber 0.4 g; sodium 180 mg
Percent calories from: protein 7 percent; fat 85 percent; carbohydrate 8 percent

Lemonade Dressing

This deceptively simple dressing is dazzling in taste and incredibly versatile. Children love it because it is mild and sweet. You'll love it because it is quick and easy. Try it on tender lettuce, vegetables, and especially on fruit salads. Because it is fat free, it's perfect for dishes with rich ingredients, such as nuts or avocado. Good sweetener choices are agave nectar, brown rice syrup, and pure maple syrup. You also can use frozen fruit juice concentrate as the sweetener to create a delightful fruity taste. This recipe is a snap to double, triple, or quadruple!

> ¼ cup fresh or frozen lemon juice
> 2 to 4 tablespoons liquid sweetener of your choice

In a small bowl, whisk together the lemon juice and sweetener until emulsified.

Per 2 Tablespoons: calories 40; protein 0.1 g; carbohydrate 11 g; fat 0 g; dietary fiber 0.1 g; sodium 1 mg
Percent calories from: protein 1 percent; fat 0 percent; carbohydrate 99 percent

Tossed Vinaigrette

This dressing is made directly in the bowl on top of the salad. It's the easiest way to dress a salad to suit your family's taste.

> Virgin olive oil
> Wine vinegar
> Lemon juice (fresh or frozen)
> Salt and pepper
> Optional seasonings (fresh or dried herbs, crushed garlic)

Sprinkle a little oil over the salad. Start with 1 or 2 tablespoons, depending on the size of the salad. Toss until everything is very lightly coated. Sprinkle on the vinegar and a little lemon juice, a pinch of salt, and pepper to taste. If you like, add a light shower of fresh or dried herbs and crushed garlic. Toss well so everything is evenly distributed. If done properly, there should be no puddle in the bottom of the bowl. Taste a piece of lettuce and adjust seasonings, if necessary.

Beets-All Salad Dressing

Makes 2½ cups

Children like bright colors and are attracted to this nutritious dressing. If you omit the second half cup of water, this makes a great dip for veggies. Here's a tip to simplify peeling beets. First, steam or boil the beet until it is soft, then cool it immediately by placing it in cold water. The skin slips off in your hand. If you prefer, drained, canned beets may be used as an alternative to fresh.

½ cup water
½ cup raw sunflower seeds
1½ teaspoons fresh oregano (or ½ teaspoon dried)
1½ teaspoons fresh thyme (or ½ teaspoon dried)
1½ teaspoons fresh basil (or ½ teaspoon dried)
3 tablespoons tamari or Bragg Liquid Aminos
3 tablespoons fresh or frozen lemon juice
¼ cup olive oil or flaxseed oil
1 boiled, peeled beet, chopped (about ¾ to 1 cup)
½ cup water

Blend ½ cup water and the sunflower seeds until smooth. Add herbs, tamari, lemon juice, oil, and beet, and blend until smooth. Blend in remaining ½ cup water. More water may be added if too thick.

Per 2 Tablespoons: calories 49; protein 1 g; carbohydrate 1 g; fat 5 g; dietary fiber 0.5 g; sodium 153 mg
Percent calories from: protein 9 percent; fat 81 percent; carbohydrate 10 percent

Variations
- Replace beet with a chopped raw (or cooked) carrot to create a flavorful, sandy-golden–colored dressing.
- For a soy-free version, replace the tamari with 3 tablespoons balsamic vinegar and add ¾ teaspoon salt.

Nutti Sauce

This delectable sauce is a terrific way to inspire children to eat their veggies. Serve it as a dipping sauce for lightly steamed vegetables; it's also great over pasta, whole grains, salad, or cooked greens.

> ½ cup peanut butter or almond butter
> ¼ cup balsamic vinegar
> ¼ cup ketchup
> ½ cup water, as needed

Cream together nut butter, vinegar, and ketchup. When well blended, whisk in just enough water to create a pourable sauce. Store leftovers in the refrigerator for three to five days. Thin with additional water before serving, if necessary.

Per 2 Tablespoons: calories 72; protein 3 g; carbohydrate 4 g; fat 5 g; dietary fiber 1 g; sodium 112 mg
Percent calories from: protein 14 percent; fat 64 percent; carbohydrate 22 percent

Tangy Dijon Apricot Sauce

Makes ⅓ cup

This delightful, speedy recipe is scrumptious with tofu sticks, steamed veggies, and Veggie Rice Rolls (page 298) as a dipping sauce. Kid-tested and approved!

> 3 tablespoons fruit-sweetened apricot jam
> 1 tablespoon Dijon mustard
> 1 tablespoon balsamic vinegar

In a small bowl, stir together all ingredients until well combined. Let rest for 10 to 15 minutes before serving, if time permits, to allow flavors to blend.

Per 2 Tablespoons: calories 57; protein 0.2 g; carbohydrate 14 g; fat 0.1 g; dietary fiber 0.2 g; sodium 129 mg
Percent calories from: protein 1 percent; fat 1 percent; carbohydrate 98 percent

Ranch-Style Dressing and Dip

Makes about 2 cups

An irresistible dipping sauce for raw or steamed veggies, as well as a luscious salad dressing and topping for baked potatoes.

1½ cups silken tofu, crumbled (12 ounces)

¼ cup virgin olive oil

¼ cup fresh or frozen lemon juice

¼ cup water

2 to 4 tablespoons minced onion

2 teaspoons dried tarragon

1 teaspoon dried dillweed

½ to 1 teaspoon crushed garlic

½ teaspoon salt

¼ teaspoon pepper

Combine all ingredients in a blender and process until smooth and creamy.

Per 2 Tablespoons: calories 48; protein 2 g; carbohydrate 1 g; fat 4 g; dietary fiber 0.1 g; sodium 81 mg
Percent calories from: protein 17 percent; fat 77 percent; carbohydrate 10 percent

Nippy Flax Dressing

This thick dressing can be made with a combination of flax and olive oils, or with either alone. Made entirely with flaxseed oil, a tablespoon provides more than 5 grams of omega-3 fatty acids. You may adjust seasonings a little by adding another dash of Tabasco or using a little less.

¾ cup flaxseed oil, or a combination of flaxseed oil and olive oil
¼ cup balsamic vinegar
2 tablespoons tamari
1 teaspoon Dijon mustard
6 drops Tabasco sauce
1 tablespoon fresh basil, packed
½ teaspoon dry oregano (or 1½ teaspoons fresh)
1 teaspoon sweetener (such as rice syrup or maple syrup)

Place all ingredients in a blender and blend until smooth. Store refrigerated in a sealed jar for up to a week.

Per Tablespoon: calories 94; protein 0 g; carbohydrate 1 g; fat 10 g; dietary fiber 0 g; sodium 135 mg
Percent calories from: protein 1 percent; fat 94 percent; carbohydrate 5 percent

SALADS

Build Your Bones Salad

Makes 6 cups (with broccoli, 7 cups)

When using kale in a salad, first place each leaf on a cutting board, fold the leaf in half lengthwise, and remove the stem, using a knife. Then slice the leafy portion matchstick thin. A 2-cup portion of this salad, with a little Sesame Tahini Salad Dressing (page 289), provides about as much calcium as a half cup of milk or fortified soymilk. As a bonus, however, the calcium present in these greens is about twice as well absorbed as that in milk. Folate, a vitamin needed for cell division, is present in substantial amounts in greens.

> 2 cups kale or collards, stem removed and thinly sliced
> 2 cups chopped napa (Chinese) cabbage
> 2 cups torn romaine lettuce
> 1 cup small broccoli florets (optional)
> ½ cup grated carrot

In a large bowl, toss together all ingredients until well combined.

Per Cup: calories 21; protein 2 g; carbohydrate 4 g; fat 0.3 g; dietary fiber 1 g; sodium 29 mg
Percent calories from: protein 25 percent; fat 9 percent; carbohydrate 66 percent

Five-Day Salad

Makes 20 cups

Would your family eat more salad if it were instantly available? A good trick is to assemble a huge salad every four or five days. Then, it's always ready when you are. Preparation is a pleasant activity when shared by two people or when listening to a favorite radio program. Removing excess moisture makes the salad last longer, so use a salad spinner, shake the lettuce leaves, or pat them dry. Toss the salad in a large container, such as a 14-inch diameter metal bowl. Store it in a couple of large, well-sealed containers (such as Tupperware), and it will last for four or five days.

> 5 large leaves kale (about 3 cups chopped)
> 8 large leaves romaine lettuce (about 4 cups chopped)
> 5 leaves napa (Chinese) cabbage (about 3 cups chopped)
> ¼ head red cabbage (about 2 cups chopped)
> 1 big stalk broccoli (about 2 cups chopped)
> ½ small head cauliflower (about 2 cups chopped)
> 3 to 4 carrots (about 3 cups chopped)
> 1 sweet red bell pepper (about 1 cup chopped)

Remove stem from kale and chop matchstick thin. Tear or cut lettuce into bite-size pieces. Cut napa cabbage leaves in half lengthwise, and slice into ¼-inch strips. Slice red cabbage into thin slices. Cut broccoli and cauliflower into bite-size florets. (Stem of broccoli can be peeled and diced.) Slice carrots and cut red bell pepper into ¼-inch strips. Toss all in bowl.

Per Cup: calories 23; protein 1 g; carbohydrate 5 g; fat 0.2 g; dietary fiber 2 g; sodium 19 mg
Percent calories from: protein 20 percent; fat 7 percent; carbohydrate 73 percent

Veggie Rice Roll

Makes 1 roll (multiply as needed)

This is one way to get children of any age to enjoy salad. Creating the rolls is great fun as a shared activity just before dinner (don't mind if anyone nibbles) or even at a birthday party. Older children can also prepare the filling materials, so set up one with a grater, carrot, and plate; another with the cucumber, paring knife, and cutting board; and so on. When the fillings are prepared and set out, everyone can make his or her own roll. Sauce can be spread inside the roll and also put in small bowls for dipping. You may provide just one sauce—such as barbecue sauce, plum sauce, Nutti Sauce (page 293), Sesame Tahini Salad Dressing (page 289), Tangy Dijon Apricot Sauce (page 294), or Ranch-Style Dressing (page 295)—or you may offer several choices.

> 1 rice paper sheet or spring roll skin (about 8½-inches)
> Warm water in large (e.g., 14-inch diameter) bowl
> ⅓ cup cooked brown rice
> 1 tablespoon sauce, or to taste
> 3 slices avocado
> 2 strips plain or marinated tofu
> 2 tablespoons grated carrot
> ¼ cup alfalfa sprouts or chopped lettuce

Dip rice paper sheet in water for 5 seconds, then place on a cutting board. Pat with dry cloth to absorb excess water. Place rice on center of paper, then cover with sauce, avocado, tofu, carrot, and sprouts. Fold right and left margins of rice paper toward the center. Then fold up the bottom margin. Fold top margin down, using a bit of pressure to seal the roll.

Per Roll, Without Dipping Sauce: calories 230; protein 11 g; carbohydrate 30 g; fat 8 g; dietary fiber 4 g; sodium 142 mg
Percent calories from: protein 18 percent; fat 31 percent; carbohydrate 51 percent

Warm Vinaigrette Potato Salad

Makes about 6 cups

This light, uncomplicated potato salad is a pleasant change from mayonnaise-laden versions. It's a good choice to make when schedules are hectic and appetites are soaring. For finicky children, the onions and parsley may be omitted. Serve this in traditional barbecue fashion as a side dish with baked beans and veggie dogs or veggie burgers on buns, or try it Southern-style alongside a large mound of steamed kale or collard greens mixed with black-eyed peas.

6 medium thin-skinned potatoes (red, white, or gold)
¼ to ⅓ cup virgin olive oil
2 tablespoons wine vinegar
Salt and pepper
½ cup minced red onion, or 6 thinly sliced scallions
3 tablespoons minced fresh parsley

Cut potatoes into cubes or bite-size chunks, making about 6 cups. Steam until tender, then transfer to a large bowl. For the dressing, whisk together oil, vinegar, salt, and pepper. Pour over the warm potatoes. Add onion or scallions and parsley. Mix gently. Serve warm.

Per Cup: calories 190; protein 4 g; carbohydrate 27 g; fat 9 g; dietary fiber 3 g; sodium 2 mg
Percent calories from: protein 8 percent; fat 40 percent; carbohydrate 52 percent

Tricolor Quinoa-Corn Salad

Makes about 6 cups

Quinoa is a high-protein, low-allergenic, gluten-free grain that is mild in flavor and very adaptable. It is important to rinse it thoroughly before using in order to remove its bitter coating called *saponin*, which is a naturally occurring insect repellent. Because the grain is so small, place it in a fine mesh strainer and then rinse it well under running water while stirring with your fingers.

2 cups water
1 cup quinoa, rinsed well and drained
½ teaspoon salt
2 cups cooked corn kernels
1 sweet red bell pepper, cut into small dice
½ cup thinly sliced scallions
3 to 4 tablespoons virgin olive oil
3 tablespoons fresh or frozen lemon juice
2 teaspoons Dijon mustard
Salt and pepper

In a heavy saucepot, bring water to a boil over high heat. Stir in quinoa and salt, cover, and reduce heat to low. Cook for 15 minutes. Remove from heat and let rest, covered, for 5 minutes. Fluff with a fork and transfer to a large bowl. Stir in corn, bell pepper, and scallions. In a small bowl, whisk together olive oil, lemon juice, and mustard. Pour over the quinoa and vegetables and toss gently. Season with salt and pepper to taste. Serve warm or thoroughly chilled.

Variation

Use half olive oil and half flaxseed oil.

Per Cup: calories 144; protein 3 g; carbohydrate 19 g; fat 7 g; dietary fiber 2 g; sodium 244 mg
Percent calories from: protein 8 percent; fat 44 percent; carbohydrate 48 percent

Rainbow Rice and Bean Salad

This tantalizing, eye-appealing, veggie-packed salad is a meal in itself and makes enough for a crowd. If you have a small family, transfer leftovers to a large, well-sealed container, and store in the refrigerator for four or five days.

> 2 cups water
> 1 cup brown rice, rinsed and drained
> ½ teaspoon salt
> 3 medium carrots, finely chopped or grated
> 2 cups cooked black beans, drained
> 1 medium zucchini, cut into small dice
> 1 cup cooked or raw fresh corn
> ½ to 1 cup minced fresh herbs, packed (use basil, cilantro, dill, or parsley)
> ⅓ cup oil-packed sun-dried tomatoes
> 3 to 4 tablespoons virgin olive oil
> 2 to 3 tablespoons fresh or frozen lemon juice or wine vinegar
> Salt and pepper

In a heavy saucepot, bring water to a boil over high heat. Add rice and salt, cover, and reduce heat to low. Cook undisturbed for 45 minutes. Remove from heat and let rest, covered, for 10 minutes. Fluff with a fork and transfer to a large bowl. Add remaining ingredients, and toss gently. Season with salt and pepper to taste. Serve warm or thoroughly chilled.

Per Cup: calories 265; protein 8 g; carbohydrate 43 g; fat 8 g; dietary fiber 7 g; sodium 196 mg
Percent calories from: protein 12 percent; fat 25 percent; carbohydrate 63 percent

Raw-Raw Vegetable Platter

Do your children say "No!" to veggies? That's often the case when it comes to cooked vegetables served at mealtime. Give up the "Don't eat between meals" rule, and use this approach that works in homes across North America. Simply cut up a big plateful of any veggies listed below, and set it on a kitchen counter before dinner. Don't say a word about it. As everyone comes by to see what's for supper, you'll find the pile will vanish. Your family will get all those vitamins, antioxidants, phytochemicals, and fiber without a complaint. Serve the raw veggie platter as an after-school snack, at mealtimes, as a TV snack, or a pretty party platter. You may want to combine it with one of the dips or spreads in the previous section.

- asparagus tips
- broccoli florets
- carrot sticks
- cauliflower florets
- celery sticks
- cherry tomatoes
- cucumber discs
- green peas in pods
- red, yellow, orange, and green pepper strips
- snow pea pods
- zucchini strips or coins

For the more adventurous, here are a few others:
- jicama sticks
- parsnip sticks
- turnip strips
- mushrooms, whole or sliced
- green onion strips

Per Cup: calories 37; protein 2 g; carbohydrate 8 g; fat 0.2 g; dietary fiber 3 g; sodium 20 mg
Percent calories from: protein 19 percent; fat 5 percent; carbohydrate 76 percent

Warm Sesame Noodles

Makes about 10 cups

Children, teens, and adults often see the world quite differently, but one thing they almost always agree on is this irresistible noodle salad. Although it is best served warm or at room temperature, chilled leftovers make an awesome packed lunch or picnic meal. Toasted sesame oil has a lovely flavor and aroma; for economy you may use a combination of regular sesame oil and the toasted oil.

> 1 pound dry whole-wheat, spelt, or brown rice noodles
>   (linguini, fettuccine, or spaghetti)
> 3 tablespoons toasted sesame oil
> ½ pound snow peas, trimmed
> ½ cup sesame tahini
> 2 tablespoons balsamic vinegar
> 1 teaspoon crushed garlic
> 1 teaspoon sweetener of your choice
> Salt and cayenne pepper (optional)
> ¼ cup water, more or less as needed
> 1 English cucumber, diced or cut into half-moons
> 2 scallions, thinly sliced

Cook noodles in boiling water until al dente. Drain in a colander, refresh under cold running water, and drain again. Transfer to a large bowl and toss with sesame oil (this will help keep the noodles from sticking together). While pasta cooks, blanch snow peas in boiling water for 1 minute. Drain, cool, and cut into thirds or quarters. Set aside. In a medium bowl, cream together tahini, vinegar, garlic, sweetener, salt, and cayenne pepper to taste, if using. Beating with a fork, add just enough water to make a thick but pourable sauce. Pour over cooked noodles, add reserved snow peas, cucumber, and scallions, and toss gently but thoroughly. Adjust seasonings, if necessary. Serve warm or at room temperature.

Per Cup: calories 283; protein 10 g; carbohydrate 40 g; fat 11 g; dietary fiber 7 g; sodium 11 mg
Percent calories from: protein 13 percent; fat 33 percent; carbohydrate 54 percent

Salad of Chickpeas, Tomatoes, and Walnuts

This quick and wholesome salad first appeared in *Vegan Deli,* by Joanne Stepaniak. It is a tribute to the amazing flavor combinations we can create with the most simple ingredients.

> 2 cups drained, cooked chickpeas
> 1 medium tomato, chopped
> ¼ cup walnuts, broken into pieces
> ¼ cup raisins
> ¼ cup minced fresh parsley
> 2 tablespoons fresh or frozen lemon juice
> 1 tablespoon olive oil
> Salt and pepper

Combine all ingredients in a large bowl. Toss to mix well. Adjust seasonings, if necessary.

Per Cup: calories 283; protein 10 g; carbohydrate 39 g; fat 11 g; dietary fiber 9 g; sodium 14 mg
Percent calories from: protein 14 percent; fat 34 percent; carbohydrate 52 percent

Simple Sprouting

Sprouts are packed with vitamins, antioxidants, and other protective phytochemicals. Sprouting increases the availability of zinc and other minerals in legumes, grains, nuts, and seeds. Sprouting is an easy way to get fresh foods during northern winters or where little produce is available. They add texture and flavor to salads, sandwiches, and stir-fry. Sprout care is so simple that it may become a favorite occupation of young children.

Basic care involves keeping sprouts moist while providing drainage and air circulation. Sprouts are healthiest when rinsed often and drained well, so set them on a kitchen countertop near a sink. In warm weather, sprouts mature more quickly and require more frequent rinsing to keep them cool and free of mold or bacterial growth. Hot direct sunlight can "cook" them, so shade is better. Alfalfa sprouts and sunflower greens require some light in order to become green; for these a balance of sun and shade works well.

Your basic equipment is wide-neck quart jars, inexpensive sprouting lids (available at many health food stores), and a tray or bowl in which you will set the jar, upside down and at an angle. You also may use sprout bags or an automatic sprout-growing tray. With any of these, follow the same general method summarized in Table 11.2 on page 307 for a few favorite seeds or lentils.

After this basic introduction, you may wish to graduate to more advanced sprouting. We'd suggest you get a good sprouting guide, such as *The Sprouting Book*, by Ann Wigmore, Avery Publishers, New York, 1986.

TABLE 11.2

Sprouting Summary

In a jar, soak lentils or seeds for the time specified. Then drain, rinse, and set jar upside down and at a 45° angle (the angle allows air circulation). Rinse sprouts twice a day by filling the jar with water and allowing it to overflow. Then drain and again set at 45° angle. At harvest, rinse (with alfalfa sprouts, rinse off seed hulls), drain, place in a clean glass jar or plastic bag, and refrigerate. Sprouts will last up to a week.

Legume or Seed	Soaking Time, Hours	Amount Dry, for Quart Jar	Length at Harvest, Inches	Days Until Ready	Tips and Comments
Lentils	12	½ cup	¼ to ¾	3–5	Try regular (green, brown, or gray) lentils and the smaller French lentils. Grow to both short and longer lengths.
Mung beans	12	¼ cup	1½	3–5	The long mung bean sprouts of Chinese cooking are grown away from light and under a little pressure; here we give just the basic sprouting method.
Alfalfa seeds	4–6	2 tbsp.	1 to 1½	4–6	To develop chlorophyll and make sprouts green, place in light 1 to 2 days before harvest.
Unhulled Sunflower seeds	12	¾ cup	5–8	7	After a week, harvest these delicious greens with scissors or a sharp knife.

To make sunflower greens (below), seeds that are still in their hulls are first soaked for 12 hours, left to drain for another 12 hours, rinsed, and then scattered on top of an inch of topsoil on a tray. A temperature of 65–75°F is best. The sprouting seeds are sprinkled with water daily for a week. To exclude light for the first 3 days, the tray is covered with paper or placed in a dark cupboard. For days 4 through 7, the tray is moved to an area with indirect light.

ENTRÉES

African Stew

Makes 6 cups

This nutrition-packed stew is an excellent source of iron, copper, magnesium, manganese, potassium, folate, niacin, thiamin, vitamins A, B_6, and C, plus it provides selenium, zinc, and vitamin E. Its best feature, however, is that children love the creamy, peanut-butter–based sauce, and the whole family will enjoy the combination of flavors. Vegetable stock can be made easily using stock cubes or powder. (From *Cooking Vegetarian*, by Vesanto Melina and Joseph Forest.)

> 1 onion, chopped
> 1 tablespoon olive oil
> 4 cups vegetable stock or water
> 2 cups peeled, diced sweet potatoes or yams
> 1 cup cooked or canned chickpeas
> 1 cup brown rice, dry
> ¼ teaspoon salt (optional)
> ¼ cup peanut butter
> 2 cups chopped collard greens or kale (stems removed)
> 2 tablespoons fresh or frozen lemon juice
> ½ teaspoon pepper
> Dash hot chili sauce or chipotle sauce (optional)

In a large saucepan over medium heat, sauté onion in oil for 5 minutes or until beginning to brown. Add stock, sweet potatoes, chickpeas, rice, and salt (if using); bring to a boil, then lower heat and simmer for 45 minutes. In a small bowl, blend peanut butter and ½ cup of hot liquid from stew to make a smooth paste. Stir peanut butter mixture into stew along with kale and cook for 5 minutes. Stir in lemon juice and pepper, and add hot sauce to taste (if using). Serve over rice or with fresh bread or rolls.

Per Cup: calories 309; protein 9 g; carbohydrate 49 g; fat 10g; dietary fiber 6 g; sodium 75 mg
Percent calories from: protein 12 percent; fat 27 percent; carbohydrate 61 percent

Grandma's Noodles

Makes 6 cups

This noodle dish is the inspiration of grandmother Shirley Hunting, whose family includes three generations of vegans. Preschoolers often prefer bland food, and this has proven to be a creamy, soothing favorite for lunch and supper. Even when very young, children enjoy the process of adding "sprinkles."

8 ounces (½ pound) noodles (parsley-garlic flavored or plain)
15 fluid ounces nondairy creamy corn soup
10 ounces frozen corn
1 tablespoon dried onion flakes
2 tablespoons nutritional yeast flakes

Optional Garnishes or Sprinkles

- additional nutritional yeast flakes
- finely chopped vegetables (such as green pepper, tomatoes, or parsley)

Cook noodles according to package directions or until tender. Meanwhile, place soup, corn, onion flakes, and 2 tablespoons nutritional yeast flakes in a blender and process until smooth. In a saucepan, warm blended corn soup mixture. Drain cooked noodles and add noodles to corn soup. If there's a delay in adding the noodles to the soup mixture, add a little olive oil to noodles to keep them from sticking together. Serve with optional garnishes that can be sprinkled over each serving to taste.

Per Cup: calories 223; protein 9 g; carbohydrate 44 g; fat 2 g; dietary fiber 3 g; sodium 27 mg
Percent calories from: protein 15 percent; fat 8 percent; carbohydrate 77 percent

Cheez-A-Roni

Most children are especially fond of noodles, and elbow macaroni in a creamy, cheesy-tasting sauce always seems to top the list of their favorites. This one has juicy tomato chunks in it and a delicious high-protein sauce. No one will guess it's made from beans, which makes it a terrific way to get wholesome food into picky eaters! If anyone in your house is sensitive to wheat or gluten, this recipe can be adapted easily to suit his or her needs. Just use rice or corn pasta instead of wheat macaroni.

> 2 tablespoons olive or safflower oil
> 1 large onion, finely chopped
> 1 teaspoon crushed garlic
> 28-ounce can diced tomatoes, undrained
> 1 recipe (2 cups) Gee Whiz Spread (page 273)
> 2 to 3 tablespoons nutritional yeast flakes
> 1 teaspoon salt, or to taste
> ¼ to ½ teaspoon pepper
> Large pinch cayenne pepper (optional)
> 3 cups (12 ounces) dry macaroni or other tube pasta (such as penne)

Heat oil in a very large saucepan over medium-high heat. When hot, add onion and sauté until tender and medium brown (adjust heat as necessary so onion doesn't burn). Stir in garlic and cook for 1 minute longer. Add undrained tomatoes and stir. Then stir in the prepared Gee Whiz Spread, nutritional yeast flakes, salt, pepper, and cayenne (if using), and mix well. Simmer gently, stirring often, for about 10 to 15 minutes. Meanwhile, cook pasta according to package directions. Drain well. Stir hot pasta into simmering sauce and combine gently but thoroughly.

Tip

As this dish cools, or if there are leftovers stored in the refrigerator, the macaroni will absorb much of the moisture from the sauce. If you want to make the mixture more saucy, add a little tomato juice, plain nondairy milk, water, or 1 or 2 chopped, fresh tomatoes when you reheat it.

Per Cup: calories 326; protein 14 g; carbohydrate 52 g; fat 8 g; dietary fiber 9 g; sodium 595 mg
Percent calories from: protein 17 percent; fat 21 percent; carbohydrate 62 percent

Chili with Veggie Wieners

Makes 8 cups

Vitamin C–rich tomato, onion, and bell peppers help us to absorb the iron from the beans and veggie wieners. One cup of this recipe provides 14 grams of protein and 3 milligrams of iron.

1 cup diced onion (or 1 small onion, diced)
1 tablespoon olive oil
1 cup each of diced carrot, celery, green pepper
2 cloves garlic, minced (½ teaspoon crushed)
2 cups vegetable stock or water
2 cups cooked or canned pinto or kidney beans, drained
2 cups chopped fresh or canned tomatoes
¼ cup tomato paste
1 cup corn
1 teaspoon each of ground cumin, dried basil, chili powder
¼ teaspoon pepper
6 veggie wieners, cut in eighths
Salt to taste

In a saucepan over medium heat, sauté onion in oil until beginning to brown, then add carrot, celery, green pepper, and garlic, and heat for another 5 minutes, stirring occasionally. Stir in stock, beans, tomatoes, tomato paste, corn, cumin, basil, chili powder, and pepper. Bring to a boil, then reduce heat, cover, and simmer 15 minutes. Add veggie wieners and salt, cook another 5 minutes, and then serve over brown rice, over a sliced Kaiser bun, or with crusty rolls.

Per Cup: calories 180; protein 14 g; carbohydrate 27 g; fat 3 g; dietary fiber 8 g, sodium 302 mg
Percent calories from: protein 30 percent; fat 13 percent; carbohydrate 57 percent

Chilibean Topping

This chili-style sauce is chock-full of flavor and healthful protein. It makes a delightful topping for any kind of pasta or cooked grain. It also can be used to make open-face "sloppy joe" sandwiches using crusty rolls or soft buns. Best of all, it is ready to serve in under 15 minutes! (Adapted from *Table for Two,* by Joanne Stepaniak.) Note that canned tomatoes and tomato paste come with or without salt, so if you use salted versions, adjust added salt to taste.

28-ounce can whole tomatoes, with juice

15-ounce can red kidney or pinto beans, drained

2 green bell peppers, diced

¼ cup unsalted tomato paste

2 tablespoons mild chili powder

½ teaspoon salt (or to taste)

½ teaspoon ground cumin

½ teaspoon garlic powder

¼ cup water

2 tablespoons cornstarch

Place tomatoes and their juice in a 4-quart or larger saucepan. Break tomatoes apart with your hands or the side of a wooden spoon. Stir in beans, peppers, tomato paste, chili powder, salt, cumin, and garlic powder. Mix well. Bring to a boil, reduce heat, cover, and simmer 10 minutes, stirring occasionally. Combine water and cornstarch in a small cup. Stir until well dissolved. Stir into tomato-bean mixture. Cook, stirring constantly, until thickened and bubbly, then cook 1 minute longer. Serve at once.

Per Cup: calories 157; protein 7 g; carbohydrate 31 g; fat 1 g; dietary fiber 10 g; sodium 583 mg
Percent calories from: protein 18 percent; fat 7 percent; carbohydrate 75 percent

Pasta and Dogs

This dish is a favorite with children and adults alike. It tastes great, is nutritious, and is a snap to prepare, even at the last minute. The secret to its special flavor is browning the onions until they are very dark and caramelized.

> 2 tablespoons olive or safflower oil
> 2 cups finely chopped onions
> ½ cup tomato paste
> 1½ cups water
> 1½ tablespoons sweetener of your choice
> ½ cup water
> 2 tablespoons cornstarch
> 1 pound bow-tie pasta, cooked and drained
> 6 to 8 veggie dogs, cooked and sliced in ¼-inch rounds
> Salt and pepper

Heat oil in a large pot. When hot, add onions and sauté until dark brown and tender. Add tomato paste, 1½ cups water, and sweetener. Mix well. Combine ½ cup water and cornstarch in a small cup. Stir until well dissolved. Stir into onion mixture. Bring to a boil, stirring constantly. Reduce heat and cook until sauce is thickened, stirring constantly. Add cooked pasta and veggie dogs, and mix gently but thoroughly. Season with salt and pepper to taste. Serve hot.

Per Cup: calories 258; protein 17 g; carbohydrate 38 g; fat 4 g; dietary fiber 3 g; sodium 223 mg
Percent calories from: protein 27 percent; fat 13 percent; carbohydrate 60 percent

Protein-Rich Stir-Fry

Makes 3½ cups

The marinade that is used here for chickpeas, tofu, tempeh, seitan, or vegetarian "chicken" adds a sweet and gingery taste. If you and your children like plenty of ginger, use the higher amount. Some prefer almost no ginger, so adjust ginger and tamari in the marinade to suit your family's taste. Seitan is a product developed from wheat protein (gluten) by Chinese Buddhist monks five hundred years ago; it has a meat-like texture.

> 1½ cups cooked chickpeas, or cubed firm tofu, tempeh, seitan,
>   or vegetarian "chicken"
> 1 to 2 tablespoons olive or sesame oil
> 1 medium white, yellow, or red onion, thinly sliced
> 2 medium carrots, sliced diagonally
> 3 cups broccoli florets and peeled and sliced stems

Marinade

> 2½ tablespoons tamari
> ½ to 1 tablespoon peeled, finely minced ginger (or to taste)
> 1 tablespoon rice syrup or corn syrup

In a jar with lid or a bowl, combine marinade ingredients: tamari, ginger, and syrup. Add chickpeas, cubed tofu, tempeh, seitan, or vegetarian "chicken." Shake jar or stir bowl contents so pieces are covered with marinade. Allow mixture to marinate for at least ½ hour, shaking or stirring occasionally. Heat a wok or cast-iron skillet to high temperature. Add oil and sauté onion until golden brown (about 2 minutes). Add carrots and cook until just beginning to soften (about 2 minutes). Add marinated mixture and broccoli and cook until broccoli is just tender and everything is warmed through (about 2 minutes more). Serve over brown rice, noodles, or millet.

Per Cup: calories 221; protein 10 g; carbohydrate 35 g; fat 6 g; dietary fiber 9 g; sodium 762 mg
Percent calories from: protein 18 percent; fat 23 percent; carbohydrate 59 percent

Crispy Tofu Fingers

Makes 3 4-ounce servings, about 6 slices each

This recipe has had astounding success in turning people of all ages into tofu fans. These tofu fingers can be used as the high-protein part of a dinner, as appetizers, or in sandwiches. When you're invited for a meal with nonvegetarians and want to take along the ingredients for a well-accepted meat alternative, this simple recipe is a winner. Some people like tofu soft, others like it dry, so experiment a little. (From *Becoming Vegetarian*, by Vesanto Melina, Brenda Davis, and Victoria Harrison.)

2 tablespoons tamari
½ cup nutritional yeast flakes
1 teaspoon salt-free or regular Spike seasoning
12 ounces extrafirm or firm regular tofu, cut into ¼-inch slices
Olive oil to oil pan, as needed

Preheat a frying pan over medium heat. Pour the tamari into a soup bowl. In a second bowl, mix together the yeast flakes and seasoning. Dip the tofu slices first into the tamari and then into the seasoned yeast, coating both sides. Place oil in pan, then fry coated tofu, browning on one side (about 2 minutes), then turning to brown the other side (about 2 minutes).

Per ⅓ Recipe: calories 222; protein 21 g; carbohydrate 11 g; fat 12 g; dietary fiber 5 g; sodium 599 mg
Percent calories from: protein 35 percent; fat 47 percent; carbohydrate 18 percent

Seasoning Variations

Instead of Spike, try ginger, garlic, or curry seasoning.

Baked Version

Instead of frying, place coated tofu slices on a baking sheet misted with nonstick cooking spray (for easiest cleanup) or lightly wiped with oil. Bake at 350°F for 20 minutes.

Per ⅓ Recipe, Baked: calories 182; protein 21 g; carbohydrate 11 g; fat 8 g; dietary fiber 5 g; sodium 599 mg
Percent calories from: protein 43 percent; fat 35 percent; carbohydrate 22 percent

Simple Nori Rolls

Makes 24 or 48 pieces

Teens and younger children have great fun making nori rolls; for this reason we have given the larger batch size for use with a party crowd. Traditional Japanese sticky white rice holds the rolls together particularly well; however, brown rice also may be used. The rolls are made using a bamboo sushi mat that is just larger than the sheet of dried nori, a mild-tasting sea vegetable that is rich in healthful minerals. The mat helps keep pressure uniform during the rolling process and protects the nori from being torn. Bamboo mats, along with less familiar ingredients in this recipe, are available from Asian markets. Choose your favorites from the fillings and garnishes listed below. Wasabi is a hot horseradish that can make your eyes water; use just a tiny amount until you find out if you like it.

For four 8-inch rolls/24 pieces (6 slices per roll):
3 cups freshly cooked Japanese white sticky rice (sushi rice) or brown rice
4 sheets dry or toasted nori sea vegetable (see Note on next page)

For eight 8-inch rolls/48 pieces (6 slices per roll):
6 cups freshly cooked Japanese white sticky rice (sushi rice) or brown rice
8 sheets dry or toasted nori sea vegetable (see Note on next page)

Choose three or more of the following fillings:

For 4 Rolls		For 8 Rolls
1 cup	grated carrot	2 cups
4 ounces	marinated or plain tofu	8 ounces
½	avocado, thinly sliced into strips	1 whole
½	red pepper, sliced into thin strips	1 whole
4	long, ¼-inch-thick slices cucumber	8
3 tablespoons	steamed spinach	⅓ cup
3 tablespoons	vegan mayonnaise	⅓ cup
2 tablespoons	thinly sliced pickled ginger	¼ cup
2 tablespoons	sesame seed sprinkles or gomasio	¼ cup

Optional Garnishes

        Thinly sliced pickled ginger
        Sesame seed sprinkles or gomasio
        Tamari (for dipping)
        Wasabi horseradish powder mixed with a little water to form a
            thick paste

Set out all ingredients in bowls or on small plates on the counter or table, along with a bowl of water. Place a sheet of nori on a bamboo sushi mat (make sure the bamboo "rungs" run horizontally). Place ¾ cup of rice on the nori and spread rice evenly to the right and left edges, and to the bottom edge closest to you, leaving a 1-inch strip of nori free of rice at the top of the nori sheet (the edge farthest from you). In a thin strip along the bottom edge of the nori, from left to right, layer a portion of the fillings you have selected (carrot, tofu, avocado, red pepper, cucumber, spinach, mayonnaise, ginger, and/or sesame seeds). Dip your finger into the bowl of water and moisten the top edge of the nori sheet that is free of rice. This wet edge will be used to "glue" the finished roll. Using both hands and firm pressure, lift the edge of the bamboo mat that is closest to you. Roll until nori roll is formed into a thick log, pressing edge to seal the roll closed. Repeat to assemble the other rolls.

    Place each roll on a cutting board, seam side down; using a sharp serrated knife, cut each into 6 equal pieces. Arrange nori roll pieces on a platter, along with optional garnishes. Serve tamari in a small bowl for dipping.

Note

Toasting makes nori sweeter. If your nori sheets do not come pretoasted (this should be stated on the package), you can toast them yourself. (This step is optional.) Just wave each sheet over a flame for a few seconds until it changes to a deep green color. Be careful not to get it too close to the flame or it will burn. The nori will soften and become pliable when the hot rice is spread on it.

Per 8-Inch Roll*: calories 185; protein 8 g; carbohydrate 33 g; fat 3 g; dietary fiber 3 g; sodium 189 mg
Percent calories from: protein 17 percent; fat 13 percent; carbohydrate 70 percent

*Nutritional analysis done with carrot, tofu, and red pepper filling.

Colorful Kabobs

Makes 8 to 9 10-inch kabobs

Kabobs are colorful, tasty, and lots of fun to make. Although they're especially welcome at a barbecue, you also can make them any time you like by browning them under the broiler. They can be served on a bed of rice or in a pita pocket. Extrafirm tofu has been pressed to remove much of the water; it holds its shape well on the 10-inch metal or bamboo skewer. Cut all the veggies into pieces about ¾ to 1 inch across, and cut the tofu into slightly smaller pieces, about ½ inch. Leftover marinade can be served on kabobs or rice.

> ½ pound extrafirm tofu cut in ½-inch pieces
> 16 to 18 small mushrooms or 1 cup pieces (1½ ounces)
> ½ red, green, or yellow bell pepper, cut in ¾- to 1-inch slices
> 1 small zucchini, cut in slices ¼-inch thick or ¾-inch cubes
> ½ medium red or white onion, cut in ¾-inch pieces
> 8 to 9 small cherry tomatoes

Sweet and Tangy Marinade

Makes about ½ cup

> ¼ cup ketchup
> 2 tablespoons balsamic vinegar
> 2 tablespoons water
> 2 teaspoons olive oil
> ¼ to ½ teaspoon crushed garlic

Prepare marinade by stirring together ingredients in a jar with a tight-fitting lid. Add tofu, put on lid, and toss so that pieces are evenly covered with marinade. Marinate 4 to 6 hours (or overnight) in the refrigerator, tossing occasionally to coat all pieces. Starting and ending with a mushroom, place pieces of tofu alternately with one or other of the vegetables (bell pepper, zucchini, onion) on skewer, with a tomato midway along the skewer.

Under Broiler

Place kabobs on a cookie sheet or roasting pan, baste with marinade, and place 6 inches under broiler for 10 minutes; turn and baste with more marinade once.

On Barbecue or Grill

Baste with marinade, turning and basting with more marinade once. Remove when heated through and browned a little.

Per Kabob: calories 75; protein 6 g; carbohydrate 7 g; fat 4 g; dietary fiber 2 g; sodium 99 mg
Percent calories from: protein 26 percent; fat 41 percent; carbohydrate 33 percent

French Bread Pizza

Makes 4 pizzas

This high-energy pizza is both amazingly simple and incredibly scrumptious. Round out the meal with a large, mixed-vegetable salad and you'll have a quick and satisfying dinner the whole family will appreciate.

1 large loaf French bread (1 pound), cut in half widthwise
   and lengthwise
½ pound firm regular tofu, rinsed, patted dry, and crumbled
2 tablespoons tomato paste
2 tablespoons olive oil
1 tablespoon tamari
1 teaspoon ground fennel or dried basil
1 teaspoon dried oregano
1 teaspoon crushed garlic
⅛ to ¼ teaspoon cayenne pepper
Salt and pepper

Preheat oven to 450°F. Place bread (cut side up) on a dry baking sheet, pizza pan, or baking stone, and set aside. Place remaining ingredients in a food processor and blend into a smooth paste. Spread evenly over bread. Bake until tofu is hot and crust is crisp, about 10 to 15 minutes.

Per Pizza: calories 548; protein 29 g; carbohydrate 66 g; fat 20 g; dietary fiber 7 g; sodium 966 mg
Percent calories from: protein 21 percent; fat 32 percent; carbohydrate 47 percent

Building a Meal Around Baked Potatoes

It's easy to build a meal around the simple baked potato just by adding some of the nutritious and flavorful toppings listed below. The oven-baked method gives an aromatic and flavorful baked crust on the potatoes. Be sure to bake plenty to have leftovers for the next day. If you like, you may complete the meal with soup, salad, or marinated tofu.

Quick Oven-Baked Method for Potatoes

To bake in half an hour or less, cut large potatoes in halve or quarters and place them on a dry baking sheet or directly on the rack in a very hot 450° or 500°F oven. Pierce whole potatoes 3 to 4 times with a fork to let steam escape so they don't burst when cooking. The exact cooking time will depend on the size of the potatoes and potato sections. You can tell the potatoes are done when a knife, fork, or skewer can be easily inserted into the potato.

Microwave Method for Potatoes

A pierced potato may be cooked in a microwave on high for about 5 minutes, depending on the size of the potato.

Speedy Pressure Cooker Method for Potatoes

Potatoes also may be pressure cooked. Cut the potatoes into quarters. Pour the minimum amount of water required for your cooker into the pot. Place the potato pieces on a stainless steel steamer rack and put into the cooker. Bring up to high pressure over high heat. Reduce the heat just enough to maintain high pressure and cook for about 4 minutes. Let the pressure come down naturally or use a quick-release method (see the instruction manual for your cooker).

Toppings

Luscious Nutrition Enhancers
Sesame Tahini Salad Dressing (page 289)
Liquid Gold Dressing (page 290)
Ranch-Style Dressing and Dip (page 295)
Nippy Flax Dressing (page 296)

Good Gravy (page 319)
Gee Whiz Spread (page 273)
Beets-All Salad Dressing (page 292)

Quick and Easy Flavor Boosters

Salsa

Ketchup

Tomato sauce

Salt and freshly cracked pepper

Lemon pepper

Seasoned salt

Chili powder

Curry powder

Seasoning blends (such as Spike or Mrs. Dash)

Finely diced red or green pepper, tomato, or cucumber

Shredded carrot or zucchini

Lettuce greens

Dulse or kelp powder or flakes

Chopped fresh herbs (parsley, cilantro, or basil)

Veggie (soy) bacon bits

Your favorite low-fat salad dressing

Nutritional yeast flakes

Mashed avocado

Extra virgin olive oil

Flaxseed oil

Miso, thinned with a little water

Chunky Tomato Pasta Sauce

Makes 5 cups without tempeh; makes 6 cups with tempeh

This recipe calls for Italian plum tomatoes, which are flavorful and "meaty" egg-shaped tomatoes. They produce less liquid than the common globe tomato, and therefore make a richer-tasting sauce. To add more protein to the meal, include the tempeh.

> 1 tablespoon olive oil
> 2 cups chopped onions
> ½ to 1 teaspoon crushed garlic
> ¼ cup tomato paste
> 2½ to 3 pounds ripe Italian plum tomatoes, chopped
> 1 cup finely chopped or grated tempeh (optional)
> 1 teaspoon dried basil
> 1 teaspoon dried oregano
> 1 teaspoon salt
> 1 tablespoon balsamic vinegar

Heat oil in a large, heavy pot. When hot, add onions and sauté until soft. Stir in garlic and cook for 30 seconds. Then stir in tomato paste and cook for 1 minute longer. Add tomatoes, tempeh (if using), basil, oregano, and salt, bring to a boil, reduce heat, and simmer with lid partially ajar until thick, about 30 to 40 minutes. Stir in balsamic vinegar. Serve hot over pasta or rice.

Per Cup Without Tempeh: calories 111; protein 3 g; carbohydrate 20 g; fat 4 g; dietary fiber 4 g; sodium 500 mg

Percent calories from: protein 11 percent; fat 27 percent; carbohydrate 62 percent

---

Per Cup With Tempeh: calories 146; protein 8 g; carbohydrate 19 g; fat 6 g; dietary fiber 5 g; sodium 419 mg

Percent calories from: protein 19 percent; fat 34 percent; carbohydrate 47 percent

Fabulous Fajitas

Makes 4 fajitas

This quick, high-protein roll-up is as delicious as it is healthful. Use a mixture of red and green bell peppers if you want your fajitas to look as spectacular as they taste. (From *Table for Two*, by Joanne Stepaniak.)

½ pound tempeh, cut into ¼-inch by 2½-inch strips (or a mix of both)
¼ cup red wine vinegar
¼ cup orange juice
2 tablespoons tamari
2 teaspoons dried oregano
½ teaspoon ground cumin
4 whole-wheat flour tortillas
2 tablespoons olive oil
1 medium onion cut into 8 wedges, with pieces separated
1 medium red or green bell pepper, cut into ½-inch by 2-inch strips
    (or a mix of both)

Optional Toppings
Diced tomatoes
Sliced scallions
Shredded lettuce

Place the tempeh strips in a glass or stainless steel pan. In a small bowl, combine the vinegar, juice, tamari, oregano, and cumin. Pour over tempeh and toss gently. Make sure each piece is well coated on all sides. Set aside for 10 minutes to marinate tempeh. Warm tortillas in a dry skillet for about 1 minute or just until hot. Stack on a flat surface and cover with a clean tea towel to keep warm. Add 1 tablespoon of oil to skillet and heat on medium-high. When hot, add tempeh and cook until golden brown all over. Transfer to a plate and set aside. Add remaining tablespoon of oil to skillet and sauté onion and pepper until tender.

To assemble fajitas, spoon equal amounts of tempeh, onion, and pepper onto each tortilla, placing them in a strip slightly off center. Add optional toppings, if desired. Roll up each tortilla to enclose filling.

Per Fajita: calories 278; protein 15 g; carbohydrate 32 g; fat 14 g; dietary fiber 6 g; sodium 683 mg
Percent calories from: protein 20 percent; fat 39 percent; carbohydrate 41 percent

The Ultimate Burger

Veggie burgers are not only quick and easy to prepare, they can be among your most nutritious lunches and dinners, especially when served with a spread of "fixin's," such as those listed below. Everyone can create his or her own taste combinations. Browse through the refrigerator or freezer section of your supermarket or natural food store and you're likely to find a wide assortment of veggie burgers (and veggie wieners), including some that are so tasty your nonvegetarian friends and relatives who thought they'd only like meat burgers will enjoy them, too.

Fixin's
Mustard (yellow, brown, horseradish, Dijon, or others)
Mayonnaise (vegan)
Ketchup
Barbecue sauce
Pickle relish
Chili sauce
Tomato slices
Sliced dill pickles
Sliced red or white onion
Avocado slices
Lettuce
Sprouts
Sauerkraut (well drained)
Mushrooms (sautéed in a little olive oil)
Soy cheese slices
Veggie bacon (cooked in a little oil, for 1 minute on each side)

Buns

Fresh bakery rolls

Kaiser buns (whole wheat or white)

Bagels

English muffins (toasted)

Cooking Veggie Burgers

Because veggie burgers are precooked, they can be on the table in a flash. In fact, if veggie burgers are cooked too long, they will dry out or become tough. So whether you pan-fry your burgers in a little oil to brown them, grill them on the barbecue, or heat in the microwave, use a minimum of time to just heat them through.

Variation: The Ultimate Dogs

For a change from veggie burgers on hamburger buns, try veggie wieners on hot dog buns. To retain their juiciness, steam veggie wieners or simmer them in water for 3 minutes, just until heated through. To heat by microwave, place veggie wieners in a microwave-safe dish with a lid, cover the wieners with water, cover the dish with the lid, and microwave on high power for 2 to 3 minutes. Veggie wieners also can be barbecued, roasted, baked, or grilled. Simply warm them through, as overcooking will produce a drier result.

Time-Saving Tacos

For an instant meal, one of the fastest nutritionally balanced combinations you can serve is the well-loved taco. Just warm the shells and beans, set out the colorful fillings, and serve. If you prefer burritos, simply replace the taco shells with soft, flour tortillas.

> 4 hard corn taco shells, warmed in oven or microwave
> 1 cup refried beans, warmed in a skillet, vegetable steamer, or microwave
> 1 cup shredded lettuce
> 1 large, ripe tomato, chopped
> ½ to 1 ripe avocado, mashed or chopped
> ½ cup salsa or taco sauce
> ½ cup sliced pitted olives (optional)
> ½ cup grated soy cheese (optional)

Place taco shells, beans, lettuce, tomatoes, avocado, salsa, olives, and cheese (if using) in serving bowls on table, allowing for individual assembly.

Per Taco: calories 176; protein 6 g; carbohydrate 24 g; fat 8 g; dietary fiber 6 g; sodium 496 mg
Percent calories from: protein 12 percent; fat 37 percent; carbohydrate 51 percent

VEGETABLE SIDE DISHES

Great Greens

Makes about 2 cups

Kale and collards are excellent sources of calcium, yet many people are not certain how to prepare these greens. To remove stem, place kale or collard on a cutting board, fold it in half, and remove stem with a knife. Then thinly slice the leaves, to give the best texture for eating. For a festive look, 1 cup of chopped red bell pepper may be added to the kale before steaming, then tossed with seasonings and formed into a circle on a plate, to resemble a holly wreath. (From *Cooking Vegetarian*, by Vesanto Melina and Joseph Forest.)

> 6 cups thinly sliced kale or collards
> 1 tablespoon balsamic vinegar
> 1 tablespoon tamari (or add salt to taste)
> 2 tablespoons flaxseed oil or olive oil (optional)

Steam greens over medium-high heat until wilted. Drain well. In a bowl large enough to hold greens, combine vinegar, tamari or salt, and oil (if using). Add greens and toss.

Per ½ Cup: calories 118; protein 3 g; carbohydrate 11 g; fat 8 g; dietary fiber 2 g; sodium 128 mg
Percent calories from: protein 11 percent; fat 55 percent; carbohydrate 34 percent

Whipped Potatoes

Fluffy whipped potatoes are satisfying and soothing—comfort food at its very best. Adding fortified nondairy milk enhances the nutritional value of this timeless, popular dish.

> 2½ pounds baking potatoes, peeled and cut into chunks
>   (about 5½ cups chunks)
> ¾ to 1 cup hot fortified nondairy milk
> 2 to 3 tablespoons olive oil
> Salt and pepper
> Garlic powder (optional)

Place potato chunks in a large pot and cover with cold water. Bring to a boil, partially cover with lid ajar, reduce heat, and simmer until the tip of a knife can be inserted easily. Drain immediately. Put through a ricer (makes the smoothest potatoes) or mash with a potato masher. Add hot milk, olive oil, salt, pepper, and garlic powder (if using) to taste. Beat with a whisk, fork, or electric beater until light and fluffy. (Do not use a food processor as this will make the potatoes gummy.)

Variation

For a protein boost and a mild, cheesy flavor, add ½ cup nutritional yeast flakes when beating in the hot milk.

Per Cup[*]: calories 220; protein 5 g; carbohydrate 36 g; fat 7 g; dietary fiber 3 g; sodium 34 mg
Percent calories from: protein 9 percent; fat 27 percent; carbohydrate 64 percent

*Nutritional analysis done using fortified soymilk.

Oven Fries

Makes about 4 cups

French fries are much adored by children, but parents abhor their high fat content. With these simple, oven-baked potatoes, however, kids now can have their fries and eat them, too!

> 6 medium russet potatoes
> ¼ cup olive oil
> 1 tablespoon paprika
> ¾ teaspoon salt
> ¼ teaspoon each of pepper, garlic powder, turmeric

Preheat oven to 450°F. Oil two large baking sheets or line them with parchment paper for easy cleanup. Scrub potatoes well and remove any eyes and discolored areas. (Peeling is optional.) Cut into French-fry shapes and place in a large bowl. Sprinkle with oil and toss to coat evenly. Sprinkle with remaining ingredients and toss again so all pieces are evenly coated. Arrange in single layers on baking sheets. Bake until golden brown and fork tender, about 30 minutes. For more even browning, turn over once midway in the cooking cycle.

Per Cup: calories 276; protein 6 g; carbohydrate 40 g; fat 14 g; dietary fiber 5 g; sodium 437 mg
Percent calories from: protein 8 percent; fat 40 percent; carbohydrate 52 percent

Marinated Dilled Mixed Veggies

Makes about 4 cups

Having tasty, ready-to-eat veggies in the fridge is an easy way to encourage youngsters to eat them. These marinated mixed vegetables make a great snack any time of the day. They also are terrific as an appetizer, side dish, or salad enhancement, and always are a welcome addition to picnic baskets and lunch boxes.

> 2 pounds mixed broccoli florets, cauliflower florets, baby carrots
> 3 tablespoons olive oil
> 2½ tablespoons apple cider vinegar, or fresh or frozen lemon juice
> 2 tablespoons dried dillweed
> ½ teaspoon salt
> ½ teaspoon crushed garlic

Steam vegetables until tender-crisp. Refresh under cold water to stop the cooking process and retain vegetables' bright colors. Transfer to a large storage container. In a small jar, combine remaining ingredients and shake well. Pour over vegetables, cover container tightly, and shake container well to thoroughly coat vegetables with marinade. Let marinate in refrigerator for a minimum of 3 to 4 hours before serving. Store leftovers in refrigerator.

Per Cup: calories 164; protein 5 g; carbohydrate 16 g; fat 11 g; dietary fiber 6 g; sodium 364 mg
Percent calories from: protein 10 percent; fat 55 percent; carbohydrate 35 percent

CELEBRATIONS

Sensational Stuffed Squash

Makes 1 medium stuffed squash (5 to 6 servings)
or 2 medium stuffed squashes (10 to 12 servings)

In some families or groups of friends, getting together to cook is one of the best parts of a celebration. Assembling this stuffed and baked squash can be the central activity for a wonderful day spent with the people you love. Although other large winter squashes may be used, we recommend buttercup (also known as "turban squash") for this recipe. Its flat bottom, round shape, beautiful dark-green shell, and succulent, deep-orange flesh make it an impressive edible showpiece for any special occasion. Buttercup squash also is sweeter, more dense, and less watery than other winter squashes, and its skin is very tender when cooked. Serve it with Good Gravy (page 332); if you like, add cranberry sauce as well.

5 to 6 Servings		10 to 12 Servings
1	3-pound buttercup squash	2
1 cup	water	2 cups
½	large onion, chopped	1
¼ cup	white basmati rice, rinsed and drained	½ cup
¼ cup	quinoa, rinsed well and drained	½ cup
¼ cup	chopped walnuts or pecans	½ cup
¼ cup	chopped, oil-packed, sun-dried tomatoes (drained)	½ cup
2 tablespoons	chopped fresh parsley	¼ cup
1½ teaspoons	olive oil	1 tablespoon

½ teaspoon	dried basil	1 teaspoon
¼ teaspoon	dried oregano	½ teaspoon
¼ teaspoon	crushed garlic	½ teaspoon

Salt and pepper to taste

Preheat oven to 350°F. Pierce top of squash with sharp knife at 45-degree angle. Pushing knife blade away from your body, rotate blade around top of squash and remove cone-shaped top piece. Slice off any fibrous material from cone and set top aside. Using a large spoon, scoop out seeds and all the fibrous pulp from cavity of squash and discard. Place squash and top on a dry baking sheet and bake for 30 minutes. Remove squash and top from oven and set aside to cool for 15 minutes.

While squash is baking, place the water, onion, rice, and quinoa in a large pot and bring to a boil. Reduce heat to medium, cover, and simmer for 15 minutes. Remove from heat and let rest, covered, for 10 minutes. Fluff with a fork, and add remaining ingredients.

Spoon stuffing into cavity of squash until almost full. Put squash top in place and bake for 50 to 60 minutes or until a toothpick can be inserted easily into side of squash. If there is leftover stuffing, place in a small pan, sprinkle with 2 to 3 tablespoons of water, cover, and heat through for last 20 minutes of squash cooking time. Remove squash from oven and place on a warm serving platter. Slice into wedges to serve.

Per Serving: calories 267; protein 6 g; carbohydrate 45 g; fat 10 g; dietary fiber 9 g; sodium 29 mg
Percent calories from: protein 8 percent; fat 30 percent; carbohydrate 62 percent

Good Gravy

Makes about 3 cups (double batch: 6 cups)

This delicious, dark gravy came to us from Shirley and Al Hunting of Seattle. It is wheat free; however, it is equally good made with wheat or spelt flour. The optional nutritional yeast is an excellent source of B vitamins. You might want to make a double batch. It's good not only with Sensational Stuffed Squash (page 331) but also on baked potatoes, mashed potatoes, and slices of marinated tofu, so don't worry if you have leftovers. They'll be welcome!

Single Batch (3 cups)		Double Batch (6 cups)
3 tablespoons	olive oil	⅓ cup
1 cup	chickpea flour	2 cups
1 teaspoon	sage	2 teaspoons
½ teaspoon	thyme or rosemary	1 teaspoon
¼ teaspoon	black pepper (optional)	½ teaspoon
¼ cup	tamari or Bragg Liquid Aminos	½ cup
3 cups	water	6 cups
2 teaspoons	lemon juice, or more, to taste	1 to 1½ tablespoons
2 tablespoons	nutritional yeast (optional)	¼ cup

Prewarm a cast-iron fry pan or other heavy-bottomed saucepan over medium heat. Add oil, flour, sage, thyme, and pepper, constantly stirring and pressing to form a smooth mixture. Cook over medium heat until lightly toasted (this should take no more than 3 to 5 minutes). Remove from heat. Add tamari and then *gradually* add water, stirring constantly with a wire whisk or slotted spoon, mixing carefully to avoid lumps. Add lemon juice and nutritional yeast (if using). Add water if needed to thin gravy to desired consistency. Adjust seasoning.

Per ¼ Cup: calories 64; protein 2 g; carbohydrate 5 g; fat 4 g; dietary fiber 1 g; sodium 337 mg
Percent calories from: protein 14 percent; fat 52 percent; carbohydrate 34 percent

Tip
Chickpea flour, also called garbanzo bean flour, chana flour or besan, can be purchased from natural food stores as well as East Indian and Asian markets.

Variations
- Substitute spelt flour or wheat flour for chickpea flour.
- This gravy can be used as a sauce for marinated tofu. Cut 1 pound firm tofu into slices ¼-inch to ½-inch thick. Place ½ cup of tamari in a bowl and add tofu slices one at a time. Turn each slice over so it can sit for a few minutes on each side to soak up the tamari. When it turns brown, remove it from the bowl and set aside. (The tamari that the tofu soaked in can be used in the gravy recipe.) Place a layer of gravy in a baking pan, then add a layer of the tofu slices, and then pour the rest of the gravy on top. Bake, broil, or microwave for a few minutes until warmed through.

German Chocolate Cake

Makes 1 9-inch diameter round,
iced layer cake (about 12 servings)

The recipes of chef Ron Pickarski are designed to support personal health and the health of the natural environment, while at the same time tantalizing the most sophisticated taste buds. They are truly amazing! You will find his books, *Eco-Cuisine* and *Friendly Foods* (Ten Speed Press), at www.eco-cuisine.com. Ron Pickarski is a seven-time Culinary Olympics medal winner whose dishes range from the everyday to the elegant. This superb cake with Coconut Squash Icing (both recipes are from *Eco-Cuisine*) is a great way to introduce people to the delights of vegan cuisine.

1½ cups sugar
1½ cups unbleached white flour
1¼ cups whole-wheat flour
¾ cup cocoa or carob powder
2 teaspoons baking soda
½ teaspoon sea salt
2 cups water
½ cup pure maple syrup
6 tablespoons safflower or canola oil
2 tablespoons apple cider vinegar
2 teaspoons vanilla extract

Preheat oven to 350°F. In a large mixing bowl, combine sugar, flours, cocoa, baking soda, and salt, and mix well. In another bowl, combine water, maple syrup, oil, vinegar, and vanilla extract. Add wet ingredients to dry and mix well. Pour batter into two lightly oiled and floured 9-inch round cake pans. Bake for 30 minutes or until a toothpick inserted into the center comes out dry. Remove pans from oven and cool completely. Turn one layer onto a serving plate so that the bottom is facing up. Spread one-third of icing on the bottom layer. Place the top layer on the bottom layer and spread remaining icing on top. Do not ice the sides.

Coconut Squash Icing

1½ cups almond nondairy milk

¼ cup coconut milk

1 cup dried unsweetened coconut

3 tablespoons arrowroot powder dissolved in 3 tablespoons cool water

1 cup sugar

½ teaspoon vanilla extract

½ cup peeled, steamed, butternut squash

2 cups walnut pieces, ground to a medium-coarse meal

In a 2-quart saucepan, combine almond nondairy milk, coconut milk, and dried coconut, and bring to a simmer over medium heat. Remove saucepan from heat, add arrowroot-water mixture, and stir vigorously with a whisk until thickened. Add sugar and vanilla, then transfer to a food processor or blender. Add squash and walnuts, and blend until smooth. Chill for 1 hour before using.

Per Serving (¹⁄₁₂ Cake and Icing): calories 584; protein 8 g; carbohydrate 88 g; fat 26 g; dietary fiber 6 g, sodium 335 mg

Percent calories from: protein 5 percent; fat 37 percent; carbohydrate 57 percent

Lemon Teasecake

When you have a chance to visit Seattle, be certain to dine at Cafe Ambrosia (www.cafeambrosia.com). This is the recipe for one of the restaurant's scrumptious signature desserts, developed by executive chef Francis Janes. Those with allergies will be delighted to find that both crust and filling are free of eggs, dairy, wheat, and soy.

Oatmeal Cinnamon Crust

1 cup rolled oats

½ cup brown rice flour

½ cup ground walnuts

1 teaspoon cinnamon

½ teaspoon sea salt

1 teaspoon vanilla extract

3 tablespoons pure maple syrup

¼ cup safflower oil

Preheat oven to 350°F. In a large bowl, combine oats, flour, walnuts, cinnamon, and salt, and mix well. In a smaller bowl or measuring cup, combine vanilla, maple syrup, and oil, and stir well. Add liquid ingredients to dry ingredients; mix to incorporate liquid. Press firmly into an 8-inch or 9-inch springform pan. Bake for 10 to 12 minutes or until lightly browned. Cool about 30 minutes before filling.

Filling

½ cup uncooked millet

2 cups water

½ cup raw unsalted cashews

⅓ cup fresh lemon juice

⅓ cup pure maple syrup

2 teaspoons vanilla extract

1 teaspoon lemon extract

In a medium saucepan with a tight-fitting lid, bring millet and water to boil. Cover and simmer over low heat for about 50 minutes, until water is absorbed and millet is soft. While millet is cooking, place cashews, lemon juice, maple syrup, and extracts in a blender. Process on high speed for 3 minutes or until perfectly smooth. If necessary, scrape down sides of blender with spatula and process for another minute. While cooked millet is still warm, add to blender mixture. Process on high speed for another 3 minutes until creamy. Pour into cooled crust.

Cool filling and crust at room temperature for 1 hour. Place in refrigerator and chill for at least 4 hours before serving. Place plastic wrap over surface to prevent excess cracking. Teasecake will keep for about 3 days, refrigerated.

Topping (Optional)

>   8 ounces cherry preserves (fruit-juice–sweetened jam)
>   2 kiwifruit, peeled and sliced thin into rounds

Place cherry preserves in a small saucepan and stir over medium-low heat until barely softened. Spread evenly over filling that has chilled and set. When ready to serve, garnish with slices of kiwifruit.

Per ¹⁄₁₀ Cake: calories 260; protein 5 g; carbohydrate 33 g; fat 13 g; dietary fiber 3 g; sodium 120 mg
Percent calories from: protein 7 percent; fat 44 percent; carbohydrate 49 percent

DESSERTS

Sneaky Dad's Pudding

Makes 2 servings (about 1¾ cups)

Louisville lawyer John Borders created this recipe as a way to get fruits, veggies, essential fatty acids, calories, and protein into a tasty pudding that his daughter would eat. He said, "I haven't felt guilty about feeding this to my daughter Mattie almost every night, and she loves making it with me. It's a great bonding time for us. And if that weren't enough, even though she's a picky eater, she *loves* the taste." Any necessary supplements can be added; it's a delicious way to get them into little ones without a fuss.

> 1½ cups frozen strawberries
> 1 banana, broken into 4 pieces
> 1 to 2 teaspoons carob or cocoa powder
> 2 teaspoons flaxseed oil
> 3 to 5 tablespoons nut butter (preferably cashew or almond)
> 2 to 3 tablespoons orange juice (or carrot juice)
> 2 tablespoons fortified soymilk (any flavor)
> ⅛ to ¼ avocado (peeled, cut into a wedge)

Optional ingredients

> 2 tablespoons cooked diced carrots (frozen or freshly steamed)

Set your little companion up on a stool beside you, ready to toss in the ingredients and push the button. Place all ingredients in a food processor or blender. (This works best in a food processor; you might want to add a bit more juice or soymilk if you use a blender.) Blend until smooth.

Per Half Recipe: calories 336; protein 7 g; carbohydrate 40 g; fat 19 g; dietary fiber 6 g; sodium 16 mg
Percent calories from: protein 7 percent; fat 48 percent; carbohydrate 45 percent

This pudding goes a long way toward ensuring that even the pickiest of eaters gets the nutrients he or she needs. For a toddler aged one to three years (and using 3 tablespoons cashew butter for the whole recipe), a serving of this pudding provides approximately:

- the entire day's requirement for magnesium, folate, vitamin C, and essential fatty acids
- two-thirds of the requirement for copper and potassium
- half the requirement for pyridoxine and fiber, and 42 percent of the protein
- a quarter of the requirement for calories, iron, and selenium
- 17 percent of the requirement for zinc (more minerals with more nut butter)
- While this pudding is relatively high in fat, the sources of fat are near perfect!

Rice and Raisin Pudding

Makes about 3 cups

This nutritious but not-too-sweet pudding is made with arborio rice, a short-grain Italian rice with a high starch content. It is traditionally used for making *risotto*, because its starch gives this classic Italian dish its characteristic creaminess. For the same reason, arborio rice is ideal for making lusciously creamy rice pudding. Do not rinse arborio rice before using, as this will wash away the essential starch. Serve this pudding warm or chilled for breakfast, dessert, or snack time. It's a bone builder: 1 cup provides about 380 milligrams of calcium and 3 milligrams of vitamin D.

> 3½ cups fortified vanilla nondairy milk
> ½ cup arborio rice
> ¼ cup raisins
> ¼ cup pure maple syrup
> Pinch of salt
> Cinnamon (optional)

Combine the milk, rice, raisins, maple syrup, and salt in a medium saucepan, and bring to a boil. Reduce heat and simmer gently, stirring often, until rice is tender and liquid is thickened and creamy, about 45 minutes. Garnish with a sprinkle of cinnamon, if desired.

Tip

The pudding will continue to thicken as it cools. For an even creamier pudding, increase the milk to 4 cups and extend the cooking time to 1 hour.

Per Cup*: calories 423; protein 11 g; carbohydrate 84 g; fat 5 g; dietary fiber 1 g; sodium 187 mg
Percent calories from: protein 11 percent; fat 10 percent; carbohydrate 79 percent

*Nutritional analysis done using fortified vanilla soymilk.

Choco-Currant Cranberry Squares

Makes 21 squares (3½ cups mixture)

Here's an ideal combination of dried fruit, chocolate, and cereal that you can stir together in minutes.

> ½ cup syrup (rice, barley malt, corn, or maple)
> ¼ cup tahini or nut butter
> 2½ squares (2.5 ounces) semisweet baking chocolate
> ⅔ cup dried currants or cranberries, or a combination
> 1¼ cups puffed rice cereal
> 1¼ cups flaked cereal

Place syrup, tahini, and baking chocolate in the top of a double boiler and heat over boiling water until chocolate is just melted. If you do not have a double boiler, place pan directly over medium heat, watching and stirring frequently to prevent burning. Stir to mix evenly and remove from heat. Add currants and cereals and mix until well coated with chocolate mixture. Press into lightly oiled 4 × 9-inch loaf pan. Place in refrigerate or freezer for 30 minutes to set. Cut into 21 squares.

Per Square: calories 81; protein 1 g; carbohydrate 15 g; fat 3 g; dietary fiber 2 g; sodium 11 mg
Percent calories from: protein 5 percent; fat 27 percent; carbohydrate 68 percent

Variation
Fruity Chocolate Coconut Balls

Makes about 24 balls

This version works best with the stickier corn syrup, rice syrup, or barley malt syrup rather than maple syrup. Spread ⅓ cup of fine, unsweetened coconut in a wide, shallow bowl. Take a spoonful of the chocolate mixture, form into a ball about 1 inch in diameter, and roll it in coconut. Store balls in refrigerator until served. (These freeze well.)

Chocolate Mint Nut Bars

Makes 21 bars

Here's an energy-packed treat with added nutrition. If you use almonds and almond butter, it's a source of calcium. For extra zinc, make it with cashews and cashew butter. For omega-3 fatty acids, use walnuts. For economy plus protein, try peanuts and peanut butter. Rice or barley syrup (available at health food stores) and corn syrup are thick, sticky syrups; maple syrup is more liquid. You may wish to use 2.5 ounces of carob chips instead of the chocolate, and vanilla in place of mint.

½ cup syrup (corn, rice, barley malt, or maple syrup)
¼ cup seed or nut butter (such as tahini or peanut, cashew, or almond butter)
2.5 ounces (2½ squares) semisweet baking chocolate
½ teaspoon mint extract
1 cup flaked cereal (such as millet rice cereal)
1 cup puffed cereal (such as puffed rice)
½ cup chopped walnuts or other unsalted nuts

Place syrup, seed or nut butter, and baking chocolate in the top of a double boiler and heat over boiling water until chocolate is just melted. If you do not have a double boiler, you may heat pan directly over medium heat; watch and stir frequently to prevent burning. Stir to mix evenly, remove from heat, and stir in mint. Add cereals and nuts and mix until they are coated with chocolate mixture. Press into lightly oiled 4 × 9-inch loaf pan, place in refrigerator or freezer for 30 minutes to set, and cut into about 21 small bars.

Per Bar: calories 87; protein 1 g; carbohydrate 11 g; fat 4 g; dietary fiber 1 g; sodium 11 mg
Percent calories from: protein 7 percent; fat 43 percent; carbohydrate 50 percent

Variation
CocoLoco Nut Balls

Makes about 28 balls

It's easier to make balls if you have used the stickier corn, rice, or barley malt syrups rather than maple syrup. Spread ⅓ cup of fine, unsweetened coconut onto a plate or in a wide, shallow bowl. Take a spoonful of the chocolate mixture, form into a ball about 1 inch in diameter, and roll it in coconut. Store balls in refrigerator until served. (These freeze well.)

Fruit Butter Bars

Makes 12 to 16 bars

This nourishing treat is a lunch box staple as well as a wholesome dessert. (From *The Vegan Sourcebook*, by Joanne Stepaniak.)

1½ cups whole-wheat pastry flour
1½ cups rolled oats
¼ cup sugar
½ teaspoon baking soda
¼ teaspoon salt
½ cup pure maple syrup
¼ cup safflower oil
1½ cups thick fruit butter (apple, prune, or peach)

Preheat oven to 350°F. Lightly oil the sides and bottom of an 8 × 8-inch glass baking pan or mist with nonstick cooking spray for easier cleanup. For the crust, combine the flour, oats, sugar, baking soda, and salt in a large mixing bowl. Mix well. In a small bowl, stir together maple syrup and oil. Pour into oat mixture and mix thoroughly until everything is evenly moistened. Mixture will be crumbly.

Press half of mixture evenly into prepared baking pan, packing it down very firmly. Carefully spread fruit butter evenly over this base. Sprinkle rest of oat mixture evenly over fruit butter, and pat it down lightly. Bake 20 to 25 minutes, or until lightly browned. Cool on a wire rack. Slice into bars or squares.

Per Bar (¹⁄₁₂ Recipe): calories 243; protein 4 g; carbohydrate 46 g; fat 6 g; dietary fiber 3 g; sodium 105 mg
Percent calories from: protein 6 percent; fat 20 percent; carbohydrate 74 percent

The Very Best
Chocolate Chip Cookies

Makes about 32 2-inch cookies

These cookies are rich but oh-so-delicious. They are a little smaller than most cookies, but this helps them hold together better. If you like, toast the walnuts in a dry skillet or on a baking sheet until lightly brown. This will give them a deeper flavor. Leftovers (if there are any) are best stored in the refrigerator. These cookies also freeze well.

1½ cups rolled oats
1 cup whole-wheat pastry flour
1 cup chopped walnuts
1 cup semisweet chocolate or carob chips
½ teaspoon salt
¼ teaspoon baking soda
½ cup safflower oil
½ cup pure maple syrup
2 tablespoons water
2 teaspoons vanilla extract

Preheat oven to 350°F. Line two baking sheets with parchment paper (for easier cleanup). Set aside.

Place oats, flour, nuts, chocolate or carob chips, salt, and baking soda in a large mixing bowl. Stir with a wire whisk to combine. In a small bowl, place oil, maple syrup, water, and vanilla, and beat vigorously with a wire whisk until emulsified. Stir into oat mixture and mix just until everything is evenly moistened. Let rest 5 minutes.

Drop slightly rounded tablespoons of dough onto prepared baking sheets, about 1 inch apart. Dough will be crumbly. Flatten with your hand to ⅛-inch thick. Smooth edges to make each cookie uniformly round, gently pressing dough so cookies hold together.

Bake one sheet at a time on the center shelf of oven until cookies are lightly brown, about 18 minutes. Transfer to cooling rack and cool completely. Store in air-tight container in refrigerator.

Per Cookie: calories 117; protein 2 g; carbohydrate 12 g; fat 7 g; dietary fiber 1 g; sodium 84 mg
Percent calories from: protein 6 percent; fat 54 percent; carbohydrate 40 percent

Nut Butter Cookies

Makes 24 cookies

This is a superbly simple recipe that children can help to make. Use any nut butter you like, such as peanut butter, almond butter, soynut butter, or even sunflower butter.

½ cup pure maple syrup
½ cup nut butter (crunchy or smooth)
1 teaspoon vanilla extract
1 cup whole-wheat pastry flour

Preheat oven to 350°F. Oil two baking sheets, mist with nonstick cooking spray, or line with parchment paper for easier cleanup. In a large mixing bowl, cream together maple syrup, nut butter, and vanilla extract. When smooth, stir in flour to form a stiff dough. Mix thoroughly. Form into 24 walnut-size balls and place on prepared baking sheets. Flatten cookies with the tines of a fork, first in one direction and then in the opposite direction to create a cross-hatch design. (Young children especially enjoy helping with this part.) Bake one sheet at a time on the center rack of the oven for 12 minutes or until bottoms of cookies are lightly browned. Remove from oven, but let rest on baking sheet for 1 full minute. Carefully loosen and transfer to a cooling rack. Cool completely before storing.

Per Cookie*: calories 67; protein 2 g; carbohydrate 9 g; fat 3 g; dietary fiber 1 g; sodium 2 mg
Percent calories from: protein 11 percent; fat 36 percent; carbohydrate 9 percent

*Nutritional analysis done using unsalted peanut butter.

Popsoycle Heaven!

Makes 6 popsoycles (1½ cups)

Blueberry-Banana Popsoycles

½ ripe banana

½ cup fortified vanilla soymilk

¾ cup frozen or fresh blueberries

Lemon Popsoycles

8 ounces (1 cup) firm silken tofu

¼ cup fresh or frozen lemon juice

¼ cup pure maple syrup

½ teaspoon vanilla extract

Creamy Cranberry Popsoycles

¾ cup concentrated frozen cranberry punch (or sweetened cranberry, raspberry, or strawberry concentrate)

6 ounces (¾ cup) firm silken tofu

Fudgesoycles

⅔ cup fortified chocolate or carob soymilk

8 ounces (1 cup) firm silken tofu

2 tablespoons cocoa or carob powder

¼ cup pure maple syrup

Select a flavor from the four types of popsoycles listed above. Place all ingredients in a blender and puree for 1 to 2 minutes until smooth. Pour into popsicle molds. Freeze until solid.

Tips

Popsoycles may take 4 hours to freeze and be ready to eat; however, the exact time will depend on your freezer temperature. Each popsoycle can be removed from its mold by running warm water over the outside of the mold, by dipping it in warm water, or even by squeezing it in your hand for a few minutes. The number of popsoycles produced will vary with different sizes of molds.

Per Blueberry-Banana Popsoycle: calories 22; protein 0.7 g; carbohydrate 4 g; fat 0.4 g; dietary fiber 0.2g; sodium 12 mg

Percent calories from: protein 12 percent; fat 15 percent; carbohydrate 73 percent

Per Lemon Popsoycle: calories 59; protein 3 g; carbohydrate 11 g; fat 0.7 g; dietary fiber 0.1 g; sodium 25 mg

Percent calories from: protein 19 percent; fat 11 percent; carbohydrate 70 percent

Per Creamy Cranberry Popsoycle: calories 87; protein 2 g; carbohydrate 21 g; fat 0.8 g; dietary fiber 0 g; sodium 13 mg

Percent calories from: protein 8 percent; fat 7 percent; carbohydrate 85 percent

Per Fudgesoycle: calories 86; protein 4 g; carbohydrate 15 g; fat 2 g; dietary fiber 0.7 g; sodium 33 mg

Percent calories from: protein 17 percent; fat 17 percent; carbohydrate 66 percent

Strawberry Popsoycles

Makes 4 popsoycles (about 1 cup)

These are easily made using a 6-ounce container of soy yogurt. Instead of fruit plus a sweetener, you may use sweetened frozen fruit.

¾ cup fruit-flavored soy yogurt
¾ cup frozen or fresh strawberries
2 tablespoons pure maple syrup

Place all ingredients in a blender and puree for 1 to 2 minutes until smooth. Pour into popsicle molds. Freeze until solid.

Per Strawberry Popsoycle: calories 74; protein 2 g; carbohydrate 13 g; fat 2 g; dietary fiber 1 g; sodium 4 mg

Percent calories from: protein 12 percent; fat 21 percent; carbohydrate 67 percent

Resources

There are countless vegan and vegetarian Web sites and numerous books, publications, and organizations that support and encourage an animal-free diet and lifestyle. Although we are able to list only a fraction of the resources that are available, we hope what we have included will provide a springboard for you and your family.

Where to Find Information

Authors' Web Sites

Grassroots Veganism, the Web site of Joanne Stepaniak, author and speaker, contains a comprehensive archive of frequently asked questions on a wide variety of issues related to vegetarianism and the vegan lifestyle. The site also includes interviews, essays, an advice column on compassionate living, recipes, a discussion board, and information about Joanne's books and seminars.

Web site: www.vegsource.com/joanne

Vesanto Melina's Web site gives vegetarian food guides, extensive lists of scientific references for her nutrition books, *Becoming Vegetarian* and *Becoming Vegan*, low-fat recipe lists for *Cooking Vegetarian*, and information about Vesanto's consultations and seminars.

Web site: www.nutrispeak.com

Cookbooks for Children and Teens

Bates, Dorothy, and Suzanne Havala. *Kids Can Cook: Vegetarian Recipes*. Summertown, Tenn.: Book Publishing Company, 2000. (reading level: ages 9–12)

Bates, Dorothy R., Bobbie Hinman, Robert Oser, and Suzanne Havala. *Munchie Madness*. Summertown, Tenn.: Book Publishing Company, 2001. (reading level: teens and up)

Butts, Lauren, and Donna Shields. *Okay, So Now You're a Vegetarian: Advice and 100 Recipes from One Vegetarian to Another*. New York: Broadway Books, 2000. (reading level: teens and up)

Crist, Vonnie Winslow, and Debra Wasserman. *Leprechaun Cake and Other Tales*. Baltimore: Vegetarian Resource Group, 1995. (reading level: ages 8–11)

Krizmanic, Judy. *The Teen's Vegetarian Cookbook*. New York: Viking Press, 1999. (reading level: teens and up)

Pierson, Stephanie. *Vegetables Rock! A Complete Guide for Teenage Vegetarians*. New York: Bantam Doubleday Dell, 1999. (reading level: teens and up)

Raymond, Carole. *Student's Vegetarian Cookbook: Quick, Easy, Cheap, and Tasty Vegetarian Recipes*. Roseville, Calif.: Prima Publishing, 2000. (reading level: teens and up)

Family Cookbooks

Bloomfield, Barb. *Soup's On!* Summertown, Tenn.: Book Publishing Company, 1997.

Brown, Judy. *The Natural Lunchbox: Vegetarian Meals for School, Work, and Home*. Summertown, Tenn.: Book Publishing Company, 1996.

Costigan, Fran. *Great Good Desserts Naturally*. Summertown, Tenn.: Book Publishing Company, 2000.

Davis, Brenda, Bryanna Clark Grogan, and Joanne Stepaniak. *Dairy-Free and Delicious*. Summertown, Tenn.: Book Publishing Company, 2001.

Gartenstein, Devra. *The Accidental Vegan*. Santa Cruz, Calif.: Crossing Press, 2000.

Gentle World. *Incredibly Delicious: The Vegan Paradigm Cookbook*. Kapa'au, Hawaii: Gentle World Publishing, 2000.

Grogan, Bryanna Clark. *Nonna's Italian Kitchen: Delicious Homestyle Vegan Cuisine.* Summertown, Tenn.: Book Publishing Company, 1998.

Klein, Donna. *The Mediterranean Vegan Kitchen: Meat-Free, Egg-Free, Dairy-Free Dishes from the Healthiest Place Under the Sun.* Thousand Oaks, Calif.: HP Books, 2001.

Kramer, Sarah, and Tanya Barnard. *How It All Vegan: Irresistible Recipes for an Animal-Free Diet.* Vancouver, B.C.: Arsenal Pulp Press, 1999.

Melina, Vesanto, and Joseph Forest. *Cooking Vegetarian: Healthy, Delicious, and Easy Vegetarian Cuisine.* Minneapolis, Minn.: Chronimed Publishing, 1998.

Muldawer, Wendy. *Better Than Peanut Butter and Jelly: Quick Vegetarian Meals Your Kids Will Love.* Ithaca, N.Y.: McBooks Press, 1997.

Null, Shelly. *Healthy Cooking for Kids.* New York: St. Martin's Griffin, 1999.

Raymond, Jennifer. *The Peaceful Palate.* Summertown, Tenn.: Book Publishing Company, 1996.

Sass, Lorna. *Lorna Sass's Complete Vegetarian Kitchen.* New York: HarperCollins, 1995.

_____. *The New Vegan Cookbook: Innovative Vegetarian Recipes Free of Dairy, Eggs, and Cholesterol.* San Francisco: Chronicle Books, 2001.

Schumann, Kate, and Virginia Messina. *The Vegetarian No-Cholesterol Family-Style Cookbook.* New York: St. Martin's, 1995.

Solomon, Jay. *150 Vegan Favorites: Fresh, Easy, Incredibly Delicious Recipes You Can Enjoy Every Day.* Roseville, Calif.: Prima Publishing, 1998.

Stepaniak, Joanne. *Table for Two: Meat- & Dairy-Free Recipes for Two.* Summertown, Tenn.: Book Publishing Company, 1996.

_____. *The Uncheese Cookbook: Creating Amazing Dairy-Free Cheese Substitutes and Classic "Uncheese" Dishes.* Summertown, Tenn.: Book Publishing Company, 1994.

_____. *Vegan Deli: Wholesome Ethnic Fast Food.* Summertown, Tenn.: Book Publishing Company, 2001.

_____. *Vegan Vittles.* Summertown, Tenn.: Book Publishing Company, 1996.

Wasserman, Debra, and Reed Mangels. *Simply Vegan.* Baltimore: Vegetarian Resource Group, 1999.

Reading and Reference Books

Bass, Jules. *Herb, the Vegetarian Dragon.* New York: Barefoot Books, 1999. (reading level: ages 8–12)

Bradley, Ann. *Cows Are Vegetarians.* Palo Alto, Calif.: Healthways Press, 1992. (reading level: ages 9–12)

Bunting, Eve. *A Turkey for Thanksgiving.* New York: Clarion Books, 1995. (reading level: ages 3–7)

Davis, Brenda, and Vesanto Melina. *Becoming Vegan.* Summertown, Tenn.: Book Publishing Company, 2000.

Krizmanic, Judy. *A Teen's Guide to Going Vegetarian.* New York: Puffin, 1994. (reading level: teens and up)

Marcus, Erik. *Vegan: The New Ethics of Eating.* Ithaca, N.Y.: McBooks Press, 2000.

Melina, Vesanto, Brenda Davis, and Victoria Harrison. *Becoming Vegetarian.* Summertown, Tenn.: Book Publishing Company, 1995.

Messina, Virginia, and Mark Messina. *The Vegetarian Way.* New York: Crown Trade Paperbacks, 1996.

Pilkey, Dav. *'Twas the Night Before Thanksgiving.* New York: Orchard Books, 1990. (reading level: ages 3–7).

Robbins, John. *The Food Revolution: How Your Diet Can Help Save Your Life and the World.* Berkeley, Calif.: Conari Press, 2001.

Stepaniak, Joanne. *Being Vegan: Living with Conscience, Conviction, and Compassion.* Chicago: McGraw-Hill/Contemporary, 2000.

_____. *Compassionate Living for Healing, Wholeness, and Harmony.* Chicago: McGraw-Hill/Keats, 2000.

_____. *The Vegan Sourcebook.* Chicago: McGraw-Hill/Contemporary, 2000.

Twinn, Michael, and Arlette Lavie. *Who Cares About Animal Rights?* Wiltshire, U.K.: Child's Play International Ltd., 1992. (reading level: ages 9–12)

Vegetarian Resource Group. *I Love Animals and Broccoli Coloring Book.* Available at cost (about 15 cents) from the Vegetarian Resource Group (listed on page 355).

Vignola, Radha. *Victor the Vegetarian.* Santa Cruz, Calif.: AVIVA, 1994. (reading level: ages 3–7)

Weil, Zoe. *So, You Love Animals: An Action-Packed, Fun-Filled Book to Help Kids Help Animals.* Jenkintown, Pa.: American Anti-Vivisection Society, 1994. (activity level: ages 6 and up)

White, E. B. *Charlotte's Web.* New York: Harper Trophy, 1999. (reading level: ages 8–12)

Organizations and Online Resources

The American Dietetic Association's Vegetarian Nutrition Dietetic Practice Group
Provides information sheets on its Web site about vegetarian nutrition for children, athletes, and pregnant women, and on specific nutrients (iron, zinc, and fats). www.andrews.edu/NUFS/vndpg.html

The American Vegan Society
Teaching the vegan way of life since 1960 through numerous publications and educational conferences. Annual membership includes the quarterly magazine *American Vegan*. Offers books, pamphlets, videotapes, and audiotapes by mail. P.O. Box 369, Malaga, NJ 08328; phone: (856) 694-2887; www.americanvegan.org

EarthSave International
Educates people about the cumulative impact of our food choices on our health and the environment through its chapters around the world. Membership includes quarterly newsmagazine and local publications when applicable. 1509 Seabright Avenue, Suite B1, Santa Cruz, CA 95062; phone: 1-800-362-3648; www.earthsave.org

Farm Animal Reform Movement (FARM)
Works to expose and stop animal abuse and destructive impacts of animal agriculture. Conducts several national grassroots campaigns including the Great American Meatout (March 20), World Farm Animals Day (October 2), and National Veal Ban Action (Mother's Day). P.O. Box 30654, Bethesda, MD 20824; phone: 1-888-FARM-USA; www.farmusa.org

Farm Sanctuary
Provides refuge for animals rescued from factory farms, stockyards, and slaughterhouses; wages campaigns to stop cruelty to farm animals, hosts educational conferences, offers sanctuary tours, and operates a bed and breakfast for visitors to the New York sanctuary. Farm Sanctuary East, P.O. Box 150, Watkins Glen, NY 14891; phone: (607) 583-2225; Farm Sanctuary West, P.O. Box 1065, Orland, CA 95963; phone: (530) 865-4617; www.farmsanctuary.org; www.factoryfarming.com

The Fund for Animals

Protects wildlife and domestic animals through education, legislation, litigation, and direct care at several sanctuaries. 200 West 57th Street, Suite 705, New York, NY 10019; phone: 1-888-405-FUND; www.fund.org

Humane Society of the United States (HSUS)

Encourages the humane treatment of animals and fosters respect, understanding, and compassion for all creatures and the environment. 2100 L Street, NW, Washington, DC 20037; phone: (202) 452-1100; www.hsus.org

International Vegetarian Union

Promotes vegetarianism throughout the world by supporting and connecting national and regional groups. Hosts the International Vegetarian Congress. Contact IVU for a listing of international vegetarian organizations and links to a global network of resources. www.ivu.org; youngsters will enjoy www.ivu.org/youth

Mothers and Others for a Livable Planet

Provides education and resources to support consumer choices that are health supporting, safe, and environmentally sound for families and communities. 40 W. 20th Street, New York, NY 10011; www.mothers.org

North American Vegetarian Society (NAVS)

Advances vegetarianism through its numerous publications and educational materials including the quarterly magazine *Vegetarian Voice*, available with membership. Sponsors national conferences and campaigns. Originated the annual celebration of World Vegetarian Day (October 1). Contact NAVS for a list of vegetarian organizations in North America. P.O. Box 72, Dolgeville, NY 13329; phone: (518) 568-7970; www.navs-online.org

People for the Ethical Treatment of Animals (PETA)

Works to expose, stop, and prevent animal cruelty in all its forms through public education, cruelty investigations, research, animal rescue, legislation, special events, celebrity involvement, and direct action. 501 Front Street, Norfolk, VA 23510; phone: (757) 622-7382; www.peta.org

Physicians Committee for Responsible Medicine (PCRM)

Promotes preventive medicine, encourages higher standards for ethics and effectiveness in medicine and research, advocates a plant-based diet. Offers numerous educational publications including *Good Medicine*, a quarterly magazine. 5100 Wisconsin Avenue, NW, Suite 404, Washington, DC 20016; phone: (202) 686-2210; www.pcrm.org

Tribe of Heart

Uses visual media, storytelling, and the arts to present a vision of a compassionate future. Creators of the award-winning documentary *The Witness*. P.O. Box 149, Ithaca, NY 14851; phone: (607) 275-0806; www.tribeofheart.org

United Poultry Concerns (UPC)

Promotes the compassionate and respectful treatment of domestic fowl through investigations and education. Operates a sanctuary for rescued chickens. Publishes quarterly newsletter *Poultry Press*. P.O. Box 150, Machipongo, VA 23405; phone: (757) 678-7875; www.upc-online.org

Vegetarian Resource Group (VRG)

A nonprofit organization dedicated to educating the public on vegetarianism and the interrelated issues of health, nutrition, ecology, ethics, and world hunger. In addition to publishing the *Vegetarian Journal*, VRG produces and sells cookbooks, other books, pamphlets, and article reprints. Registered dietitians and physicians aid in the development of nutrition-related publications and answer member or media questions about the vegetarian diet. P.O. Box 1463, Baltimore, MD 21203; phone: (410) 366-8343; fax: (410) 366-8804. Their award-winning Web site is an outstanding resource: www.vrg.org

Each year the Vegetarian Resource Group gives $5,000 scholarships to two graduating high school seniors who have shown courage and conviction to make a peaceful world through a vegetarian diet and lifestyle. VRG also sponsors an annual essay contest for students aged nineteen and under with $50 savings bonds awarded in three categories. Details can be found at www.vrg.org.

Vegetarian Restaurant Web Sites

Provide guides to vegetarian restaurants and bed and breakfasts around the world; www.happycow.net or www.vegdining.com

VegSource

Hosts over one hundred vegan and vegetarian Web sites and discussion boards including sites on nutrition, breastfeeding, child rearing, home schooling, lifestyle issues, weight management, exercise, organic gardening, spirituality, travel information, and much more. www.vegsource.com

Periodicals

GRRR! Magazine

GRRR! is free to youngsters. To subscribe, email education@peta-online.org Also visit the Web site www.PETAkids.com

Vegetarian Baby & Child

This magazine covers all topics related to vegetarian and vegan family life. Six issues per year. P.O. Box 519, Tuolumne, CA 95379; www.vegetarianbaby.com

Vegetarian Journal

This thirty-six-page bimonthly magazine published by the Vegetarian Resource Group contains informative articles, delicious vegan recipes, book reviews, notices about vegetarian events, product evaluations, hints on where to find vegetarian products and services, travel tips, and more. P.O. Box 1463, Baltimore, MD 21203; phone: (410) 366-8343; fax: (410) 366-8804; www.vrg.org

VegNews

North America's monthly vegetarian newspaper. Includes outstanding articles, interviews, travel guides, vegan recipes, restaurant and book reviews, event calendars, and more. P.O. Box 320130, San Francisco, CA 94123; www.vegnews.com

Breastfeeding Resources

La Leche League

Provides outstanding support for breastfeeding, including groups throughout the world; phone (U.S.): 1-800-LALECHE or (Canada): 1-800-665-4324; www.lalecheleague.org/leaderinfo.html

Videos

DVD Production. *Dr. Jane Morton's Guide to Successful Breastfeeding.* Videotransform Inc., Palo Alto, CA; phone: 1-800-253-7678 or (415) 494-1529. (20 minutes)

La Leche League International. *Breastfeeding Your Baby: A Mother's Guide.* Medela, Crystal Lake, IL. (64 minutes) (See contact information on previous page.)

Livingstone, Verity. *The Art of Successful Breastfeeding: A Guide for Mothers.* New Vision Media, Vancouver, BC; phone: (604) 689-9549. (60 minutes)

Pacific Prenatal Education Association. *Mother to Mother: Love, Science, and Breastfeeding.* Pacific Prenatal Education Association, Maple Ridge, BC; phone: (604) 462-0457. (30 minutes)

Growth Charts for Infants

These are Internet links for charts for the weights and length of infants as they grow from birth to thirty-six months of age. These are the same charts that are used at health clinics and were developed by the National Center for Health Statistics in collaboration with the National Center for Chronic Disease Prevention and Health Promotion (2000). Use of the charts is described on page 195. The charts can also be found on pages 198 to 201 as Figures 9.1 to 9.4.

Boys 0–36 months, weight
www.cdc.gov/nchs/about/major/nhanes/growthcharts/set1/chart01.pdf

Girl 0–36 months, weight
www.cdc.gov/nchs/about/major/nhanes/growthcharts/set1/chart02.pdf

Boys 0–36 months, length
www.cdc.gov/nchs/about/major/nhanes/growthcharts/set1/chart05.pdf

Girls 0–36 months, length
www.cdc.gov/nchs/about/major/nhanes/growthcharts/set1/chart06.pdf

(Note that we refer to infant "length" rather than height or stature because the baby is not standing for the measurement.)

Where to Find Products

Mail-Order Products

Bob's Red Mill

A vast offering of legumes, heirloom beans, common and uncommon grains, and stone-ground, whole-grain flours, unique flour blends, meals, cereals, and pancake and waffle mixes. Many products are ideal for children and adults with wheat or gluten allergies. 5209 S.E. International Way, Milwaukie, OR 97222; phone: 1-800-349-2173; www.bobsredmill.com

Diamond Organics

A beautiful and impressive variety of fresh organic fruits and vegetables shipped direct to your home. Also carries organic pantry staples such as dried beans, grains, dried fruit, pasta, and flours, as well as fruit and vegetable samplers, gift baskets, fresh organic breads, and organic vegetable oils. P.O. Box 2159, Freedom, CA 95019; phone: 1-888-674-2641; www.diamondorganics.com

Gold Mine Natural Foods

A large selection of organic legumes, organic grains, heirloom beans and grains, a wide variety of macrobiotic foods, and hard-to-find cooking equipment. 7805 Arjons Drive, San Diego, CA 92126; phone: (619) 537-9830 or 1-800-475-FOOD; www.goldminenaturalfood.com

Mail-Order Catalog

Extensive roster of vegan and vegetarian cookbooks as well as a huge inventory of nonperishable vegan and vegetarian pantry staples including tofu, nutritional yeast, meat substitutes, sweeteners, baking supplies, salad dressings, condiments, nut butters, mixes, and more. P.O. Box 180, Summertown, TN 38483; phone: 1-800-695-2241; www.healthy-eating.com

Pangea

A dazzling assortment of vegan items including hard-to-find vegan products such as nonleather shoes and accessories, clothing, jackets, hats, ties, gloves, first-aid and personal care products, specialty chocolates and candies, gift baskets, makeup, wallets, purses and briefcases, T-shirts, candles, cleaning products, food staples, books, bumper stickers, and novelty items. 2381 Lewis Avenue, Rockville, MD 20851; phone: (301) 816-9300 or orders: 1-800-340-1200; www.veganstore.com

Vegan Essentials

A plethora of vegan products for health, home, and spirit including leather alternatives, hemp goods, jewelry, chocolates and sweets, vitamins and supplements, products for babies and children, books, fragrances and body oils, sun care products, pantry essentials, and more. 7722 W. Menomonee River Parkway, Wauwatosa, WI 53213; phone: (414) 607-1953; www.veganessentials.com

Vegan Street

Vegan Street specializes in quality, original vegan message gear on stylish organic cotton clothing, as well as buttons, bumper stickers, and other unique products designed to get out the word. P.O. Box 477898, Chicago, IL 60647; phone: (866) 55-VEGAN; www.veganstreet.com

Supplements

(reliable vegan and vegetarian vitamin and mineral supplements)

Freeda Vitamins

Provides an almost entirely vegan line of multivitamin-mineral supplements (the few exceptions contain vitamin D_3). Freeda Vitamins, New York, NY; phone: 1-800-777-3737.

SISU

Provides an excellent multivitamin-mineral supplement, SISU Vegi-Mins, and SISU Liquid Calcium, Magnesium, and Vitamin D (ergocalciferol). SISU, Vancouver, BC; phone: (604) 420-6610; www.sisuhealth.com

Long-Chain Omega-3 Fatty Acids

(completely vegetarian/vegan, derived from marine microalgae and packaged in vegetable-based gelcaps)

Genestra Neurogen

This DHA–rich microalgae-based oil comes from Seroyal, Toronto, ON; phone: 1-800-263-5861.

O-Mega-Zen3

This DHA–rich microalgae-based oil comes from OmegaTech and is packaged by NuTru, Lincolnwood, IL; phone: (847) 982-1101; www.nutru.com or www.nutru.com/omega.htm

Note: You can obtain organic flaxseed oil (a source of short-chain omega-3 fatty acids) in veggie caps from Health from the Sun, P.O. Box 840, Sunapee, NH 03782; phone: 1-800-447-2249; www.hfts.com

Making the Most of School and Camp

School Meals

Berkoff, Nancy. *Vegan in Volume.* Baltimore: Vegetarian Resource Group, 2000. (Book includes recipes and chapter on school foods.)

U.S. Department of Agriculture (USDA). *Community Nutrition Action Kit.* phone: (703) 305-1624 or write USDA, 3101 Park Center Dr., Room 802, Alexandria, VA, 22302 (no charge).

_____. *Toolkit for Healthy School Meals.* Toolkit includes several vegetarian and vegan meals and lists vegetarian commodities (such as canned beans, peanut butter, frozen vegetables, canned and frozen fruit, cornmeal, and flour) that schools are expected to use. Cost is $25; however your school food service department is likely to have a copy. www.nal.usda.gov/fnic/schoolmeals

Wasserman, Debra, and Reed Mangels. *Vegetarian Quantity Recipes Packet* (School Foods Packet). Baltimore: Vegetarian Resource Group, July 1991; updated 2001. For many other helpful resources, search www.vrg.org under "school lunch" or call (410) 366-8343.

Alternatives to Dissection in School

The American Anti-Vivisection Society

Dedicated to the elimination of animal use in research, product testing, and education. Offers pamphlets, videos, and educational materials. 801 Old York Road, #204, Jenkintown, PA 19046; phone: (215) 887-0816; www.aavs.org

Vegetarian Camps

Au Grand Bois Vegetarian Summer Camps

A holistic, heart-centered camp experience for children, grown-ups, and families of all types. Located on 565 acres of rolling hills, woods, fields, streams, and ponds, Au Grand Bois offers a wide range of crafts, nature activities, music, swimming, and noncompetitive games in a safe, caring environment. Lactovegetarian food, always with a vegan option. Can accommodate most food allergies. Their own organic gardens supply fresh greens and vegetables. Ladysmith, QC, Canada J0X 2A0; phone: (819) 647-3522; www.agb.ottawa.com

Legacy International's Global Youth Village

Offers a dynamic blend of workshops and recreational activities for youths, ages fourteen to eighteen, and staff from around the world. A micromodel of the world community filled with the music, laughter, food, arts, and aspirations of our one diverse humanity. Here future leaders expand their minds, skills, and horizons. With trust, cooperation, and enthusiasm, they cross barriers of ethnicity and race, gender and religion. Meals are vegetarian (natural foods; no sugar) with an international flair; a poultry dish is served twice a session. Can accommodate special dietary restrictions. Accredited by the American Camping Association; phone: (540) 297-5982; www.globalyouthvillage.org

Youth for Environmental Sanity (YES!)

Educates, inspires, and empowers young people to join forces for social justice and environmental sanity. Offers weeklong summer camps with delicious plant-based meals for young people ages fifteen to thirty. 420 Bronco Road, Soquel, CA 95073; www.yesworld.org

References

Chapter 6

American Academy of Pediatrics Work Group on Cow's Milk Protein and Diabetes Mellitus. "Infant Feeding Practices and Their Possible Relationship to the Etiology of Diabetes Mellitus." *Pediatrics* 94 (1994): 752–54.

American Dietetic Association and Dietitians of Canada. "Vegetarian Nutrition." In *Manual of Clinical Dietetics*, 159–176. Chicago: American Dietetic Association, 2000.

Appleby, P. N., M. Thorogood, J. I. Mann, and T. J. Key. "The Oxford Vegetarian Study: An Overview." *American Journal of Clinical Nutrition* 70, supplement 3 (September 1999): 525S–531S. Online at: www.ajcn.org/cgi/content/full/70/3/525S

Davis, B., and V. Melina. *Becoming Vegan.* Summertown, Tenn.: The Book Publishing Company, 2000.

ESHA Research. *The Food Processor Nutrition and Fitness Software.* Salem Ore.: ESHA Research, 2001. www.esha.com 1-800-659-3742

Fogarty, A., and J. Britton. "Nutritional Issues and Asthma." *Current Opinion in Pulmonary Medicine* 6, no. 1 (January 2000): 86–89. Review.

Green, T. J., R. M. Issenman, and K. Jacobson. "Patients' Diets and Preferences in a Pediatric Population with Inflammatory Bowel Disease." *Canadian Journal of Gastroenterology* 12, no. 8 (November–December 1998): 544–49.

Haddad, E., J. Sabaté, and C. Whitten. "Vegetarian Food Guide Pyramid: A Conceptual Framework." *American Journal of Clinical Nutrition* 70 (1999): 615–19S.

Havala, S. *Good Foods, Bad Foods: What's Left to Eat?* Minneapolis: Chronimed Publishers, 1998.

Health Canada. *Canada's Food Guide to Healthy Eating.* Minister of Supply and Services Canada, 1992. (Cat. No. H39-252/1992E)

Heaney, R. P., M. S. Dowell, K. Rafferty, and J. Bierman. "Bioavailability of the Calcium in Fortified Soy Imitation Milk, with Some Observations on Method." *American Journal of Clinical Nutrition* 71, no. 5 (May 2000): 1166–69.

Hermon-Taylor, J., T. J. Bull, J. M. Sheridan, J. Cheng, M. L. Stellakis, and N. Sumar. "Causation of Crohn's Disease by Mycobacterium Avium Subspecies Paratuberculosis." *Canadian Journal of Gastroenterology* 14, no. 6 (June 2000): 521–39. Review.

Kahn, L., C. W. Warren, W. A. Harris, J. L. Collins, K. A. Douglas, M. E. Collins, B. I. Williams, J. G. Ross, and L. J. Koble. "Youth Risk Behavior Surveillance—United States, 1993." In "Center for Disease Control (CDC) Surveillance Summaries." *Morbidity and Mortality Weekly Report* 44, SS–1 (March 24, 1995): 1–56. www.cdc.gov/mmwr/preview/ind95_ss.html

Lucarelli, S., T. Frediani, A. M. Zingoni, F. Ferruzzi, O. Giardini, F. Quintieri, M. Barbato, P. D'Eufemia, and E. Cardi. "Food Allergy and Infantile Autism." *Panminerva Medica* 37, no. 3 (September 1995): 137–41.

Messina, M., and V. Messina. *The Dietitians' Guide to Vegetarian Diets.* Gaithersburg, Md.: Aspen Publishers, Inc. 1996.

Messina, V. K., and K. I. Burke. "Position of the American Dietetic Association: Vegetarian Diets." *Journal of the American Dietetic Association* 97, no. 11 (November 1997): 1317–21.

Neumark-Sztainer, D., M. Story, M. D. Resnick, and R. W. Blum. "Correlates of Inadequate Fruit and Vegetable Consumption Among Adolescents." *Preventive Medicine* 25 (1995): 497–505.

Pena, A. S., and J. B. Crusius. "Food Allergy, Coeliac Disease, and Chronic Inflammatory Bowel Disease in Man." *The Veterinary Quarterly* 20, supplement 3 (1998): S49–52. Review.

Physicians Committee for Responsible Medicine, ed. *Healthy Eating for Life to Prevent and Treat Cancer.* New York: John Wiley and Sons, 2002.

Sabaté, J., ed. *Vegetarian Nutrition.* Boca Raton, Fla.: CRC Press, 2001.

Trumbo, P., A. A. Yates, S. Schlicker, and M. Poos. "Dietary Reference Intakes: Vitamin A, Vitamin K, Arsenic, Boron, Chromium, Copper, Iodine, Iron, Manganese, Molybdenum, Nickel, Silicon, Vanadium, and Zinc." *Journal of the American Dietetic Association* 101, no. 3 (March 2001): 294–301.

U.S. Department of Agriculture. *U.S. Food Guide Pyramid,* 2000. Online at www.health.gov/dietaryguidelines/dga2000/DIETGD.PDF, page 15.

World Cancer Research Foundation and the American Institute for Cancer Research. *Food, Nutrition, and the Prevention of Cancer: A Global Perspective.* Washington, D.C.: American Institute for Cancer Research, 1997.

World Health Organization Study Group on Diet, Nutrition, and the Prevention of Noncommunicable Diseases. *Diet, Nutrition, and the Prevention of Chronic Diseases.* Geneva: World Health Organization Technical Report Series 797, 1991.

Young, V. R., and P. L. Pellet. "Plant Proteins in Relation to Human Nutrition and Amino Acid Nutrition." Paper presented at the 2nd International Congress on Vegetarian Nutrition, Arlington, Va., June 29, 1992.

Chapter 7

American Dietetic Association. "Position of the American Dietetic Association: Promotion of Breast-Feeding." *Journal of the American Dietetic Association* 97, no. 6 (June 1997): 662–66.

Barry, D. *Babies and Other Hazards of Sex.* Emmaus, Pa.: Rodale Press, 1984.

Buck, G. M., J. E. Vena, E. F. Schisterman, J. Dmochowski, P. Mendola, L. E. Sever, E. Fitzgerald, P. Kostyniak, H. Greizerstein, and H. Olson. "Parental Consumption of Contaminated Sport Fish from Lake Ontario and Predicted Fecundability." *Epidemiology* 11 (2000): 388–93.

Carnielli, V. P., D. J. Wattimena, I. H. Luijendijk, A. Boerlage, H. J. Degenhart, and P. J. Sauer. "The Very Low Birth Weight Premature Infant Is Capable of Synthesizing Arachidonic and Docosahexaenoic Acids from Linoleic and Linolenic Acids." *Pediatric Research* 40, no. 1 (July 1996): 169–74.

Committee on Nutrition, American Academy of Pediatrics. *Pediatric Nutrition Handbook.* 4th ed. Elk Grove Village, Ill.: American Academy of Pediatrics, 1998.

Dagnelie, P. C., W. A. van Staveren, A. H. Roos, L. G. Tuinstra, and J. Burema. "Nutrients and Contaminants in Human Milk from Mothers on Macrobiotic and Omnivorous Diets." *European Journal of Clinical Nutrition* 46, no. 5 (May 1992): 355–66.

Davis, B., and V. Melina. *Becoming Vegan.* Summertown, Tenn.: The Book Publishing Company, 2000.

ESHA Research. *The Food Processor Nutrition and Fitness Software.* Salem Ore.: ESHA Research, 2001. www.esha.com 1-800-659-3742

Fisher, J. O., L. L. Birch, H. Smiciklas-Wright, and M. F. Picciano. "Breast-Feeding Through the First Year Predicts Maternal Control in Feeding and Subsequent Toddler Energy Intakes." *Journal of the American Dietetic Association* 100, no. 6 (June 2000): 641–46.

Gillman, M. W., S. L. Rifas-Shiman, C. A Camargo, Jr., C. S. Berkey, A. L. Frazier, H. R. Rockett, A. E. Field, and G. A. Colditz. "Risk of Overweight Among Adolescents Who Were Breastfed as Infants." *Journal of the American Medical Association* 285, no. 19 (May 16, 2001): 2461–67.

Hebbelink, M., and P. Clarys. "Physical Growth and Development of Vegetarian Children and Adolescents." In *Vegetarian Nutrition,* edited by J. Sabaté, pages 173–193. Boca Raton, Fla.: CRC Press, 2001.

Kramer, F. M., A. J. Stunkard, K. A. Marshall, S. McKinney, and J. Liebschutz. "Breast-Feeding Reduces Maternal Lower-Body Fat." *Journal of the American Dietetic Association* 93, no. 4 (April 1993): 429–33.

Jensen, C. L., M. Maude, R. E. Anderson, and W. C. Heird. "Effect of Docosa-hexaenoic Acid Supplementation of Lactating Women on the Fatty Acid Composition of Breast Milk Lipids and Maternal and Infant Plasma Phospholipids."

American Journal of Clinical Nutrition 71, supplement 1 (January 2000): 292S–99S.

Johnson, P. "Vegetarian Diets in Pregnancy and Lactation." In *Vegetarian Nutrition*, edited by J. Sabaté, pages 195–219. Boca Raton, Fla.: CRC Press, 2001.

Lust, K. D., J. E. Brown, and W. Thomas. "Maternal Intake of Cruciferous Vegetables and Other Foods and Colic Symptoms in Exclusively Breast-Fed Infants." *Journal of the American Dietetic Association* 96, no. 1 (January 1996): 46–48.

Mangels, A. R. *Vegetarian Diets During Pregnancy, Lactation, and Infancy.* Online at: vrg.org/family/adatranscript.htm

Mangels, A. R., and V. K. Messina. "Considerations in Planning Vegan Diets: Infants." *Journal of the American Dietetic Association* 101, no. 6 (June 2001): 670–77.

Messina, M., and V. Messina. *The Dietitians' Guide to Vegetarian Diets.* Gaithersburg, Md.: Aspen Publishers, Inc., 1996.

Messina, V. K., and K. I. Burke. "Position of the American Dietetic Association: Vegetarian Diets." *Journal of the American Dietetic Association* 97, no. 11 (November 1997): 1317–21.

Monte, W. C., C. S. Johnston, and L. E. Roll. "Bovine Serum Albumin Detected in Infant Formula Is a Possible Trigger for Insulin-Dependent Diabetes Mellitus." *Journal of the American Dietetic Association* 94, no. 3 (March 1994): 314–16.

Murtaugh, M. A. "Optimal Breast-Feeding Duration." *Journal of the American Dietetic Association* 97, no. 11 (November 1997): 1252–54.

Noren, K. "Levels of Organochlorine Contaminants in Human Milk in Relation to the Dietary Habits of the Mothers." *Acta Paediatrica Scandinavica* 72, no. 6 (November 1983): 811–16.

Sanders, T. A., and S. Reddy. "The Influence of a Vegetarian Diet on the Fatty Acid Composition of Human Milk and the Essential Fatty Acid Status of the Infant." *The Journal of Pediatrics* 120, no. 4 (April 1992): S71–S77.

Strom, B. L., R. Schinnar, E. E. Ziegler, K. T. Barnhart, M. D. Sammel, G. A. Macones, V. A. Stallings, J. M. Drulis, S. E. Nelson, and S. A. Hanson. "Exposure to Soy-Based Formula in Infancy and Endocrinological and Reproductive Outcomes in Young Adulthood." *Journal of the American Medical Association* 286, no. 7 (August 15, 2001): 807–14.

Thomas, J., and F. R. Ellis. "The Health of Vegans During Pregnancy." *The Proceedings of the Nutrition Society* 36, no. 1 (May 1977): 46A.

Tryggvadottir, L., H. Tulinius, J. E. Eyfjord, and T. Sigurvinsson. "Breastfeeding and Reduced Risk of Breast Cancer in an Icelandic Cohort Study." *American Journal of Epidemiology* 154, no.1 (July 1, 2001): 37–42. World Health Organization. Exclusive Breastfeeding www.who.int/child-adolescent-health/NUTRITION/infant_exclusive.htm

Chapter 8

Committee on Nutrition, American Academy of Pediatrics. *Pediatric Nutrition Handbook.* 4th ed. Elk Grove Village, Ill.: American Academy of Pediatrics, 1998.

Davis, B., and V. Melina. *Becoming Vegan.* Summertown, Tenn.: The Book Publishing Company, 2000.

ESHA Research. *The Food Processor Nutrition and Fitness Software.* Salem Ore.: ESHA Research, 2001. www.esha.com 1-800-659-3742

Hahn, N. I. "Why Children and Parents Must Play While They Eat: An Interview with T. Berry Brazelton, M.D." *Journal of the American Dietetic Association* 93, no. 12 (December 1993): 1385–87.

Hebbelink, M., and P. Clarys. "Physical Growth and Development of Vegetarian Children and Adolescents." In *Vegetarian Nutrition,* edited by J. Sabaté, pages 173–193. Boca Raton, Fla.: CRC Press, 2001.

Joneja, J. V. *Dietary Management of Food Allergies and Intolerances.* Vancouver, B.C.: J. A. Hall Publications, 1998.

Mangels, A. R. *Vegetarian Diets During Pregnancy, Lactation, and Infancy.* Online at: vrg.org/family/adatranscript.htm

Mangels, A. R., and V. K. Messina. "Considerations in Planning Vegan Diets: Infants." *Journal of the American Dietetic Association* 101, no. 6 (June 2001): 670–77.

Messina, M., and V. Messina. *The Dietitians' Guide to Vegetarian Diets.* Gaithersburg, Md.: Aspen Publishers, Inc., 1996.

Messina, V. K., and K. I. Burke. "Position of the American Dietetic Association: Vegetarian Diets." *Journal of the American Dietetic Association* 97, no. 11 (November 1997): 1317–21.

Monte, W. C., C. S. Johnston, and L. E. Roll. "Bovine Serum Albumin Detected in Infant Formula Is a Possible Trigger for Insulin-Dependent Diabetes Mellitus." *Journal of the American Dietetic Association* 94, no. 3 (March 1994): 314–16.

Murtaugh, M. A. "Optimal Breast-Feeding Duration." *Journal of the American Dietetic Association* 97, no. 11 (November 1997): 1252–54. World Health Organization. Exclusive Breastfeeding www.who.int/child-adolescent-health/NUTRITION/infant_exclusive.htm

Chapter 9

American Dietetic Association. "Dietary Guidance for Healthy Children Aged 2 to 11 years—Position of American Dietetic Association." *Journal of the American Dietetic Association* 99 (1999): 93–101.

Breier, D., and R. Mangels. *Vegan and Vegetarian FAQ: Answers to Your Frequently Asked Questions.* Baltimore: The Vegetarian Resource Group, 2001.

Davis, B., and V. Melina. *Becoming Vegan.* Summertown, Tenn.: The Book Publishing Company, 2000.

Dickie, N., and A. Bender. "Breakfast and Performance in School Children." *The British Journal of Nutrition* 48 (1982): 483–96.

ESHA Research. *The Food Processor Nutrition and Fitness Software.* Salem Ore.: ESHA Research, 2001. www.esha.com 1-800-659-3742

Hebbelink, M., and P. Clarys. "Physical Growth and Development of Vegetarian Children and Adolescents." In *Vegetarian Nutrition,* edited by J. Sabaté, pages 173–193. Boca Raton, Fla.: CRC Press, 2001.

Messina, M., and V. Messina. *The Dietitians' Guide to Vegetarian Diets.* Gaithersburg, Md.: Aspen Publishers, Inc., 1996.

Messina, V. K., and K. I. Burke. "Position of the American Dietetic Association: Vegetarian Diets." *Journal of the American Dietetic Association* 97, no. 11 (November 1997): 1317–21.

Nicklas, T. A., B. Weihang, L. S. Webber, and G. S. Berenson. "Breakfast Consumption Affects Adequacy of Total Daily Intake in Children." *Journal of the American Dietetic Association* 93 (1993): 886–91.

Toews, J., and N. Parton. *Raising Happy, Healthy, Weight-Wise Kids.* Toronto: Key Porter Books, 2000.

Chapter 10

Barnard, N. D. *Foods That Fight Pain.* New York: Harmony Books, 1998.

Barnard, N. D., A. R. Scialli, D. Hurlock, and P. Bertron. "Diet and Sex-Hormone Binding Globulin, Dysmenorrhea, and Premenstrual Symptoms." *Obstetrics and Gynecology* 95, no. 2 (February 2000): 245–50.

Davis, B., and V. Melina. *Becoming Vegan.* Summertown, Tenn.: The Book Publishing Company, 2000.

Dorfman, L. *The Vegetarian Sports Nutrition Guide.* New York: John Wiley and Sons, 2000.

ESHA Research. *The Food Processor Nutrition and Fitness Software.* Salem Ore,: ESHA Research, 2001. www.esha.com 1-800-659-3742

Gingras, J. "Body Image Dissatisfaction: A Framework of Development and Recommendations for Dietitians." *Canadian Journal of Dietetic Practice and Research* 59, no. 3 (1998): 132–37.

Messina, M., and V. Messina. *The Dietitians' Guide to Vegetarian Diets.* Gaithersburg, Md.: Aspen Publishers, Inc., 1996.

Messina, V. K., and K. I. Burke. "Position of the American Dietetic Association: Vegetarian Diets." *Journal of the American Dietetic Association* 97, no. 11 (November 1997): 1317–21.

Sabaté, J., ed. *Vegetarian Nutrition.* Boca Raton, Fla.: CRC Press, 2001.

Toews, J., and N. Parton. *Raising Happy, Healthy, Weight-Wise Kids.* Toronto: Key Porter Books, 2000.

Chapter 12

ESHA. *The Food Processor Nutritional Analysis Program.* Salem, Ore.: ESHA Research, 2001. 1-800-659-3742; www.esha.com/foodpro.htm

Index

Warm Sesame Noodles, 304
Warm Spiced Milk, 248
Warm Vinaigrette Potato Salad, 300
washing
    cutting boards, 99–100
    dishes, 109
    fruits and vegetables, 109
    hands, 92–93, 112–13
water activity, defined, 99
water intake, 128, 157–58, 223
weaning, 160, 173, 174, 176, 191, 195
Web sites. *See* Internet Web sites

weight management, 224–25
    bulking up, 227–28
weight management, for adolescents,
        224–25, 227–28
Wheat-Free Minipancakes, 258
whey, 60
Whipped Potatoes, 328

yeast, nutritional, 153

zinc, 132, 133, 137, 143
    breastfeeding and, 166–67